De La War Bay

Cape Hinlopen

Annapolis

Queens T.

London

Lewis

Upper Marlboro

Vernon

Oxford   Bolingbroke

Choptank River

arles Town

Patuxen River

MARY LAND

ck River

Stratford Hall

St. Mary's

Tangier Islands

Somerset

Leeds

Damned Quarter

Rappahannock River

This line was run
27 May 1688

Chesapeake Bay

rton

Urbanna

De La War

Atlantic Ocean

York River

burg

Gloucester

York   Fort

York   Fort

Cape Charles

Jamestown

Cobham

Hampton

Fort George

Cape Henry

Norfolk

Suffolk

BOOKS BY MARSHALL W. FISHWICK:

Virginia: A New Look at the Old Dominion
The Virginia Tradition
American Heroes: Myth and Reality
General Lee's Photographer
Rockbridge County, Virginia: An Informal History (editor)
Virginians on Olympus
Isle of Shoals
The Face of Jang

VIRGINIA: A New Look at the Old Dominion

A REGIONS OF AMERICA BOOK

Virginia: *A NEW LOOK AT THE OLD DOMINION*

MARSHALL W. FISHWICK

HARPER & ROW, PUBLISHERS

New York, Evanston, and London

Contents

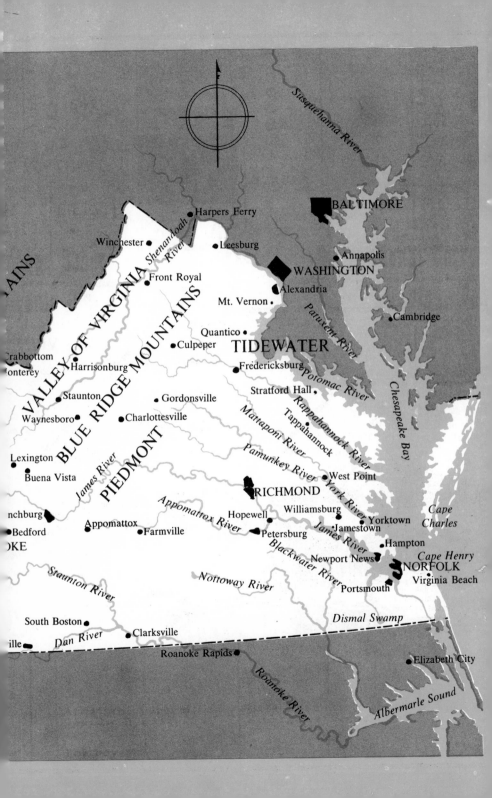

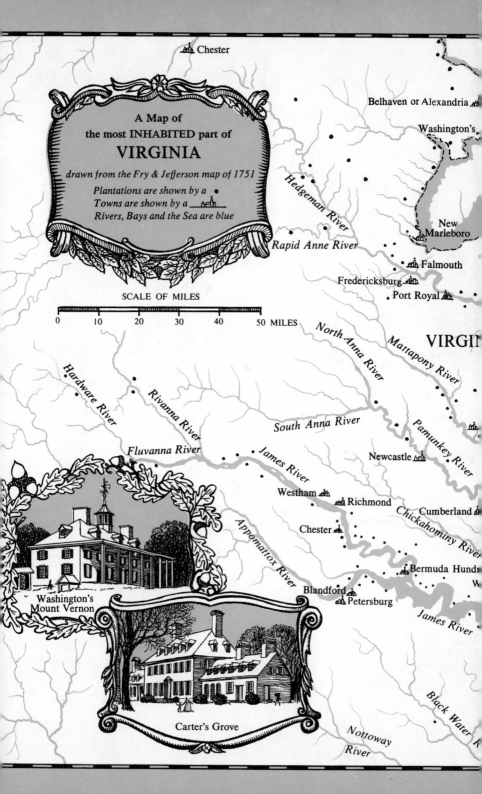

🏠 Chester

Belhaven or Alexandria 🏛

Washington's

**A Map of
the most INHABITED part of
VIRGINIA**

drawn from the Fry & Jefferson map of 1751

Plantations are shown by a •
Towns are shown by a 🏛
Rivers, Bays and the Sea are blue

New Marleboro

Hedgeman River

Rapid Anne River

🏛 Falmouth

Fredericksburg 🏛

Port Royal 🏛

SCALE OF MILES

0   10   20   30   40   50 MILES

North Anna River

Mattapony River

VIRGI

Hardware River

Rivanna River

South Anna River

Pamunkey River

Fluvanna River

James River

Newcastle 🏛

Westham 🏛

🏛 Richmond

Chickahominy River

Cumberland

Appomattox River

Chester 🏛

Bermuda Hundr

Washington's
Mount Vernon

Blandford •
🏛 Petersburg

James River

Carter's Grove

Black Water R

Nottoway River

De La War Bay

Annapolis

Queens T.

London

Cape Hinlopen

Lewis

Upper Marlboro

Mount Vernon

Oxford Bolingbroke

Charles Town

Choptank River

MARY LAND

Patuxen River

Patowmack River

Stratford Hall

St. Mary's

Tangier Islands

Somerset

Leeds

Damned Quarter

NIA

This line was run 27 May 1688

Rappahannock River

Walkerton

Chesapeake Bay

Urbanna

De La War

York River

Atlantic Ocean

Walkerton

ed

lliamsburg

Gloucester

York

Fort

Jamestown

Cape Charles

Cobham

Hampton

Fort George

Cape Henry

Norfolk

Suffolk

iver

VIRGINIA
THE OLD DOMINION STATE

ALLEGHENY MOUNT

White Sulphur Springs

Clifton Forge

Covington

Bluefield

Pearisburg

ROAN

Radford

Pulaski

Appalachia

Norton

Wytheville

Harlan

Big Stone Gap

MOUNTAIN EMPIRE

Martinsville

Bristol

Dan

Clinch River

Kingsport

Mt. Airy

J.O'H. COSGRAVE II

SCALE OF MILES

0   10   20   30   40   50 MILES

Acknowledgments

Many people in and out of the state have helped me with this book. I should like to thank them all, and pay special homage to six gentlemen who make it such a pleasure to be in the academic world: Ralph Gabriel, James Leyburn, Marion Junkin, Francis Simkins, Louis Rubin, Jr., and Carl Carmer. I wish this were worthy of them.

Some of this material has appeared in different form in *Saturday Review, American Heritage, American Quarterly, Shenandoah, Commonwealth,* and the *Virginia Magazine of History and Biography,* and is used here with permission. Generous grants from the Rockefeller Foundation and the Southern Fellowships Fund helped with the research. I am grateful.

MARSHALL W. FISHWICK

Lexington, Virginia

Prologue

I am fond of Virginia. My native state is "her," not "it," to me. My feeling for her is complex, bound up with my feeling for the Virginians who share my name and my history. The land here is good. I have walked on it, dug it, owned it, and I know. Being here is being home. Going away is being lonesome for the blue mountains, the softness, the modest elegance, the slow, sure pace. Going away is being with people who do not regulate their lives in accordance with the code which exists not in our books but in our hearts. Outsiders point out that ours is not the noblest or wisest of codes. Knowing this, we still keep it, because it is ours, honorably and decently come by. We want to preserve its good points and amend the bad; we cannot do more, and we would not do less.

Like most Virginians, I have British ancestors. Being more deliberate than heroic, they set sail not with the Elizabethans but the Victorians. They arrived too late for Jamestown, Yorktown, or Appomattox. Once settled, they quickly adopted the code and bred well-indoctrinated Virginians. My parents sent me to the public schools, and to Mr. Jefferson's University in Charlottesville. They even encouraged me to go abroad and do graduate work in New England. In due time I returned to teach at General Lee's University in Lexington and to write this book.

This will explain, in part, my angle of vision. I have not written an objective history of my state. Even if I could (impossible feat),

I am not sure that I would. For Virginia can only be understood in terms of its mythology. What Virginians *think* they are has a lot to do with what they have become. Neither the people nor their historians have been bound by the tyranny of facts. There is the Virginia that was, the Virginia that ought to have been, the Virginia that is, and the Virginia that might have been. What people say and believe about all four is the Virginia tradition.

I have tried to write about that. Because most Virginia histories are strong on what might have been, and weak on what is, I have tried to follow truth, wherever it might lead; to investigate some of the areas not usually mentioned. This has caused me to condemn and, at times, to despair. Virginia's saga has taken on so many aspects of folklore that it is now largely academic to try to separate fact from legend. The historian trained to trust documents and expert opinion comes eventually to realize that the ultimate authority in Virginia history is *vox populi*. He comes to realize that the Old Dominion's story is saturated with pride; that mores have been elevated above the law, and bigotry has been tacitly and legally authorized. He discovers that citizens of this state—many, but not all, of them colored—have been lashed and lynched, and that when the atomic age began, Virginia's convicts were still being shackled with chains. He knows that if he drives for half an hour along any Virginia road, he will see poverty and degredation unreported in the tabulated records of man's inhumanity to man.

My job is to understand and describe the four Virginias we have just named; to make a picture and paint a character—not to preach, to prove, or to flatter.

No simple task, this. Virginia history is encrusted with sentimentality and clichés. Many men and organizations, with high, middle, and low motives, labor to keep the crust thick. The hardest job has been to break through that crust. I do not for a moment claim that by making this effort I have escaped my Virginia heritage; the very act of rebellion has made me more conscious of it than ever.

The crust-breaker must start by pointing out that many accepted versions of the state's history are not true, and many true versions are ignored. Many of the relics are not genuine; many of the restorations are not authentic. No matter how many Southern belles bedeck the state's tourist literature, Virginia is not "in the heart of Dixie." The northern tip of Virginia is further north than Indianapolis; the western tip is further west than Detroit. Virginia's history and its heroes are not like those of Deep South states, though the racial and religious prejudices usually described as Southern are deeply ingrained here. No one in his right mind would say Virginians act or talk like Yankees.

Actually the Old Dominion is at the crossroads of two regional cultures, flirting coyly with both from time to time, but marrying neither. In her uniqueness and coyness she resembles the virgin Queen Elizabeth, for whom she was named.

Despite her veneer of pink-coated fox hunters and smiling house servants, Virginia has been for a century one of the poorer states of the Union. Saddled with a leadership which does not lead, she has fallen behind in many essential services. The one item she has never been short of, however, is great memories.

At first the colony stretched from one ocean to the other. The western land that she ceded was regained, in part, when she sent out the men and the ideas that conquered it. If there is any state whose pride approaches that of Virginia, it is Texas. Virginians assume that Texans will not be so rash as to challenge their superiority; if they do, they remind the bumptious Westerners that they would have no state had no such Virginians as Stephen Austin, Sam Houston, and Big Foot Wallace established it for them.

When the Virginia colony became a commonwealth, her territory still stretched northwest of the Ohio River and west of the Mississippi. She ceded enough land to the Union to become the Mother of States. Kentucky was not cut off until 1792, nor West Virginia until 1863. The area left, present-day Virginia, contains over 40,000 square miles. It is roughly triangular, the base being the southern boundary which stretches from the sea west for 450 miles. To the north the line follows the Potomac River; to the west it lies on the crest of the Alleghenies. There is still enough of Virginia to cut across the grain of eastern America.

The state is not, and can never be, monolithic. Before the British came there were three distinct cultures here, requiring interpreters for intercommunication. The main pull in the Union has been north versus south, but Virginia's main tension has been east versus west. On this truism Virginia history rests.

But there are several wests. The frontier was a dynamic, not a static, thing. The map of Virginia is a mosaic of different regions, varied resources, and remembered histories. Hundreds of detailed studies of individual pieces or small areas in the mosaic have been made. To see the total picture, we must generalize. The paradox of the general history is that it must sacrifice accuracy to achieve clarity.

Traditionally all Virginia is divided into three parts: Tidewater, Piedmont, and a region of ridges and valleys. The eastern third is called Tidewater because tides ebb and flow in the wide muddy rivers which cut the area into peninsulas or necks and empty into the Chesapeake Bay. Between the Potomac and Rappahannock is the Northern Neck; between the Rappahannock and York is the Middle Peninsula; between the York and the James is land called simply the Peninsula. The neck jutting down from Maryland on the other side of the Chesapeake Bay is the Eastern Shore.

Tidewater is flat, sandy, and hot. Its western boundary is the fall line, where the streams tumble from high hard rock to the softer rock of the plain. Rivers have not been navigable beyond this, and the boundary is economic as well as geographic. Those who believe the old adage—gentlemen and clams end at the fall line—insist that it is social, too.

The third of Virginia just west of Tidewater is the Piedmont. The word means "foot of the mountains." This fertile, undulating land widens from forty miles near the Potomac to 185 miles at the North Carolina border. Swift-moving upper courses of the Tidewater rivers drain the land which was covered with thick forests before the white men came.

The Piedmont was the early eighteenth-century frontier. Above its western edge the ancient rounded Blue Ridge Mountains, part of the Appalachian system, rise abruptly. Actually a ridge in the northern part of the state, the mountains fan out into a rugged plateau of uplands and ravines further south. The gaps in the Blue Ridge have been important to Virginia history. Settlers, railroads, and highways have penetrated the three water gaps (Potomac, James, Roanoke) and eight wind gaps (Snickers, Ashby, Manassas, Thornton, Thoroughfare, Fishers, Swift Run, and Rockfish).

Beyond the Blue Ridge is the Valley of Virginia, extending from the Potomac River to the Tennessee border and forming a natural highway from north to south. People use the term "Valley" loosely, while geologists insist that there are six separate valleys. As is generally true in such matters, the people are winning out. The largest and best known of the six valleys is the Shenandoah, which extends from Harpers Ferry to Botetourt County, and is drained by the Shenandoah River. Southwest of it are the other five—Fincastle, Roanoke, New River, Holston, Clinch, and Powell—each with its own history, ecology, and memories. The soil of all has been formed from limestone, and is very fertile. Grasslands that nourished buffalo now feed great herds of cattle.

West of the Valley of Virginia the up-slanting Allegheny Mountains create the most rugged and inaccessible region of the state. These ridges parallel the Blue Ridge, but they are higher. Here live the hillbillies, often parodied but seldom understood, on a frontier never conquered.

One more term is essential in our basic geographical vocabulary —southwest Virginia. Here nineteen counties spread from Roanoke 260 miles west to Cumberland Gap. This is the Mountain Empire, isolated by the Blue Ridge, the Alleghenies, and the Cumberlands. Being so cut off, it has maintained many early characteristics to the present.

For decades most Virginia histories have exhibited a noticeable bias. They have dealt largely with the eastern half of the state and the first half of her history. Tidewater plantations have appealed to the state's historians, but not Allegheny cabins. They have celebrated men who fought redcoats, but ignored those who fought redskins. The significance of the frontier has been minimized. Yet the history of eastern Virginia cannot be understood without a knowledge of men and events to the west. Significantly, it was western and not northern Virginia which refused to follow the Richmond secessionists in 1861.

One of my goals is to cover, so far as space allows, as much of Virginia history, in space and time, as is possible. Of course three and a half centuries cannot be packaged, like frozen vegetables, and put into neatly labeled cartons. The real art of the historian is selectivity. Choosing what to use in a study of a state which has been as meticulously described, as much praised, and as much misunderstood as Virginia is no easy task. Undoubtedly I have made errors of judgment as well as of fact. But the errors are unintentional and the interpretation is inevitable. I would not want to claim more, or less, than this.

Finally, there is the question of why one should attempt yet another book about the best documented of our state histories. I know of no better answer than James Branch Cabell's: "I too have set about the task which is laid upon every native Virginian author, and have started to put together a book of homage to the remarkable Commonwealth of Virginia."

1 Into Denser Green

MYTHICAL BROWS WE SAW RETIRING—LOTH,
DISTURBED AND DESTINED, INTO DENSER GREEN.
GREETING THEY SPED US, ON THE ARROW'S OATH:
NOW LIE INCORRIGIBLY WHAT YEARS BETWEEN.—*Hart Crane**

The moment was rigged for remembrance. Halberdiers, pikemen, sailors, and trumpeters were gathered, bedecked in seventeenth-century costumes. Bishops with puffed sleeves, politicians with silk hats, and officials with authoritative bearing looked on. The *Susan Constant,* the *Godspeed,* and the *Discovery*—twentieth-century replicas of the seagoing originals of 300 years before—rode in the water. Their time of christening had come.

As flashbulbs popped and cameras cranked, a high-born lady stepped forward, sipped red wine from a silver goblet, and poured the remainder on the deck, part to the north and part to the east, part to the south and part to the west. "I christen thee *Discovery,* and wish thee all success," she said. Then the other two sailing ships had their brief, bright moments of glory.

December 20, 1956. With pride and pageantry the Commonwealth of Virginia launched the celebration of her three hundred and fiftieth birthday.

What took place between the christening of the first *Discovery* in 1606 and the second in 1956 is the subject of this book.

How can we explain the complicated forces that sent three ships

* From "The Bridge," in *The Collected Poems of Hart Crane* (Liveright Publishing Corp.) Copyright 1933 Liveright Publishing Corp.

from England to Jamestown? How can we untangle the skein of man, myth, and malaria of that first century, now that the men and malaria have gone, leaving only the elusive myth behind? How can we summarize the thoughts and deeds of thirty-five decades?

Knowledge of the result ruins the composition of history. The only remedy is to look at events, so far as possible, through the eyes of contemporaries from whom the future was concealed.

Try to imagine how it was when the breathless stir in the Elizabethan age gave way to an age of commerce and organization, and the plucky English swarmed over the world. By 1606 Spain was toppling from her pinnacle. The Dutch, French, and English were beginning a struggle which the English were destined to win. Veiled and virgin, the New World was luring Europe on when she was most credulous into realms of gold.

Try to imagine how Master George Percy felt when he wrote in his logbook: "April 26, 1607. About foure a clock in the morning wee descried the Land of Virginia."

God knows it was time. In sullen December the three small ships had started out, the largest only a hundred tons burden, the smallest twenty. There was so little space between decks that men had to crawl into the living quarters. Because of "unprosperous winds," the ships had anchored for six weeks in the Downs, a roadstead off Kent. Crammed into primitive steerage, impatient with the wind, denied even the semblance of privacy, the voyagers' smiles soon turned to snarls. Chaplain Robert Hunt was so ill that it looked as if he would die within twenty miles of his home, before they were fairly started. But he lived, and the ships sailed in early February, as a blazing star (Halley's comet) lighted up the heavens. Westward they went, past the Great Canary Islands, until in March the ships "fell with the Iland of Mataneio" (Martinique). On March 27 they went ashore on Guadeloupe, where they found a spring with hot water that "caused a piece of Porke to be put in it to be boyled" in half an hour.

In April they stopped at Mona and Monito, where bird eggs were "as thicke as drops of Hale." Northward they sailed, until the terrible storm of April 21 so discouraged Captain John Ratcliffe that he "rather desired to beare up the helme to returne for England." But they sailed on, and five days later the three ships and 104 men and boys—all of them sick to death of the sea—were lying off the southern cape of Chesapeake Bay.

This was the Promised Land.

They were ravished with its loveliness: a warm, soft-voiced spring-green landscape, dotted with sassafras and scarlet-colored snakewood, smelling of wild strawberries and hart's tongue. Giant dogwood petals were as bright as cockscombs in the spring. Sea swallows, cormorants, and pelicans darted over the water; moor hens, lapwings, and green plovers hovered about the land. There was gushing water, and good things to eat. Instantly they forgot their toil and hunger as they looked at the firm land, the full-bellied clouds, and the wild cavorting birds. They wanted to go ashore, throw rocks at those birds, to poke and pry in childish wonderment. They wanted to let little flat crabs run over their toes, and squeeze the juice out of eglantine berries. They wanted to own and master this land.

The jubilation, so justly earned, was short-lived. On their first trip ashore, the adventurers were attacked by Indians, "creeping upon all fours from the Hills, like Beares, with their Bowes in their mouthes." The voyagers drove them off and hurried back to their ships. That night Captain Christopher Newport opened the sealed box put aboard in London. In it were their official instructions. In the perspective of time we know, though they did not, that the box should have been labeled "Pandora's." For years to come, confusion would reign.

The orders named seven men to the Council in Virginia—Christopher Newport, Edward Maria Wingfield, Bartholomew Gosnold, John Ratcliffe, John Martin, George Kendall, and John Smith. The battle for power commenced. It would seesaw back and forth among these seven men, and others who came. Always in the background there would be three sounds: water lapping on the land, mosquitoes buzzing through the night, and men groaning as they prepared to die.

Instructed to elect a president from its own number, the Council chose Wingfield. He decided to disembark on a low malarial island up the river. On May 14, 1607, the men went ashore with their belongings. It would have been hard to find a worse place to settle. Both the river and the town were named after King James. The men turned to and built a fortified town in the form of an isosceles triangle. The base extended 400 feet along the river, and the shorter sides met in the woods. The Virginia adventure was under way.

There had been earlier abortive attempts. Sir Humphrey Gilbert, with a 1583 proprietary patent from Queen Elizabeth, had tried to organize a colony and failed. So had Sir Walter Raleigh, who lost both his Roanoke Island colony and his head. But the dream did not die with such disasters; it was far too patriotic and profitable for that. The 1588 English victory over the Spanish Armada cleared the sea lanes for English expansion. The 1606 charter to the London Company sent to sea the tiny ships which landed at Jamestown and secured for England a permanent hold on the area Raleigh had named Virginia after the virgin Queen Elizabeth.

Pleased with the spring-intoxicated beginning, Captain Newport sailed for England in June, promising to return with supplies as soon as possible. No one worried much about the fact that the provisions he left could sustain the newcomers only thirteen or fourteen weeks. They would find food and plant crops. This was a right fair venture.

When summer and malaria came, what they planted were the bodies of their dead comrades. The daily record began to read like this:

The sixth of August, there died John Asbie, of the bloudie Fluxe.
The ninth day, died George Flowre, of the swelling.
The tenth day, died William Bruster, Gentleman, of a wound given by the Savages. . . .
The fourteenth day, Jerome Alikock . . . of a wound; the same day, Francis Midwinter and Edward Moris, Corporall, died suddenly.
The fifteenth day, there died Edward Browne and Stephen Galthorpe.

In the morning bodies were dragged out of the crude cabins, which were "worse than naught," to be buried "like Dogges."

Bartholomew Gosnold, best-liked of all the Council members, died in August. The following month the desperate survivors ousted Wingfield and put Ratcliffe in command, but the "disgustfull brawls" continued. Bitter and frequent were the charges and countercharges. "He reporteth that I do slack the service and do nought but tend my spit and overn and pot," sickly John Martin wrote of Wingfield, "but he hath starved my son."

As the wrangling and turmoil continued in 1608, the burden of command centered in the most colorful and controversial of the early Virginians. About him, no one could be neutral. This "subjugator of nine and thirty kings"—characteristically, his own phrase —could and can be admired or detested, but not ignored. Captain John Smith, as John Fiske was later to comment, is one of those persons about whom historians are apt to lose their tempers.[1] *

---

* The superior figures refer to notes, which will be found in a section beginning on page 284.

Smith's was the rough-and-tumble world of the professional soldier. Left an orphan in 1594, the fifteen-year-old lad was apprenticed to Thomas Sendall, a wealthy merchant. He ran off to the Low Countries and became a soldier of fortune. In 1601 he joined the Austrians against the Turks, who were regarded then as the chief threat to Christendom. His own accounts of the next few years abound with heroic and incredible deeds. Smith tells of rescuing a besieged town by perfecting a pyrotechnic signal system, of inventing "fiery Dragons," incendiary bombs which streaked the sky with flame, and of beheading three Turkish warriors in Transylvania. For this, he says, the English College of Heralds gave him a coat of arms with the motto "Vincere est Vivere"—to conquer is to live. Although historians have tended for some time to consider Smith's history to be a mixture of fact and fiction, recent research indicates that instead of being the Impostor General, he was a surprisingly accurate and detailed chronicler.[2]

By 1604 Smith was back in England. Only twenty-six years old when the Virginia Company received its patent, he was employed for the 1606 Jamestown sailing, and chosen one of the Council members. En route he was imprisoned and sentenced to death for mutiny. His gallows were actually built on Nevis among the Summer Islands; but as Smith later reported, he "could not be persuaded to use them." Though brought ashore in irons at Jamestown, he was allowed to sit with the Council later on.

John Smith was never one to sit for long. Soon he was exploring, procuring food, bargaining with the Indians. He spent the summer of 1608 searching out the country to the north and west. Later on, he told how he was captured, condemned to death by Chief Powhatan, and saved at the last moment by the Princess Pocahontas. Elected president of the Council in the fall of 1608, Smith settled down to govern the colony.

Whether or not he saved the settlement, he certainly alienated most of its leaders. When he took over, only sixteen days' subsistence diet remained, but Smith bullied friend and foe, Indian and settler, into surviving the winter. He pulled the colony through.

Meanwhile, the London backers were successful in obtaining from King James a new charter on May 23, 1609. The joint-stock company was continued; but the government of Jamestown would be taken from the Council and given to "one able and absolute Governor." Men could argue about how able John Smith was; no one denied that he was absolute. He left a unique mark on the early years of settlement.

Severely wounded on one of his expeditions, Smith returned to England in October, 1609, and was succeeded by George Percy. He would never again see Virginia, "my wyfe, to whom I have given all," as he described the land. Percy, Radcliffe, and others drew up the charges which sent the wounded Smith home in disgrace; but it was Edward Maria Wingfield who vouched that Smith had "told him plainly how he lied," thus starting the interminable debate over the Captain's veracity. The argument points to deeper, broader problems, such as class consciousness. Smith, son of a tenant farmer, was dealing with, and sometimes ruling, men like the aristocratic Wingfield and George Percy, eighth son of the Earl of Northumberland. One charge stated that Smith "did not show due regard for Gentlemen." He seems at worst a scrabbler after glory, plagued by a persecution complex arising from his low birth and small stature.

Full of oaths and conceits, quick to anger but quicker to forgive, bush-bearded "Captain Jack" managed to catch the imagination of those who came after that. More important, he was able, as Carl Carmer has pointed out in *The Susquehanna,* to link in his own experience the popular attitudes of four centuries. In Hungary he was the romantic medieval champion of the jousting tourney. In Virginia he was the complete Elizabethan—poet, philosopher, man of action. Smith's account of the giant Susquehannock Indians whom he met at the mouth of their river at least pointed toward the next century's delight in the "natural man" and the "Noble Savage."[3] This stepchild of Ulysses never doubted, up to his dying day, that he could accomplish the legendary; perhaps because, on some occasions, he did. He saw strange seas, talked with wonderful people, and lived through an epic.

Whether the Pocahontas rescue story was true or not, it entranced posterity. The swashbuckling Smith, aided by a beautiful Indian princess, founded a nation and made the dream of an English colony a reality. This summary has proved so useful and satisfying that it is deeply embedded in American history. Pocahontas' story is a fairy tale come to life. She is Cinderella in doeskin. At the center of stirring events, she risked her own life to save the brave Smith, and was rewarded for her fidelity. As John Rolfe's wife she went to the Court of St. James as a princess, and there outshone all the celebrated royal beauties. At the end is the tragic note. She suffered a premature and unexpected death, and was mourned on both sides of the ocean.

Though he published his first account of Virginia in 1608 (critics have made much of the fact that it does not mention Pocahontas' rescue) most of Smith's writing was done later. His most important book, *The Generall Historie of Virginia, New England, and the Summer Isles,* appeared in 1624. Euphuistic and partisan, it was nevertheless as accurate as most Elizabethan histories, and brought him some fame in his final years. Such fame did not improve his fortune. He died leaving behind only eighty pounds, twenty of which he directed should be spent on his funeral.

After Smith's departure in 1609, the colony had two months' supply in the store and ten months to wait for a possible harvest. Relief from home would not come until spring, if at all. The Starving Time was upon them.

The daily ration, a half pint of corn, "contained as many worms as grains." Men bartered their clothes and blankets for a capful of corn, and paid for their folly by freezing to death. Percy was too sick to enforce the laws. Houses were torn down for firewood, and even the palisades were burned. The gates of the fort, no longer barred, swung back and forth in the cold winter nights.

Starving settlers ate boots, shoes, or any other leather, and were "gladd to make shift with vermin." They crawled to the woods to catch snakes or dig up roots with their hands. A small group turned traitor and sailed off on the *Swallow,* bringing Jamestown to its nadir of despair. Men "licked upp the bloode which had fallen from their weak fellowes." One demented wretch killed his wife and ate her before the murder was discovered.[4] With sardonic Elizabethan humor, Captain Smith thought the episode worth commenting on when he wrote his history. "Whether she was better roasted, boyled, or carbonado'd, I know not," he speculated. "But such a dish as powdered wife I never heard of!"

History has few specters to outdo what finally happened. Men whose skull bones showed through pinched faces dug corpses out of their graves and ravenously ate them stewed with roots and herbs.

Then, miraculously, two ships appeared. Sir Thomas Gates, who with the survivors of two shipwrecked vessels had spent nine months on Bermuda, finally built two small vessels (the *Deliverance* and the *Patience*) to finish the voyage. Instead of the 500 settlers he expected to find at Jamestown, three were 65 "anatomies," staring

out with terror-stricken eyes and making pathetic sounds with their
feeble voices: "We are starved! We are starved!" Gates fed them and
formulated his plans to abandon the island of disease and death.
The poor wretches who had gone through the winter wanted not
only to leave but also to burn the memory-haunted, blood-soaked
village first. Gates decided against this, ordering every man, "at the
beating of a drum, to repair aboard." Embark they did, in early
June, when the chances for return to England seemed brightest.
With luck they might meet a fishing vessel off Newfoundland. After
three years of sometimes foolish, often courageous effort, the English settlers of Virginia were giving up. Raleigh's first colony had
been lost; this one had been starved out.

Had there been a stout breeze the morning Gates set sail, he would
soon have cleared the Cape and moved out into the troughs of the
deep salt sea. At this point Chance, who always plays a hand at Clio's
card table, held a high trump. There was no breeze. The tiny ships
could not move. They anchored off Hog Island in the James River.
Lord De la Warre, who was standing through the Capes en route
to Jamestown, intercepted Gates. Fresh and ambitious, full of myth
rather than malaria, De la Warre and his companions had no idea
of escorting their predecessors home. "Turn back!" De la Warre
ordered. Despite the "groans, curses, and great grief," Gates' force
turned back. The first English-speaking colony in the New World
was not destined to die.

The new arrivals could hardly believe what they saw at the
fort. Only gross mismanagement and indolence could have brought
about such conditions, De la Warre decided; iron discipline would
make a reoccurrence impossible. Among the new rules posted for
all to see were these:

Anyone caught stealing food was to have his ears cut off. A second
offense drew a year as a slave in the galleys. For speaking dis-
respectfully to the new Governor, doing anything "against the
known articles of the Christian faith," or accumulating three un-
excused absences from the Sunday service, the penalty was death.
These were the days of the "Egyptian slavery and Scythian cruelty."

Not that Lord De la Warre gave up the prerogative and pageantry
of his position. In days of utter privation and agony, he attended
church at Jamestown with "a guard of fifty Halberdiers in his
Lordship's Livery, fair red cloaks, on each side and behind him.
The Lord Governor sat in the choir, in a green velvet chair, with
a velvet cushion before him."[5] Many settlers counted it as one of

their few blessings when De la Warre returned to England the next spring, leaving George Percy as deputy Governor. Not capable of dealing with the harrowing circumstances, Percy took the *Trial* out on a fishing expedition; instead of returning with the good catch, he sailed on to London in ignominious fashion.

This left control in the hands, or rather the fists, of Sir Thomas Dale, who as Marshal of Virginia had come over a few months earlier with 250 settlers. Dale not only confirmed the strict code of martial law but also added thirty-two new articles which would have made Spartans blanch. He did not even allow the hamstrung colonists to "doe the necessities of nature" except a quarter mile or more outside the stockade. Since venturing out involved not only the possibility but probability of an Indian attack, and since a person out on this mission could hardly defend himself, it must have created inhibitions enough to challenge the most adept phrase-makers.

Homo sapiens is a tough animal; the settlers of Jamestown survived Dale and the other leaders. After several years of crop failures, they abandoned the technique of broadcast seeding used in Great Britain and adopted the hill-planting method of the Indians. The soil on the hills was stirred and loosened, but that in the intervening spaces was not broken. Corn, squash, and a variety of beans (white, red, black, spotted) were frequently grown on the same hill.[6] If the Indian's military might almost wiped out the colony, his agricultural skill saved it.

Always in the background, during the early years, was the spirit and intelligence of Sir Edwin Sandys, liberal leader of the British Parliament and initiator of representative government in America. He drafted the 1609 document for the London Company, the more liberal 1612 charter, and the 1618 "Great Charter of Privileges, Orders, and Laws." King James thought poorly of all this and, prior to an election, instructed London Company members to "choose the Devile if you will, but not Sir Edwin Sandys." The English monarch eventually annulled the company's charter in 1624, converting Virginia into a royal colony. By then representative government was firmly entrenched in Jamestown. So were the other guarantees listed in the "Great Charter": settlers could own their own land, taxation was restricted, martial law and common holding were forbidden, "corporacouns" or counties were set up. Such changes were prompted by the desire to make the colony a financial success, to increase the population, and to bolster the settlers' sagging morale. When Argall returned to Virginia in 1618 as deputy Governor in charge, he re-established good relations with Opechanca-nough, the most powerful Indian leader. In his other actions he was less successful, and the highhanded Argall slipped away from the colony a few days before the recently knighted Sir George Yeardley returned as Governor of Virginia.

Soon after his arrival Yeardley issued a call for a meeting of a General Assembly of the colony. It met for six hot days in the "quire of the church" at Jamestown. The members of the eleven duly constituted plantations who attended suffered from "extreme heat both past and likely to ensue," but stayed long enough to plant the seeds from which the tree of liberty would later spring. This first representative assembly in America, composed of Burgesses sitting with the Governor and Council, continued to meet until King James gave it his full sanction in 1628. In August, 1619, the first Negroes were brought to Virginia by a Dutch ship, beginning a momentous chapter in the history of the state and nation. On November 17, 1619, the Virginia Company approved a plan to send over 100 young maids to become wives. Jamestown was not to be a military but a family outpost. On December 30, the English Parliament passed a law forbidding the planting of tobacco in England and Ireland. Virginia was to concentrate on the tobacco market, without Old World competition.

Not all the major disasters were past. The Indians grew ever more restless, and found a cunning leader in Opechancanough. On the fatal Friday morning of March 22, 1622, they staged a violent attack, slaughtering a third of the settlers. Except for the advance warning of Chanco, a converted Indian boy, Jamestown might have been wiped out. There had been talk of a school to Christianize the Indians. From now on the program was to exterminate them.

Disease, famine, ignorance, bad luck, pride, broken promises, and discord continued to take their toll. Of the 14,000 colonists who had come over since 1607, about 13,000 had died by 1622. No war or plague in history—not even the Black Death—took a higher percentage of lives than were lost in this first generation.

Dark years would return, but none darker than the initial fifteen. "Scientific" historians, reacting against the earlier romanticized accounts which glossed over the blood and anguish, have argued that they were almost totally black; that the first Virginians were "dissipated men of the world, still smelling of the stews and grog-shops of London," whose survival was an incredible stroke of luck.[7] It is time to revise such revisionists.

The settlement of Jamestown was a triumph of the human spirit. Despite the many blunders (some pathetic, others inexcusable), the men who came to the malarial island planted the cornerstone of a new nation, and planted it well. Their motives ranged from base to magnificent. "Good Master" Hunt, the first Anglican minister to arrive, preached the Gospel, administered the sacraments, and shared the suffering of his flock—"yet none did ever hear him repine of his loss." In circumstances more grim than glorious, George Sandys managed to translate the last ten books of Ovid's *Metamorphoses* expertly enough to win the praise of both Pope and Dryden. Colonists whose names are forgotten worked and died so that others might follow them and live.

Not all the days were dark. Some were smiling and shimmering, filled with air soft as pinfeathers. The winters were bleak, but the springs were meadow-green. The woods were full of "pease, pumpions, and chinquapins." On lazy autumnal days, the tables sagged with the meat of wondrous and succulent birds and beasts. Tears gave way to laughter and loving and good talk of home.

Gradually "home" meant Jamestown, not distant Kent or Sussex. Men stopped looking toward the sea and turned their gaze westward.

If those fifteen years had not implanted in the English colonists a faith stronger than hunger and death, Virginia never would have survived. Individuals fell; the settlement and the long hope endured.

Standing back far enough from the daily drabness, one sees that the dominating color at early Jamestown was not black but dense green. With all its faults, this land would grow as Europe could never grow. Here were fields beyond numbering, and unfenced green pastures. This was indeed the Brave New World, and these were the wondrous people in't.

2 *A Second Start*

After the Great Massacre of 1622, Virginia had a second wind and a second start. The following year a broadside ballad called "Good Newes from Virginia" appeared on the streets of London, relating in doggerel verse the punitive expeditions against the Indians, measures taken to strengthen the Jamestown colony, and the optimism and courage with which settlers faced the future. The last verse urged bold Englishmen to strike out for the New Land:

> Thus wishing God will turne the mindes
> of many for to come:

> And not to live like dormise still
> continuall keeping home.

> Who ever sees Virginia
> this shall he surely find:

> What's fit for men, and more and than
> a country man most kind.[1]

Settlers began to replace original wattled cottages, which the sun pierced through until they were hot as stoves, with more comfortable structures. Richard Chesley's 1621 hut measured only twelve by fourteen feet: he wanted more room. By 1625, row houses, and ten years later a sturdy State House, appeared in Jamestown.

We know from the 1625 census that Jamestown could boast of a church, guardhouse, three storehouses, a merchant's store, and thirty-three houses. Ten of the colony's forty boats were there, along with four pieces of ordnance, adequate supplies of ammunition, thirty-six suits of armor, and seventy swords.

Europeans were most concerned not with what the colony had, but what it grew—strong, sweet tobacco, as pleasant as any under the sun. The tobacco being imported by England from Spain brought eighteen shillings a pound in 1619; as Virginia's production went up, the price went down. Later on, cotton would be king. Now it was tobacco.

Not only the economy but the history, politics, and society of the colony were shaped by tobacco. Because of it, the plantation came into prominence and the planter into power. John Rolfe pioneered in the cultivation of the plant. There were no centuries of experience to draw upon, so problems had to be worked out by trial and error in the wilderness. When planters learned to cure the plant by suspending it on lines, production soared. Whereas only 20,000 pounds were shipped overseas in 1619, 60,000 went out in 1622 and half a million in 1627. Here was the currency of Virginia's survival.

England was the double gainer from the increase. Very little tobacco is used in the raw state, and the processing was done in the mother country. It was estimated that one Virginian engaged in tobacco growing kept three Englishmen employed. In addition, the royal government derived considerable revenue from tobacco products resold on the European market.

Tobacco quickly became Virginia's medium of exchange, acceptable for goods, services, and the payment of debts. Salaries were fixed in pounds of tobacco. In spite of fluctuations in price, tobacco production continued to rise. This was a soil-exhausting crop, and later generations would struggle with worn-out land. The rule for early colonists was "Plant!" They frequently neglected to grow grain, which they hoped they would be able to obtain by gift, barter, or seizure from the Indians, so they could raise more of the leaf which brought as much per pound as grain brought per bushel. A 1633 law required gunsmiths, carpenters, joiners, brickmakers, and turners to stick to their trades and not to plant tobacco.

Because of this economic inducement and a British mercantile policy that encouraged the production of raw materials, the settlers moved out to establish what were variously called "plantations," "hundreds," or "colonies." The earliest of these were plain, often crude places. Life was precarious, and death was always close at hand. The colonists were long on land and short on man power. Consequently the land was badly misused. Year after year men sowed the same crop in identical spots until diminishing yields forced them to new land. A typical plantation would have a large expanse of virgin forest, a restricted area of cultivated land, and several abandoned fields.[2]

The economy was explosive and uncontrolled, and the cry was for more man power. The population, which had been less than 2,500 in 1619, passed 8,000 in 1640 and 40,000 in 1670. As the place names show—Kent, Portsmouth, Isle of Wight, Surrey—many newcomers were from southern England. Eastern and central Englishmen came too, naming Warwick, York, Northampton, and Norfolk. Except for two Indian adaptations, the first county names were English: Accomack, Charles City, Charles River, Elizabeth City, Henrico, James City, Warwick River, and Warrosquyoake.

By 1625 England had a new King and Virginia a new form of government. The charter of the London Company was voided as control moved into the hands of the King. Charles I would appoint a royal Governor who would enforce laws, command the militia, and dispose of land. The General Assembly, meeting at the Governor's bidding, needed his consent to pass laws or stay in session. The Governor would also appoint justices of the peace and county sheriffs. The justices of the peace in each county would form the county court and appoint local officials, completing the web of government.

Obviously, the Governor was a person of power. When he was as opinionated and quick-tempered as Sir John Harvey, the King's appointee in 1629, anything was likely to happen. Harvey, said one of his enemies, "walked among the colonists as he did the deck of a ship," and retaliated against one dissenting Council member by knocking out his teeth with a club. Nonetheless, the Council would not be bullied. In the record for April 28, 1635, is this notation: "Sir John Harvey thrust out of his government."

There were various causes for the revolt against Harvey. More accusations have been hurled at him by later historians than by his contemporaries.[3] Our scholars have seized on any evidence of discontent as an anticipation of our later-day War of Independence.

Apparently the revolt against Sir John did not spring from the people, but from certain Council members. In any case, Charles I did not favor such treatment for his governors, and sent Harvey back for a second term before replacing him in 1639 with the more conciliatory Sir Francis Wyatt.

In 1634 Benjamin Symmes left eight cows and two hundred acres to support a free school for children in Elizabeth City and Kecoughtan parishes, allowing Virginians to claim the first one within the present limits of the United States. Not that the colony believed in democratic education or a democratic society. Governor Wyatt's successor, Sir William Berkeley, thanked God that there were no public schools and printing presses in his colony.

This often-quoted remark is hardly a fair one with which to introduce the most beloved and long-enduring of the seventeenth-century governors. Member of a distinguished family, Berkeley was a graduate of Oxford and the Inns of Court, a writer, and a favorite of the King. He served a total of twenty-five years as royal Governor, ending in much less happy circumstances than those under which he began. In recent years, however, the Dr. Jekyll and Mr. Hyde interpretation of Berkeley's career has been questioned by revisionist historians.

The good feeling which characterized the first years of Berkeley's regime was altered first by the Great Massacre and Indian War which opened in 1644, and then by the struggle for prerogative in England which culminated with the beheading of Charles I in 1649. A 1646 treaty with the Indians promised them rights which the white men refused to give, despite Governor Berkeley's honest and courageous efforts to enforce the agreement. For a while Indian affairs were subservent to the struggle for power at home. Berkeley's sentiments, and those of his colony, were strongly with the royal cause. He refused to recognize the rule of Oliver Cromwell, and went so far as to invite Charles II to live in Virginia. Fully occupied with home problems, Parliament took no military action against the upstart colony. The embargo slapped on Virginia was rendered ineffective when Berkeley sought and secured business with other colonies and with the Dutch. Cromwell eventually sent two commissioners, Richard Bennett and William Claiborne, to "reduce" Virginia. A compromise resulted. Cromwell and the Council of the Commonwealth were to exercise veto power over the colonial assembly. The Burgesses, however, were to choose their own Governor and Council. When Bennett became acting Governor in 1652, Sir William retired temporarily to his plantation, Green Spring, hoping for better days.

Those days came with the 1660 Restoration of Charles II. Berkeley ordered the sheriffs of all counties to proclaim the new King, and to cause all writs and warrants to be issued in His Majesty's name. Virginia's Assembly decreed that January 30, the day Charles I was beheaded, should "be annually solemnized with fasting and prayers that our sorrowes may expiate our crime and our teares wash away our guilt." May 29, on the other hand, the day of Charles II's birth and Restoration, was to be a holy day, celebrated "in testimony of our thankfulnesse and joy."

Charles II was not unmindful of such loyalty. Because Virginia had stood by the Stuarts when other dominions had deserted, he decreed that Virginia should be called the "Old Dominion." To the title the state has clung proudly and tenaciously ever since.

If English conditions improved, Indian affairs deteriorated. For this the white settlers seem largely to blame. The story of Colonel Edward Hill's 1656 expedition is all too typical. When several hundred Indians were reported to have moved down from the mountains near the falls of the James, the Assembly ordered Hill and a hundred men to remove them peacefully, making war only in self-defense. Although the Indians had come to trade, Hill perfidiously had five of the chiefs who came to parley slain—an act which even one of Hill's associates branded "hellish treachery and anti-christian perfidy more to be detested than any heathenish inhumanity." Worse yet, the chief Tottopottomoy, who lost his life fighting bravely for the English, was rewarded by having the very land he owned extorted from him and his successors.

In 1662 Sir William Berkeley assumed the post of Governor for the third time. Age and misfortune had withered his hopes. Instead of being rewarded for his devotion, he was snubbed when he returned to court in London. His pleas for revision of the mercantile policies which were working considerable hardship on the people of Virginia received little sympathy. "Why," asked Berkeley, "should 40,000 Virginians be impoverished to enrich little more than forty merchants, who being the only buyers of our tobacco, give us what they please for it, then sell it how they please?" He asked, but no one answered.

This lack of sympathetic understanding in London offices was to grow, and with it the colonists' determination to strike out on their own. But before Britain was to face a revolution, the loyal Governor of Virginia would meet one on the very soil he had protected so stanchly for the Crown. Sir William Berkeley boarded a ship and made the long voyage to Virginia, where, to his amazement and chagrin, a full-scale uprising occurred right under his royalist nose.

His adversary was Nathaniel Bacon, an Oxford graduate who had not been in Virginia long when he became the center of a storm of protest against royal policy. The Indian issue was at stake. An unauthorized attack on the friendly Susquehannocks in the winter of 1675 brought on a series of raids of retaliation. Hoping to restore peace, Governer Berkeley ordered an investigation. The officials whom he appointed actually organized a military expedition and killed the Susquehannock chiefs under a flag of truce. This crime caused Berkeley to announce that anyone who proceeded against the Indians without his commission would be hanged as a rebel.

Bacon, whose property had been attacked, would have none of this. "If the redskins meddle with me, damn my blood but I'll harry them, commission or no commission!" he stated. They meddled and he harried. Berkeley branded Bacon and his men traitors, and the break was made.

Evaluating Bacon's Rebellion has proved difficult for colonial historians. Unfortunately, there is little contemporary printed material about the outbreak to examine. Research has been based on two pamphlets which William Harris published in London in 1677: *Strange News from Virginia* and *More News from Virginia*. Drawing upon these, and the official British reaction to Berkeley's severe measures, most writers have come to picture Bacon as a reformer and Berkeley as an oppressor. They have glorified Bacon's memory and made him the torchbearer of the American Revolution a century later. Seventeen novels have been written about the affair. In them Bacon appears as a Virginia Robin Hood, defending the weak against the strong and the poor against the rich. Efforts were made to glorify Bacon in the 1957 celebrations at the Jamestown Festival.

But new sources have been found which put the matter in a different and less romantic light. The Sir Henry Coventry papers, in the library of the Marquis of Bath, dispute the long-accepted version of the uprising.[4]

It was Bacon's men, not Berkeley's, who were highhanded with Indian affairs. The Governor refused Bacon's demand for a commission on the grounds that attacks on neighboring subject Indians would disarrange Virginia's defenses, which depended on the subject Indians acting as buffers against the "foreign" tribes. The notion that the Rebellion was an attempt at political reform cannot be documented. Most of Bacon's followers had records of oppression of the Indians. The only laws in which they were interested were those authorizing attacks on the red men who blocked their expansion. Many historians have failed to see that the aggressiveness of the frontiersmen was the major cause of the Rebellion.

Thus Thomas Perkins Abernethy seems justified in calling Nathaniel Bacon an "indulged only son" who lacked the restraining influence of maturity and experience.[5] Even if he had won the Rebellion, he would have had to rule by force rather than with the consent of his fellow Virginians. The idea that the Rebellion was a "class struggle" between big and little planters is disproved by examining the large grants held by certain of the participants. Moreover, there was little similarity between conditions in the 1670's and the 1770's, when the success of the colonies meant the triumph of the notion that government must rest upon the consent of the governed.

Why then was London so unsympathetic to Berkeley's actions? One reason is that the rebel view of the dispute reached London ahead of the Governor's. Another is that Giles Bland, a Bacon lieutenant, and Thomas Povey, his friend, were influential figures at court and in English commercial circles. Povey stood well with the Secretary of State, Sir Joseph Williamson. Thirdly, the King's Commissioners sent to Virginia to ascertain the facts exceeded their instructions, hampered Berkeley in his post-Rebellion activities, and condemned him without hearing all the evidence. The Commissioners' report, and the ignorance of the London official who approved it, resulted in censure of Berkeley.

One reason Bacon's case has been viewed with such sympathy, despite the documentary evidence, is that his was a stirring tragedy, played out with dash and daring. The rebellious planter had a hot anger, a righteous sword, and a turn of phrase that was stirring and almost Shakespearean: "If ever you have fought well and bravely, you must do so now. They call us rebels and traitors, but we will see whether their courage is as great as their pretended loyalty. Come on, my hearts of gold! He who dies in the field of battle dies in the bed of honor!"

His men came on, drove Berkeley into exile, and burned James-town. Bacon went off to gather further support. Overcome by the passion of action and of feeling, he became "sick of a flux," and died unexpectedly in October, 1676. In the hands of a mediocre follower, Colonel Ingram, the Rebellion disintegrated. Governor Berkeley, who had been "shut up in the Ark," reassumed control and meted out vengeance. He executed more men than had been killed in the entire Civil War, prompting King Charles' often quoted remark: "That old fool has hanged more men in that naked country than I did for the murder of my father."

After Berkeley there were ten other seventeenth-century English executives who served with varying degrees of success. Throughout the period the Established Church was the Anglican. Although more moderate in policy than some other Protestant denominations, it was no model of tolerance, even after the Toleration Act of 1689. The Virginia Council was proud to report in 1629 that "noe papists have beene suffered to settle amongst us," and strong feeling against Maryland Roman Catholics hung on for decades. There was little liberal blood in the veins of such Anglican clerics as Richard Buck, William Wickham, or Alexander Whitaker, though it must be ad-mitted that the persecutions of the Puritans under Berkeley were primarily for political reasons. The Established Church was too much under lay control to be characterized as a strong coercive force. Its chief contribution may have been a common-sense attitude which not only enabled the Church to survive but also implanted its methods as well as its theology upon generations of Virginians.

As their resources increased, the colonists moved out of their dark medieval houses into more comfortable quarters. The transitional period was the last quarter of the seventeenth century. The end toward which they worked was only gradually defined: symmetrical brick homes, two rooms deep and two stories high, neat and orderly in design.

There was a more formidable obstacle than civil strife and hous-ing in the settlers' path—the devil. Almost all seventeenth-century Englishmen believed in His Satanic Majesty and the witches and sorcerers who served him. King James himself published in 1597 his *Daemonologie,* a powerful reassertion of the reality of Satan's hosts. The way to compensate for major and minor calamities was to seek out and destroy the black magicians. British law was explicit as to legal procedures and punishment.

The settlers firmly believed they had not brought the devil with them, but that he was already in Virginia, motivating and inspiring the Indians. Again and again their early literature insisted that their chiefs, priests, idols, and ceremonies were demoniac. Captain John Smith tells how his captives "entertained him with most strange and fearful Conjurations:

> As if neare led to hell
> Amongst the Devills to dwell."

Writing from the infant colony, good Master William Crashaw assured his English readers that "Satan visible and palpably raignes there, more than in any other known place of the world."[6]

In the 1620's the "great witches" ceased to be exclusively Indian. The first recorded case in which a white woman was accused of witchcraft developed in September, 1626. Goodwife Joan Wright, who lived in Surrey County across the river from Jamestown, was charged by a number of people with practicing black arts. Elizabeth Gates testified that the accused put spells on chickens and "threatened her maide she said she would make her dance naked and stand before the Tree!" But the evidence did not seem to Governor Yeardley and the Grand Jury sufficient to warrant conviction. Actual trials of accused persons, and civil suits by individuals defamed as witches, continued for decades. Nothing approaching the "witchcraft delusion" which rocked New England ever occurred, however. While fifty-five persons were being put to torture and twenty were being hanged for allegedly marketing their souls in Salem, Massachusetts, Virginians were doing nothing more severe than dunking Grace Sherwood in Lynnhaven Bay.

Why Mistress Sherwood should have made a compact with Satan, and why hers is the best-known story in the annals of Virginia witchcraft, is difficult to say. She was no withered crone, but the prosperous daughter of a landowner and carpenter named John White. Her husband, Master James Sherwood, was a respectable figure, and her three sons were quite normal. Nonetheless, disquieting whispers started. Before long, they mounted into a crescendo of doubts and accusation.

The Gisburne's cotton crop was blighted, and their pigs acted in a queer manner. Then Elizabeth Barnes claimed she was ridden about by Grace Sherwood, who brought her home and left "out of the Key hole or crack of the door like a black Catt." As if that weren't enough, Grace crossed over to Currituck Sound in an eggshell, and tied it by a single thread to a nearby tree.

Determined to squelch such stories, the Sherwoods brought suit against various defamers. Undoubtedly the ill will growing out of the litigation was responsible for much of the trouble that followed.[7]

Mistress Sherwood won her case against "Luke Hill and Uxor," charging that Hill's wife had "assaulted, bruised, maimed, and barbarously beaten her." Seeking revenge, Luke Hill brought suit on February 6, 1706, against Grace "for suspition of witchcraft." When she refused to appear in court, and when several sworn evidences were made against her "by which doleful things very likely appear," the court requested that "as many antient and knowing women as possible search for titts, spotts, and marks." This was done. Nine ancient women all declared on oath that "she is not like ye nor noe other women yet they know of, having two things like titts on her of a black coler, being blacker than rest of her body."

A worried community referred the matter to the General Court in Williamsburg, which promptly labeled the evidence too general and remanded the case to the county court. After much debate, it was decided to give Grace the water test. Water, being pure, would refuse to receive into its depths the body of a tainted living person, Thus, if an accused person were cast into a pool and sank, he or she must be innocent. If such a person floated, this was incontrovertible evidence of guilt. So Virginians—and Europeans— of that day reasoned.

On July 10, 1706, Grace Sherwood was taken to a spot on Lynnhaven Bay, known ever since as Witch Duck Point. She was bound, rowed out into the bay, and pushed overboard. From the crowd on the shore came gasps and cries. She floated! Worse yet—if local storytellers are to be believed—lightning flashed, thunder roared, and a deluge drenched the spectators, who fled in consternation.

Back to ye common gaol went poor Grace, "to be secured in irons or otherwise where she shall remain till such time as otherwise directed." Months later she was released, and the witch story inexplicably ends. We do know that she wrote her will in 1733 and died in 1740. If she was never cleared of the charge of witchcraft, she was never convicted of it. She lived almost eighty years and, unlike some New England ladies similarly accused, she died a natural death.

Other Virginia ladies faced difficulties for different reasons. Poor Martha Burwell, a Williamsburg belle, decided to reject Governor

Nicholson's suit and marry a man more to her liking. If the marriage were consummated, swore the Governor with a very wounded ego, he would cut the throat of the bridegroom, and probably those of the clergymen and issuing justice as well. When this didn't faze young Martha, he threw in half a dozen more throats, including those of her father and brothers.

Martha Burwell was unaware that the female is the weaker sex. She went right ahead with her marriage. No throats were cut; but it was noted by visitors to the Governor's Palace that His Excellency made a "Roaring Noise."[8]

Thus did the men—and women—gain control of Virginia. Instead of being, as Michael Drayton had proclaimed in his poem, "earth's only paradise," the place was proving for many "a miserie, a ruine, a death, and a hell" as well. Jubilation and rejoicing had been followed by dejection and starving. On many occasions Virginia's green grass was covered with red blood.

Yet the central thread of the colony's early history is clear. Those who came, no matter what their backgrounds, wrested the land from the forest, the wild beasts, and the Indians. Most of them were not squires or aristocrats but city-bred Englishmen, often in poor straits. Their readjustment to the New World and the climate was agonizing. So was that of thousands of African Negroes who were torn from their homeland and imported without even the advantage of language onto an alien shore. They too made Virginia.

Still, the seventeenth century ended auspiciously. The 1688 Glorious Revolution, which exiled James II and brought William and Mary to the throne, greatly benefited Virginia. The new Parliamentary Bill of Rights meant as much or even more to Englishmen in Virginia as to those at home. Early Virginians were proud of their connections with Mother England. "Good families," noted the Reverend Hugh Jones, "live in the same neat manner, dress after the same modes, and behave themselves exactly as the gentry in London." This is the central fact about the cultural pattern that developed in the Old Dominion which was more loyal to the Crown than England herself.

If, as recent writers have stressed, aristocracy was not the actuality in early Virginia, it was certainly the ideal, never fully realized, but eagerly sought after. In that search, rare and fine things were uncovered.

After earlier failures, a college was chartered in 1693 and named for the new monarchs, William and Mary. This institution, with a central building from the office (if not the pen) of Sir Christopher Wren, provided an intellectual focus and a symbol of growing status for the colony. But tobacco continued to foot the bills. All along the shores of the James, the York, and the Rappahannock, the crop thrived. When the Edict of Nantes was revoked in 1685, the first largy body of continental Europeans, French Huguenots, came to add their skill and labor to the common pool. By 1700, twenty-three counties fringed the Chesapeake, with 5,000 taxpayers and a total population of about 70,000.

When in the closing years of the century the Jamestown State House burned, the Assembly moved temporarily to the buildings of the College of William and Mary, at the Middle Plantation. The students worked hard and ate well. School hours ran from seven to eleven o'clock in the morning, and from two to six in the afternoon. The housekeeper had instructions to serve fresh meat as well as salt meat, and "twice a week as well as Sunday, pie and puddings must show themselves on the table." She was also told to see that "Suppers be not as usually made up of different Scraps." Perhaps because the higher, healthier location pleased him, perhaps because Jamestown was soaked with so much bitter memory and blood, Governor Francis Nicholson urged the people to place the new capital at the Middle Plantation, and they did. In honor of King William, the town was named Williamsburg. Up to now it had been only a scattered settlement of houses, but plans were drawn for laying out a suitable capital. Because of the many ravines, Governor Nicholson was not able to lay out the streets in the form of the letters W and M, as he wished. Instead, he favored one wide, splendid thoroughfare, the Duke of Gloucester Street. Though Jamestown was only a few miles away, the seat of authority was moving inland and westward.

With the new capital came new hope. Children growing up in this distant outpost of English civilization were profoundly shaped by the impact of the American experience and landscape. This wild and gigantic continent was a world away from well-ordered, cozy, feudal Europe. This was tense, terrifying country, bathed in searing bright light. All around was land, to be grasped from nature or nature's surrogate, the Indian. All over the land were trees, to be burned and destroyed. Virginians no longer felt like menial servants of hereditary lords, but lords of the American earth in their own right.

Perhaps the greatest achievement of the early years was the creation of the family farm, where men could own land in fee simple; own and till it, live in peace, and enjoy the fruits of their labor.

The settlers wanted an active, not a passive, role in the political and economic destiny. The power they had they intended to exercise. They had got out of the habit of being pushed around. As yet they were not defiant; but they were determined. Their attitudes colored the literature and oratory of the late seventeenth century. An example is the valedictory address made by a young student at the 1699 May Day exercise at the College of William and Mary.

"Methinks," he said, "we see already that happy time when we shall surpass the Asiatician in civility, the Egyptians in geometry, the Phoenicians in arithmetic, and the Chaldeans in astrology. O happy Virginia!"[9]

3 *Eden, in Fact*

THE WHOLE FAMILY PIGG'D LOVINGLY TOGETHER ON THE FLOOR.
William Byrd, Journey to the Land of Eden

Any young Virginian would have been agog.

There were chickens with extra legs, women with three breasts, a baby whose head measured thirty-six inches around, and a horse small enough to fit in a lady's lap. And where was Will Byrd's lady? Not at the Bartholomew Fair, where such monsters might be viewed, but visiting in far-off Ireland. His anguish was both eloquent and literary, as his July 20, 1703, letter in his "Facetia" proves: "The instant your coach drove away, madam, my heart felt as if it had been torn up by the roots, and the rest of my body as if severed limb from limb. . . . Could I at that time have been convinced that the only pleasure I had in the world was leaving me, I had hung upon your coach and had been torn in pieces sooner than have suffered myself to be taken from you!"[1]

Because he was an eighteenth-century gentleman, young Byrd's reason soon returned, and he conveyed to "Facetia" some of the London gossip which always delighted him. Phizinini had said she would marry Sir Christopher—"I cannot but think what greasy doings there will be betwixt them in the dog days." Mrs. Barlow had accepted Lord Guilford—"and the gods alone can tell what will be produced by the conjunction of so much fat and good humour!"

Will Byrd made, as well as conveyed, spicy gossip. Ladies of good and bad repute were his downfall. He met them in London's bagnios, picked them up on the streets, or chased them in St. James's Park. Notoriously promiscuous, he was not above taking to the grass with a *fille de joie* whom he had picked up on the street. All of these matters he recorded meticulously in his diary.[2] Sent over from Virginia when he was seven, Byrd made several trips back and forth before settling in London as colonial agent, so that he became quite at home in England. "Facetia" must have thought he could out-British the British.

In January, 1705 a letter arrived from Virginia with news that changed everything. His father, William Byrd I, was dead. Young Will's carefree days were over.

For a generation his father had been one of the most influential and respected people in America. Coming to Virginia as an English youth, the senior Byrd had inherited considerable land on both sides of the James from his Uncle Stegg. Marrying Warham Horsemanden, a Royalist refugee, had further enhanced his position. Hard-working, capable, affluent, he was known as "Captain Byrd" in his early twenties. Hot-blooded, too, he joined Bacon's rebels, withdrawing just in time to escape disaster. His son and namesake was born in 1674. Moving up from the House of Burgesses to the Council of State and Auditor Generalship, the elder Byrd was the colony's leading Indian authority. He went to Albany to sign the 1685 treaty with the Iroquois. As his ventures in land, fur, and slaves prospered, his reputation flourished, and he was elected president of the Council of State. Death came suddenly in his early fifties.

Consequently young Will Byrd came home to take over. Sturdily built, he had deep-seated eyes, a broad forehead, and a large nose. His mind was rapierlike, his curiosity limitless. Explorer, church-man, *bon vivant*, linguist, scientist, William Byrd II saw and thought as much as any American who died before the Revolution.

Young Will convinced his neighbors to send him to the House of Burgesses. Next he persuaded beautiful, fiery Lucy Parke to marry him. She was the daughter of the gallant rake Daniel Parke, who fought with Marlborough on the Continent and brought the news of the victory at Blenheim to Queen Anne. Daniel Parke's daughter inherited some of her father's temperament, and there were many family quarrels in the Byrd household. Byrd seemed rather proud of his victories at such times, as this diary entry for February 5, 1711, indicates: "My wife and I quarrelled about her pulling her brows.

She threatened she would not go to Williamsburg if she might not pull them; I refused, however, and got the better of her and maintained my authority . . ."

Trips to Williamsburg were a necessary part of his life, since Byrd was elevated to the Council of Virginia in 1708—a job which marked the epitome of political and social prominence. Still in his early thirties, William Byrd had definitely arrived.

During most of his adult life he kept a shorthand diary of his daily routine, recording in detail all the facts and actions. Portions covering the years 1709 to 1721, never intended for any eyes but his, make one of the most fascinating documents in Virginia history. As we go through the entries of the Old Dominion's Pepys, we realize what a remarkable person Byrd was—a witty, urbane aristocrat equally at home in English drawing rooms, coffeehouses, Virginia's Council of State, or various assorted boudoirs. A single diary entry, such as this one for November 2, 1709, shows us a planter, and a plantation, far removed from the stereotype featured in standard history books and novels:

I rose at 6 o'clock and read a chapter in Hebrew and some Greek in Lucian. I said my prayers and ate milk for breakfast, and settled some accounts, and then went to court where we made an end of the business. We went to dinner about 4 o'clock and I ate boiled beef again. In the evening I went to Dr. B-r-t's, where my wife came this afternoon. Here I found Mrs. Chriswell, my sister Custis, and other ladies. We sat and talked till about 11 o'clock, and then retired to our chambers. I played at (r-m) with Mrs. Chriswell and kissed her on the bed till she was angry and my wife also was uneasy about it, and cried as soon as the company was gone. I neglected to say my prayers, which I should not have done, because I ought to beg pardon for the lust I had for another man's wife. However, I had good health, good thoughts, and good humor, thanks be to God Almighty.

He found time for more serious undertakings, such as building Westover, one of the colony's finest homes. Byrd and his neighbors strove for no new architectural theory. They copied the English, who borrowed from an Italian Renaissance which modeled itself on Rome and Greece. Georgian manor houses were fourth-hand copies which would have disturbed Plato in his quest for reality. But then, it was on Wren, not Plato, that a gentleman depended for a house plan.

Christopher Wren was one of the few people who profited from London's Great Fire of 1666. His program for the reconstructed city was an impressive example of Renaissance city planning. His designs for fifty London churches virtually reconstructed English Protestant architecture. Wren's dignified symmetrical creations set new patterns. "Skilled masons and carpenters," Hugh Morrison tells us, "building smaller manors and country houses, learned enough from Wren's example to endow their modest buildings with a singular grace of form and detail."[3] So overpowering was his influence that Wren became the leading architectural influence on British America.

It is not so remarkable that the ambitious young Byrd wanted so fine a place as that he got it. Triumphant architectural solutions never come quickly or easily. Only first-rate minds can conjure up first-rate houses. As early as April 17, 1709, William Byrd noted in his diary that his men were making brick. Five years later, stonecutters from Williamsburg were working on the library chimney. Planning and building took years. There were interruptions, delays, faulty shipments. When skill was lacking, men had to be trained. Finally, on what had been uninhabited river land, Westover appeared.

Generations have not changed it much. The house grows out of a little rise a hundred yards from the broad James, a masterpiece of symmetry, proportion, and dignity. The north and south faces are almost identical. The beautiful doorways are derived from William Salmon's *Palladio Londinensis,* just published when Byrd obtained a copy. Craftsmanship throughout is of the highest order; gates and mantelpieces are notable. Westover is as English as can be: or perhaps, because of the quality of the local materials and the landscape, more aesthetically satisfying than the English.

Like most Georgian buildings, Westover was planned from the outside in. Still the interior comes off very well too. The main hallway, eighteen feet wide and off center, goes the full depth of the house. Near the end is a stairway with three runs and a balustrade of richly turned mahogany. The handsomely paneled walls of the downstairs rooms support gilded ceilings. Though less ornate, upstairs rooms are also beautiful. Underneath the house is another series of rooms, converging at the subterranean passage leading to the river. Two underground chambers, built as hiding places, are reached through a dry well. William Byrd, who took no fancy to being dry, kept them well stocked with good claret and Madeira.

In the rear, neat and detached, are the other necessary structures—overseer's and secretary's rooms, offices, smokehouse, kitchen, servants' rooms, stables. To the northwest is the formal two-acre garden.

Here grew iris, crocus, and anemone; thyme, marjoram, and phlox; roses, larkspur, and jasmine. "Colonel Byrd, in his garden, which is the finest in that country, has a summerhouse set round with Indian honeysuckles. All the summer it is continually full of sweet flowers, in which hummingbirds delight exceedingly," wrote Robert Beverley.

Visitors came to talk, to admire, to stroll. There was no such thing as an intruder at the plantations. The doors were always open. "Even if one is willing to pay," noted a Swiss traveler, Francis Louis Michel, "they do not accept anything, but are rather angry, asking whether one did not know of the custom of the country." At Westover one might find the Carters from Shirley, the Lees from Stratford, the Harrisons from Randolph, Spotswood from Germanna—even that confirmed woman-hater, John Custis, from Arlington.

Any account of Virginia should contain a short tribute to Custis' irascible memory. While others left immortal lines about life and liberty and freedom which ring in our ears, he bequeathed us words that warm henpecked hearts. With his highhanded lady he got on monstrous poorly. For whole weeks they refused to speak to each other. When they did, it was worth noting.

Once, in his anger, Custis turned and drove his carriage into the Chesapeake Bay. When his lady asked him where he was going, he shouted, "To Hell, Madam." "Drive on," she said imperiously. "Any place is better than Arlington!" In his study he composed his own epitaph, which his son executed on pain of being disowned:

> Beneath this Marble Tomb lies the Body
> of the Hon. John Custis, Esq.
> Age 71 years, and yet lived but seven years,
>   which was the space of time he kept
>   a bachelor's home at Arlington
>   on the Eastern Shore of Virginia.

Surely John Custis, had there been more room, would also have praised his visits to Westover to enjoy the dining, dancing, conversing, gossiping, and fox hunting. While there he may even have enjoyed a little game of chance; gambling was popular, even among children. Young Sally Fairfax was so expert at checks (a game played with peach seeds) that she defeated her own mother. This explains the entry Sally wrote in her diary for January 6, 1772: "There came a woman and a girl today. Mama bought 3 old hens from them, and gave them to me. That reduced her debt she owed me, which was 5 and nine pence, to 3 and nine pence."[4]

There were balls, fairs, parlor games, fish feasts, and barbecues. Even christenings sometimes brought on a week-long celebration. Here, as a matter of demonstrable fact, was the basis of the later legendary "Virginia hospitality," founded not so much upon the desire to imitate the European gentry as upon the social needs of isolated groups.

This hospitality should not be equated with frivolity or dalliance. Entertaining friends was seldom the chief item in the daily life of William Byrd. As soon as he awoke he read Latin, Greek, or Hebrew before breakfast. Books were not hard to come by at Westover; there were over 3,600 volumes in his library, dealing with theology, philosophy, drama, poetry, law, and science.[5] There was a librarian, the amusing Mr. Proctor, to care for them. Almost every line William Byrd wrote proved his intimate knowledge of the works of distinguished thinkers and writers of the past.

Nor was all the talk about London scandal and hairdos. Great political and military decisions were made in plantation drawing rooms. The vigor and brilliance of the age are in part an outgrowth of its conversation. Talk, talk, talk, far into the night—it sharpened wits, punctured arguments, and clinched decisions. America talked her way into a Revolution and independent nationhood. Much of that talk originated in Virginia. It hasn't yet entirely gone out of fashion.

Some phrases, especially in the taverns, groggeries, and ordinaries, "which were the poor man's Bacchanalian Mansions," were not very nice. In these places of crude conviviality, rum, toddy, flip, and oaths abounded. Jonathan Boucher commented on "the forward intrusion which subjects you to hear obscene Conceits and broad Expression; and from this, there are times when no sex, Rank, or Conduct can exempt you."

Men and women quarreled publicly, and scandal was never hard to come by. "The noblest ornaments of society were sometimes drunk in public," Louis Wright informs us.[6] Mrs. James Blair, wife of the highest-ranking official of the Church of England, was habitually tipsy. Daniel Parke threatened to drag her bodily from the Bruton Parish Church, both because of her gossip and of her husband's charge that Parke had committed adultery. There are aspects of the real Williamsburg's past which are not stressed by the restoration guides.

William Byrd had no grounds for complaints about his neighbors' conduct. He was no model for a Sunday-school class. On October 4, 1718, for example, he called upon a certain Mrs. A-l-n. Finding her absent, he seduced the maid. Eventually Mrs. A-l-n came home; Byrd completed the evening by seducing her. Not quite; for after that he went home and ate a plum cake.

Despite these earthy failings, the society prospered. Although they were not aware of characteristic twentieth-century clichés like "group dynamics" and "sense of community," the colonials exemplified them. They were constantly visiting, refuting, and assisting one another. Tidewater was governed by a system of benevolent paternalism. There was so much intermarriage among the leading families that a sort of Shintoism inevitably resulted. The essential jobs—sheriff, justice of the peace, vestryman, colonel of the militia, member of the House Council—stayed in the family. Whether attained through birth, friendship, or marriage, the support of the gentry was the way to social and political advancement.[7] With it, a candidate had no trouble succeeding.

All this being perfectly understood by those in power, successful marriages were much sought after. That both Washington and Jefferson married rich widows is a significant fact. Ambitious young men usually found they could love a rich girl more than a poor one. Newspaper accounts were honest to the point of impropriety where marriages were concerned. One reads, for example, that handsome twenty-three-year-old William Carter married Madam Sarah Ellson, widow of eighty-five, and "a sprightly old Tit, with three thousand pounds fortune."

Wherever property went, the aristocratic pattern and the Georgian façades which could transform it into reality followed close behind. The manor houses are the unquestionable proof. Stratford (H-shaped and commanding) and Rosewell (with its mahogany balustrade from San Domingo) had been completed before Westover. Then came Gunston Hall, with cut-stone quoins and coziness; Brandon, with chaste cornices and stern beauty; Sabine Hall, named for and reminiscent of Horace's villa at Tivoli; Mount Airy, with white facings on red sandstone; Kenmore, with a mantle representing Aesop's fox-and-crow fable; and Shirley, a compact, inviting château. Carter's Grove, Berkeley, Cleve, Mount Vernon had special distinctions and beauty.[8] Pacatone, on the Yeocomico, had its own ghosts and was famous for the midnight groans, flashes, and shrieks.

But the place we seem to know best is Nomini Hall, built in Westmoreland County about 1730 by Robert Carter II. He was the son of "King" Carter, who owned 1,000 slaves, oversaw 300,000 acres, and ordered his Episcopal minister to pray for rain. Nonconformists to the marrow, the Carters often did the unpredictable. Robert Carter III not only demanded that the Episcopal chapel make way for a Baptist church; he later deserted the Baptists, and became a Swedenborgian.

Not to a Carter, but to a Yankee tutor, is the historian most indebted. Philip Fithian came to Nomini Hall to educate the second Robert Carter's children and left a fascinating diary. It tells about the life and work of colonial Virginia; the parties and politics, food and clothes, courtships and stolen kisses. Through the eyes of this young Princeton graduate, the plantation comes alive again.

Fithian tells us just how Nomini Hall was laid out. The elegant main house was seventy-six feet long, forty-four feet wide, and two stories high. One hundred yards from each corner were four matching buildings: the schoolhouse, the laundry, the stable, and the coach house. Outside the square formed by the four corner houses was a row of poplar trees, forming an avenue fifty feet wide which led to Williamsburg. Such symmetry was indicative of the thinking of the age. The Great House was the focal point of a culture; everything moved around it in orderly fashion.

We would like to peer inside and see just how the tight little world which was Nomini Hall functioned; but if we did so, our story would never move beyond 1800. There are Virginians who would ask, "And would that be so bad?" For many of them have attempted to live on in the eighteenth century, despite history's urging them on into the present. Herein lies the charm, and the tragedy, of their lives.

Yet no one should underestimate that half of Virginia history which belongs to colonial days. Excelling in agriculture and politics, it produced a unique rural aristocracy, men of intellect rather than intellectuals. Though unchallenged by industrialism and an ambitious bourgeoisie, and given to an idyllic pose, it was a hardworking society. Leisure was a myth, endless work was a reality, for both the men and the ladies.[9] They were working against time, half realizing that their plantation world would fade as quickly as it had flourished.

By the very nature of things, theirs was not a society that would produce the intellectual ferment and artistic achievement generated by urban conditions. The plantations were long on tobacco and short on intellectual stimulation. Byrd in his day, and Jefferson in his, were the exception rather than the rule. For each of them, as an eighteenth-century European visitor noted, there were dozens of gentlemen by whom "the ingenuity of a Locke or the discoveries of a Newton were considered as infinitely inferior to the accomplishments of him who knew when to shoulder a blind cock or to start a fleet horse."[10]

Wealth, status, and privilege were the Chesapeake trinity, and it was a case of three in one. Wealth guaranteed status; status conveyed privilege; and privilege insured wealth.

Though the wealth sprang largely from tobacco, it came eventually from other sources too: wheat, lumber, iron, shipbuilding, trade. Gentlemen learned to combine various activities. Carter Braxton, for example, varied his agrarian interests with the convict and slave traffic. Land speculation was widely practiced.

All this prosperity rested on the enormous success of chattel slavery, an institution which practically destroyed the yeomanry and altered Virginia from a place of independent white laborers to a community of unpaid colored servants. Negroes made up only 9 per cent of the population in 1700. This jumped to 25 per cent in 1715 and 40 per cent in 1750. The flowering of eighteenth-century Virginia was based on Negro labor.[11] The white yeomen perished, scrambled up the economic ladder, or pushed on west and south to the frontier.

What sort of life awaited them there? William Byrd was a man who wanted to find out for himself; and that is just what he did. His chance came in 1727, when on his fifty-third birthday George II appointed him one of the Virginia commissioners to survey the long-disputed Virginia-North Carolina boundary. Hard up for cash, Byrd eagerly joined Richard Fitzwilliam and William Dandridge in the task. He insisted on taking along a chaplain, because "there are many Gentiles on your frontier who never had an opportunity of being baptized." In the next spring the Virginia party met the Carolina commissioners. The group, to which various laborers and surveyors were added, had its initial tiff over where to start. Finally they were under way.

The survey was, to say the least, remarkable. No summary is as interesting as Byrd's own *History of the Dividing Line,* the culmination of his thirty-year apprenticeship to the most able English prose masters of his day.[12] For days humor and tragedy vied with each other for supremacy. Indians stole their food. The rain drenched everything and everybody, causing Byrd to swear like a trooper in His Majesty's guards. Quarrels developed between the commissioners.

To mend the rifts, Byrd arranged a party around a cheerful bowl. In the gaiety of their hearts, these eighteenth-century Rover Boys invited a tallow-faced country wench who had sprained her wrist to visit them. That was safe enough. They offered her drink "to raise her in good humor." That was dangerous. Byrd told what followed in two pithy lines: "They examined all her hidden charms and played a great many pranks. The poor damsel was disabled from making any resistance by the lameness of her hand." On a half dozen occasions, the violence offered to women was of such bizarre circumstances that Byrd recorded it; how many females fell unheralded, we know not. Before they had finished their journey, little virginal seems to have been left except the pine trees.

The survey progressed well enough until the adventurers reached the Dismal Swamp. Byrd took a quick look, saw why turkey buzzards preferred to fly around it, and decided what to do. He made a speech.

"Gentlemen," he said solemnly, "we are at last arrived at this dreadful place, which until now has been thought impassable." The surveyors and laborers looked. Byrd does not say, but probably no one was laughing now. "I make no doubt that you will convince everybody that there is no difficulty which may not be conquered by spirit and constancy. The only reason I don't share in your fatigue is the fear of adding to your burdens (which are but too heavy already) while I am sure I can add nothing to your resolution. I shall say no more but only pray the Almighty to prosper your undertaking and grant we may meet on the other side in perfect health and safety."

As his men plunged into the mucky water, he thought of one further concession. He promised to have the chaplain give them a place in the litany. The chaplain (who also chose the longer, drier route at this point) did better than that; he even "rubbed up" his gentlemen swamp-evaders "with a seasonable sermon."

In addition to swamps, the other commissioners got in Colonel Byrd's way. Fitzwilliam in particular (Byrd preferred to call him "Firebrand") riled both Byrd and Dandridge. At one critical juncture Firebrand became so annoyed that he picked up a table leg "big enough to knock down an ox," and prepared to drive Dandridge into the ground. Byrd, seeing that just now words would not help, leaped across the table, seized Fitzwilliam's arm, and barely stopped the blow.

A Carolina commissioner also rushed forward, but later than Byrd. He fell under the table Byrd upset, to the great hazard of his gouty limbs. Finally poor Dandridge realized what was happening. He thereupon saluted Fitzwilliam with a long line of titles, the most acceptable of which was "son of a whore."

Provocative as this and other Byrd treks were, we are not so much interested in the survey as in the people and conditions he met on the eighteenth-century frontier. On both this trip and a later one to survey 20,000 acres of Roanoke River bottomland, Byrd kept careful notes. His new property Byrd called the Land of Eden —perhaps because he hoped to attract immigrants to the garden spot, perhaps because Governor Eden administered Carolina at this time. For history, the best thing about it all was that it made possible the delightful account of *A Journey to Eden*.

As to the land and people between the James and the Roanoke rivers, Byrd is as blunt as can be. They were the lubbers, the thickskulls, the common buckskins. Many of the indolent males "lye abed and Snore, till the Sun has run one third of his course." Finally, having arisen and lit their pipes, they venture out under the protection of a cloud of smoke. If the weather is just right, they may even consider going out and working in the fields; but after due consideration, they generally give up the idea. "Thus they loiter away their Lives, like Solomon's Sluggard, with their Arms across, and at the winding up of the Year Scarcely have Bread to Eat. It approaches nearer to the description of Lubberland than any other," he says. The back-country people with their custard complexions are even too lazy to pick fruit off trees. They cut them down to make one harvest for all. Because they allow their cattle and swine to roam at will, "these indolent wretches during one half of the year lose the advantage of the milk of their cattle, as well as their dung, and many of the poor creatures by this ill management perish in the mire into the bargain."

So much for their diet. Of morals it would seem they had none. The surveyors had hardly begun their boundary line when they met a man who called himself a hermit—"though he forfeited that name by suffering a wanton female to cohabit with him." He ate by sending his female companion out to gather oysters from adjacent rocks, or by driving up the neighbor's cows "to moisten their mouths with a little milk." Clothes were less of a problem than food. The hermit depended mostly upon his long beard, and she upon her unkempt hair, "part of which she brought decently forward. The rest dangled behind quite down to the rump, like one of Herodotus's east Indian pigmies." Here was the real frontier, very different from the romantic idealization to be celebrated in later American mythology. The "natural men" were "wretches living in a dirty state of nature"; they were mere Adamites, "innocence only excepted." Byrd's 1733 journey to the Land of Eden fully confirmed his low opinion of his pork-eating, immoral neighbors in Lubberland. He found that "ten or a dozen people are forced to pig together in a room" and endure the squalling of peevish dirty children. The ill-fed whites broke out "into insolent and passionate expressions against the poor negroes." The dirt, the sloth, and the smells appalled him. This was the land of Eden.

Byrd mentions casually having performed an act which might have been the most significant one of his life. On September 19, 1733, having completed talks with his overseer at the falls of the James, Byrd decided to "lay out the foundation of two large cities; one at Shacco's, to be called Richmond, and the other at the point of the Appomattuck River, to be called Petersburg." The first of these projected cities, known in his father's day as "world's end," would become the capital of Virginia and the Confederacy.

Byrd could not foresee this, or surmise that a child already trying out his infant lungs on a Northern Neck plantation would grow up to lead a Revolution against Mother England. (The Washingtons were a cut below the Byrds.)

Obviously he could not have conceived of a later, larger fall-line city, named after Washington, which would be the capital of a transcontinental nation; or that Richmond and Washington would be contending capitals in a divided nation.

Eden seemed to hold his destiny. His idea was to develop and populate the vast empty area. Somehow he was never able to throw off his debts—those of his father-in-law, his family, his plantation. For years he struggled to satisfy London creditors such as Micajah Perry, known in his diary as "grasping old Mr. Perry." Desperately he set about to lure European immigrants to his unprofitable acres. To entice Swiss colonists to Eden, he assured them that the water was "as clear as crystal and as sweet as milk." A shipload set out from Europe in 1738, but was wrecked on the Carolina coast. In desperation, Byrd tried to persuade a band of Scotch-Irish to come down from Pennsylvania. Neither they nor the Germans would agree. He died with almost 180,000 acres of land to his name, wealthy in learning and grace; "but not very far short of poor," Richmond Beatty says, "in that substance which Americans had come, already, to value most."[13]

To think of Westover as an economic burden and Byrd as a failure violates our sense of poetic justice. We do not want to think of it as a place of debt and frustration, but as one of happy people, honeysuckle, and golden crops. The people and the honeysuckle were there, but so was the handwriting on the wall. Even during Byrd's lifetime, the colony's agrarian economy was decaying. In truth, though not by general admission, there was little prospect of recovery.

Nothing of quality was manufactured in eighteenth-century Virginia for general sale [Douglas Southall Freeman has pointed out]. Conditions had not greatly changed after that time of economic mockery, about 1691, when the first William Byrd, a large exporter of leaf, repeatedly directed his London agent to send him a box of smoking tobacco.

Virginians of 1750 accepted their economic disadvantage as a matter of course. They were born to it; they blindly believed they would overcome it as the Colony developed; they regarded compliance as part of their duty to a King among whose "most zealous" subjects they counted themselves.[14]

Available figures from Byrd's plantation and many others bear out Freeman's claims. In 1791, British merchants submitted claims for some £4 million against Southern planters, £2,505,000 of which were against Virginians.

Rather than view the planters as debtors, men caught in an economic dilemma, we prefer to see them as they saw themselves: proud, self-sufficient, blessed. "Like one of the Patriarchs, I have my Flocks and my Herds, my Bond-men and Bond-women, and every sort of trade and skill amongst my own Servants," William Byrd wrote an English friend. "I live in a kind of Independence of every one but Providence."

Thus did he help spread a legend which his own writings and life had specifically disproved. Probably he never thought much on the paradox. This eclectic virtuoso, like so many Virginians who followed him, refused to bow down to the tyranny of facts.

He did, however, continue to do the bizarre and unexpected. "I had my father's grave opened to see him," Byrd confides in his secret diary. "But he was so wasted there was not one thing to be distinguished. I ate fish for dinner."

4 *The Lonesome Valley*

AND STEPPING WESTWARD SEEMED TO BE
A KIND OF HEAVENLY DESTINY.—*William Wordsworth*

What a shame that the spectators consisted largely of reptiles and black bears. There the Governor stood, a-tiptoe on the crest of the Blue Ridge, his peacock plume poking a hole in the sky, his green velvet cape flapping in the fall breeze, his Russian leather boots and his eyes sparkling.

September 7, 1716. Governor Alexander Spotswood, knowing full well this was a memorable day, fondled it tenderly as it passed. By claiming this magnificent valley which the Indians called Shenandoah, the English would sever communications between French outposts to the north and those along the Mississippi. Just west of the mountains ahead lay the Great Lakes and destiny.

As sparkling as lake water was, this occasion conjured up stronger stuff. "Gentlemen," said the Governor, "let us drink a toast to King George!"

On this "for men only" outing, toasts were easily come by. Though the Williamsburg gentry involved complained of stiffness in their bones "because they had not had good beds to lie on," and had a close call with a bear, they could take consolation in the knowledge that they would not suffer from thirst. Lieutenant John Fontaine, a young Huguenot who had joined the British army and attached himself to Spotswood, listed the following provisions: "several sorts of liquor, viz: Virginia red wine and white wine, Irish usquebaugh, brandy, shrub, two sorts of rum, champagne, canary, cherry punch, cider, etc. etc." The gentlemen explorers were seemingly prepared to float the Shenandoah Valley into the British Empire.

The grand manner came naturally to Spotswood. In an age of dazzling individuals, he had won early distinction as a British officer. He had been "dangerously wounded" at Blenheim. What attracted attention was not his wound, but the fact that instead of having it treated, he rushed off to retrieve the offending cannon ball as a souvenir. For this, and other plucky feats, he was at the age of twenty-eight made a quartermaster general by Marlborough. Politically ambitious, Spotswood came to Virginia in 1710 as royal Governor. As his Council soon discovered, he could and did "swear like our army in Flanders," set up iron works, import artisans, and plot to move the Union Jack westward. He was proficient with the pen, the sword, and the flask. September 6, 1716, was definitely a day for the flask.

Champagne corks popped merrily atop the Great Blue Ridge. Fitting ceremonies were held on the peaks, one of which was named Mt. George and another Mt. Spotswood, and there was a feast of wild deer, turkey, currants, cucumbers, and grapes. The last-named item apparently set off a chain reaction which extended back to the vineyards of the Old World. After the meal, Lieutenant Fontaine tells us in his diary, "we drank the King's health in champagne, and fired a volley; the Princess in Burgundy, and fired a volley; all the rest in claret, and fired a volley. We drank the Governor's health, and fired yet another volley." By this time the valley was dancing.

On the hazy horizon a river meandered through the tall grass. To the well-plied Governor it seemed so grand a stream that he promptly named it the Euphrates. (At a later and soberer moment, the name was changed to Shenandoah.) Utilizing one of the innumerable empty bottles, Spotswood buried a paper on which was written the claim that this place was now in the possession of King George I of England. After centuries of service as an international hunting ground for Delaware, Catawba, and Shawnee Indians, the valley was to become an outpost for white Europeans.

Back in Williamsburg, Alexander Spotswood had miniature gold horseshoes made for his jolly companions. On them was inscribed "Sic Juvat Transcendere Montes." The Knights of the Golden

Horseshoe had cast a golden glow over the Valley which it would never lose.

Spotswood was not the first white man to see the Shenandoah—but he ought to have been, at least so far as popular fancy is concerned; and so, in a poetic sense, he was. Prosaic histories record that as early as 1654 Colonel Abraham Wood (who named the New River) crossed the mountains further south, as did Captain Henry Batts in 1671. They tell that the adventurous German John Lederer made three such expeditions in 1669. "A modest ingenuous person and a pretty scholar," in Sir William Talbott's words, Lederer prepared a map and account of his adventures in Latin, both of which were published in London in 1672.[1] Frenchman Louis Michelle approached the Valley from the north in 1707. There may have been others who preceded Spotswood in 1716; none, certainly, made the trip with the inimitable flourish of the Golden Knights.

Fine plumes and velvet were not standard equipment for the German and Scotch-Irish pioneers who followed in the eighteenth century. Long rifles and scalping knives were more functional. These small farmers, owning no slaves, hated the highhanded Tidewater slaveholders. They were, as Frederick Jackson Turner first pointed out, essentially Westerners, with the traditional frontier hostility to the East. The reason they would play such a small part in the Virginia tradition was that the planters who perpetuated traditions, passed laws, and wrote histories would accord them no larger one.

Indians, incensed by the invasion of their best hunting ground, fought the oncoming settlers with a peculiar ferocity, as men like George Painter found out. They raided his house near Woodstock. When he tried to escape, he was shot and his bloody body dragged back into the house, which was then set on fire. The rest of the family, and several neighbors who had sought refuge in the cellar, came out and surrendered. Four babies were hanged on trees, riddled with rifle shots, and left dangling in the wind. A stable full of sheep and cows was burned, and all the animals roasted. The remaining whites were forced to march to an Indian village beyond the Allegheny Mountains. One of the prisoners was Jacob Fisher, a plump German lad of twelve. The Indians forced him to collect a pile of faggots. These were ignited, and the boy was goaded with sharp sticks until he ran through the flames again and again. After the braves had tired of the goading, the squaws took over. Hours later, while his family watched helplessly, the screams stopped.

Bleeding from a hundred wounds, Jacob Fisher found relief in death. No wonder, when the white men were able to revenge such atrocities, they answered in kind and fed their dogs on Indian flesh.

Those who mastered the Valley were strong and resourceful. Men like Jost Hite, allegedly a baron from Alsace who sailed his own schooner over from Germany. At first he lived in a log cabin, but he soon set to work to build the first stone home in the Valley, five miles southwest of the site of Winchester. Although Governor Gooch confirmed his 100,000-acre grant, the courts ruled against it. Jost Hite didn't budge. Then Lord Fairfax, who owned most of the Northern Neck, told him to give way. Jost Hite didn't budge. Instead he plowed more fields, planted more corn, and said more prayers. He slept on a feather bed, ate sauerkraut, and kept his stock indoors all winter. When he had lived his life out, he died on his own Virginia soil and was buried in it.

Men like John Lewis, who came to Virginia from Ireland with a price on his head, having killed his landlord, Lord Clonmithgairn, in an argument over rents. He came over the Blue Ridge with thirty faithful tenants and founded Staunton in 1732. They set their rude cabins in thick grass that unrolled like gaudy carpeting. It was the best grass they had ever seen. Snowdrop, the white cow, waddled in every evening, her legs stained crimson by wild strawberries. Even the Indians, who came by full-painted, looked like fragments of rainbows or mountebanks at the Irish county fairs. There were many bad moments, but even more good ones, in John Lewis's life. Then there was the epitaph, which summed the whole thing up:

> HERE LIES THE REMAINS OF JOHN LEWIS
> WHO SLEW THE IRISH LORD
> SETTLED IN AUGUSTA COUNTY
> LOCATED THE TOWN OF STAUNTON
> AND FURNISHED FIVE SONS TO FIGHT THE BATTLES OF
> THE AMERICAN REVOLUTION

Women like Isabel Stockton, Hannah Dennis, Mary Moore, or "Mad Ann" Baily, who could "hew with an ax as good as airy man." Born Ann Hennis in Liverpool, England, Mad Ann came to Virginia in 1750 as an indentured servant. Her husband, James Trotter, was still a boy when the Indians scalped him at the battle of Point Pleasant. After the news came, Ann left her only child, William, with a neighbor, dressed in buckskins, carried a tomahawk, and hunted Indians. She found them, and began her scalp collection.

When John Baily turned up, she took time off to marry him. All the dowry she could supply was a horse, bridle and saddle, and covers enough to keep a bed warm. Soon she went back to scalping Indians.

Mad Ann's finest moment came when the Redskins laid siege to Fort Lee, a stockade outpost near present-day Charleston, West Virginia. She slipped out during the night, rode to Fort Union (near Lewisburg), and returned with enough powder to turn the contest. Not many men could have done it; none who were there even dared try. What men did do was erect a monument to her memory, on top of Hot Springs Mountain. It still stands.

Most of the settlers came down the Great Warriors Trace, used by the Iroquois coming South, and running between the Blue Ridge and the Alleghenies; others followed the Occaneechee Trace from Tidewater. The principal center of Indian trade for some time was Occaneechee Island, lying at the point where the Staunton and Dan rivers join to form the Roanoke River. From the Indians the white men learned the word Shenandoah—"Daughter of the Stars." This was the place where the Great Spirit brought the stars together to sing for joy. While they were singing one night, the Indians told in awed voices, a great rock in the mountain wall split and fell asunder. The water of the beautiful lake poured out and rushed toward the sea. The moon and stars fled away. Whenever they thought of the beautiful blue lake, they spoke in whispers.

A thousand years later the stars were again looking for a place to gather and sing. They went back to the blue mountains where they had cast their robe of light in ages past, and found the land even more beautiful than the water had been. The Great Spirit had caused a spring of water to gush out and feed the beautiful Shenandoah River. Flowers sprang up to fill the valley with their fragrance.

The white men who wrested Shenandoah from the Indians were mainly of two ethnic groups—Germans and Scotch-Irish. In the former were Palatinate Germans, Mennonites, Lutherans, and Quakers, seeking religious freedom in the New World. Coming first to Pennsylvania, they were captivated by stories of the rich "Cenantua Valley," and set out to find it. Short on material goods, they were long on faith. Temporary hardships would lead to permanent joy. "There is no man that hath left house, or brethren, or sisters, or father, or mother, or wife, or children, or lands, for my sake and the gospel's, but he shall receive an hundredfold now in this time, houses, and brethren, and sisters, and mothers, and children, and lands, with persecutions; and in the world to come eternal life."[2]

And so there was little talk of Golden Horseshoes and fancy clothing among the people in the northern half of the Shenandoah Valley. The men wore homespun clothes and shoes of coarse leather; the women, petticoats, "shortgowns," and tight calico caps, except in summer when their feet, hands, and arms were bare. Fine mowers and reapers, they worked in the grain fields alongside their men, taking their turn at the heavy labor. They hoed and plowed and sweated. Their descendants would keep house in the homes they raised on clearings carved from the forest.

"Switzer" barns were usually the finest buildings on the farms. The Germans took excellent care of their stock, housing even the pigs in winter. Hay was plentiful, so the animals emerged from the cold months in fine health. In every season the work day began before sunup. At so early an hour barefoot lads looked for a way to warm their feet. The solution was to move one of the sleepy cows and step quickly on the spot where she had lain. In a few minutes cold toes would be thawed out. Work ended at dusk.

Valley life was isolated and isolating. Mountain barriers blocked the way to the sea, and settlements were few and far between. German newspapers appeared at Winchester, New Market, Harrisonburg, and Staunton. At Singer's Glen, the first Mennonite press in America was established. There were no plantations, in the Tidewater sense of the word. For all practical purposes, this was a different world from that on the other side of the mountain.

The Scotch-Irish, who moved on south of the German settlements, were as rugged a lot as ever took the open road. They had such a fear of God in their hearts that it left no room for fear of man. They got used to being not wanted. When they were shoved out of Dundee, they went to Ulster. Unwilling to bow to the authorities there, they picked up and came to the New World. Many of them came to Pennsylvania, where most of the good land was taken. So they kept moving, down to the Valley, big and fertile and nearly empty. They kept moving, the McDowells, Alexanders, Campbells, Douglases, McCorkles, a brave, iron-veined people, beyond what would become Shenandoah, Rockingham, and Frederick counties, into Augusta, Rockbridge, and Botetourt.

Rye, oats, corn, and wheat were their chief crops. A few raised cattle and drove them to market in Winchester or Philadelphia.

Perhaps we should call them America's first cowboys. As early as 1767 we find in the *Augusta Judgments* a complaint by a farmer whose crops were overrun by the migrating tribe of William Crow. "Crow's drove," the enraged farmer reported, "increased damnable."

The Ulsterman's God was not a creature of sweetness and light, but a strong, full-blown, sinewy Overlord. Those who believed in him could stand the wear and tear of pioneering; the spirits of Calvin and Knox stalked the land.

Wolves were still howling on the ridges, and Indians stalking down the trails, when they erected their first houses of worship—simple, severe, prayer-filled buildings that could serve as forts in emergencies.

Reformation men, they were not free from all medieval superstition. Oak timber was cut at one phase of the zodiac, pine at another. Hex signs were drawn on barns, and scrollwork on documents. Each month had its "up-going" and "down-going" period. Crops that yielded their harvest were planted in the former but potatoes in the latter period. Shingles were nailed on roofs in the down-going; otherwise the roof might blow off. Every day, prayers had to go up if men were not to go down.

As early as 1738 they petitioned John Caldwell at the Presbyterian Synod in Philadelphia to "procure the favor and countenance of the Government" in religious matters. They also looked to Pennsylvania and Tidewater for occasional "supply ministers." The Reverend John Blair visited Shenandoah country in 1745. While there, he preached the Gospel with all his might and organized the congregations of North Mountain, New Providence, and Forks-of-James.[3] Families read the Bible all the way through every year. Sabbath services began in the forenoon and lasted until evening, with time out for dinner. Most of the sermons sprang from Calvin or Knox. "Speak to sad hearts, you will find them everywhere," was the guiding principle. Their minds, as well as their bodies, tended to harden up in this environment. "Dear God," began one of their prayers, "set our feet in the right way. For if we start in the wrong way, there can be no changing."

Having asked God to give them their daily bread, these Valley men set out to help Him by building grist mills. The landscape suggested it. Fast-flowing streams were everywhere, wood and limestone were plentiful for construction, and every family needed ground grain. The Valley's first communal structures, except for churches, were mills. Many of them stand today, just as they were erected, with not one stone out of place.

Building a mill took weeks or even months of labor. No machinery or standardized parts were available, only human strength and ingenuity. Except for a few parts the blacksmith might forge, everything had to be made from wood and stone. This is how they did it.

A good site was found, and a building writ got from the court. (For a while nobody bothered about writs.) Limestone foundation walls were erected, topped by a log, or perhaps a stone, superstructure. Then it was time to call in the neighbors. Everybody who could came, men, women, and children, with axes, saws, augurs, and ready muscles. The men, working in teams, hoisted the huge logs into place as the leader shouted:

"See that ye carry your corners up plumb. I couldn't stand to see 'em leaning over whopper-jawed. Easy, now. Shake it back, boys, jest a hair!"

Occasionally a handspike would slip and a log would drop. A scathing un-Presbyterian oath would go rolling across the Valley as a hand was crushed. The rest would keep on building.

Women and boys did the lighter jobs, such as fashioning shingles for the roof. To do this they sawed logs into blocks, took out the heart, and worked the slabs with frows and mallets. The boys kept busy with the ax, and the women with the kettle, so that logs and victuals were always on hand.

Then the millwright, called in for the job, was ready to take over. Under his supervision two pillars went up, one inside and one outside the basement wall, to support the wheel shaft. A section of a white oak tree, about four feet long, would be brought to the site, trued up, and punctured with morticed openings into which the hewn-oak spokes of the wheel could be inserted. Yellow locust journals, upon which the wheel revolved, were fitted into each end of the shaft. They rested on hardwood blocks topping the piers, and were lubricated with tallow.

"How we gonna git that shaft into place, mister?" a strapping farm hand might ask the millwright.

"By main strength and awkwardness, young 'un, and the muscle in yer back!"

The shaft would be put in place, arms fitted on, timbers sawed to make water buckets, millstones put into place. A hopper would be built to carry the precious golden grain to the stones, and the millrace flooded. Finally the mill would be in operation. Simple sweaty farmers would watch, silent and proud as knights at a coronation, as the first corn was ground. They didn't have to ask for whom the wheel turned. It turned for them.

The houses were as solid and functional as the mills. Stones and unhewn logs were used in what generally began as one-room structures, to grow with the family. Wooden pegs served as joints and coat hangers. Buck antlers on the wall held the family treasure —the long rifle. Wooden pegs also supported the clapboard table and stools. Around the cabin were the items that made up frontier life: the wool and the looms, the Holy Bible and Shakespeare, the moccasins and the linsey-woolsey, the short gowns and hunting shirts. On the table, depending on the rifle, might be bear meat, venison, wild turkey, or pheasant. If the family were lucky enough to have a cow grazing on the wild-pea vine and bluegrass, there was milk; if not, water would wash down the corn pone.

Though there were not many neighbors, these were neighborly people. They came together to catechize the children, marry the grown-ups, and bury the old. They liked logrollings, corn shuckings, housewarmings, sugar stirrings, quilting parties, and apple-butter bilin's. Here in this Valley love and rancor and honeysuckle and blood ebbed, flowed, mixed. This made life all of a piece, solid and compact and harsh and tender, life all the way through to bone marrows.

Not that it was all sweetness and light. There were as many scoundrels as saints on the frontier, and more that was nasty than nice. Too many histories romanticize the grit and substance out of the past. They tell you about the black side of the ledger without turning to the red. That's why no history of the Shenandoah Valley gets around to Robert Bailey.

He was a damned dasher.

He came down the Great Path as a young lad, binding himself as an apprentice to survive. He rose before the sun, fed and curried his horse, ate a piece of bread, and went to the fields to plow furrows straight and deep.

As the boy became man he found there were many things that made his heart sing: girls, women, other men's wives. They all captivated him. Robert Bailey obliged us by leaving one of the most specific and tempestuous frontier autobiographies.[4]

This Don Juan in the wilderness had a taste for the passing gilded nothings, making and losing fortunes as a gambler. Faro, Black and Red, Rolet, and Equality: take your choice, sir. He insisted that he was a sportsman. A gambler invents schemes to allure and seduce others into a contest, so that he may empty their pockets. But a sportsman is a liberal-minded gentleman, attached to amusements regardless of gain. His motto is honor; his shield is judgment. He risks what he has for the love of the thing, and not for mere vulgar victory.

When Dame Fortune smiled, Bailey squandered his substance as a meteor in the sky squanders energy. His four elegant horses that would trot at ten miles an hour. Sometimes he ran the whites before the blacks, sometimes the blacks before the whites. In winter he moved about in an elegant embossed sleigh, with a gold-corded cloak around his shoulders. "I might well have passed for a Bishop," he modestly admitted. His colored servant was dressed in scarlet livery. Beside him lay a silver trumpet which he blew frequently; if Lord Bailey met wagons, or the mail stage, they had to turn out for him.

Owning a daredevil horse and a colt out of Diomed, he raced and lived with a bold dash. No one could tame him—until he met Mrs. Turnbull. She was tall and firm and handsome, with yellow hair rolled in a knot at the back. A little devil sparkled in the corner of her blue eyes. Sometimes this devil escaped and ran all over the Valley. When it did, Bob Bailey ran alongside.

They made their triumphant way throughout the Old Dominion. He loved all thirty-seven inns in Williamsburg, but especially the Raleigh Tavern with its inscription: "Hilaritas sapientiae et bonae vitae proles"—jollity, the offspring of wisdom and good living. At the most fashionable places Bailey would invite all comers into the drawing room, "To take a bottle of Burgundy or Champagne, and at the same time to elevate Madam's vanity, which was not generally past elevation, either from intoxication or its own zenith." His taste also ran toward Jamaica spirits, Holland gin, tea, coffee, chocolate, cesse, and segards of the best qualities. The combination was not always as agreeable inside as outside his stomach. One unhappy night the bold libertine thought sure he must die. He called in the recorder of wills, made his final dispositions, and kissed Mrs. Turnbull passionately. Then he ordered a servant named Mike fetch him a bottle of chilled champagne.

"Oh, don't or you will die, suh," the servant said. Nevertheless, when sufficiently threatened, Mike obeyed. Bailey poured a full glass, drank it, and felt better. The more he drank, the better he felt; and the better he felt, the surer he was that he wanted to eat oysters.

He ordered Mike to bring in half a bushel and roast them. The patient ate these, and became thirsty. He sent Mike for another bottle of champagne. So it went.

"The next morning," Bailey confides in his autobiography, "I ordered some peach brandy and honey, which gave me a most voracious appetite. Then I ordered a beef steak and some strong coffee, and have never taken to medicine since."

He very much took to a certain Mr. Wigg, however, when that gentleman turned out Bailey's horses from a stable and put his own in their place. In addition, Wigg beat Bailey's servant boy with a club until his head was cut to pieces.

Bailey rose from the table and went to see Mr. Wigg. Though he was shaking with rage, he managed to contain himself. "By what authority did you undertake to whip my servant as you have?" Bailey asked.

"Because he's a damn'd impertinent black scoundrel. If you take his part, you are no better than himself."

That was enough. Bailey's arm went back, and Wigg went out the window so fast that he took the sash with him. Bailey followed, kicked, cursed, and cuffed his groaning opponent. He may have been a little too vigorous. Wigg was carried off and kept in bed for a week.

Consequently Wigg's brother-in-law, Colonel Barnharts, delivered a formal challenge to the Tiger of the Valley. When the Colonel demanded satisfaction, Bailey said he would have to consult a friend and find out just what to do. "Well, sir," Barnharts said, "see to it immediately," and walked off. Bailey later regretted that he didn't treat him as he had Wigg.

"Bailey, you must fight," his friend said when he heard the story. "You are a gentleman. If you don't, you'll be hissed out of Virginia. Say you're not afraid and I'll be your second."

"Well, I've never shot a duelling pistol in my life, and they say this man can hit a dollar nine out of ten times. I can't hit a tree. But I'll not be hissed. By God, I won't!"

"Then take him on at handkerchief's length." Bailey thought this fine, but Wigg would have none of it. They finally settled on twenty yards. They met at five the next morning. Wigg shot first, and missed. Bailey took deliberate aim and fired. Wigg fell. The doctor found the bullet in his arm; the limb became infected, and had to be amputated.

Eighteenth-century amputations were not pleasant. There was no real anesthetic. The doctor administered a strong slug of whisky and got four men to hold the writhing patient. "Say the psalms," he advised, and started hacking.

"I hope I will never have to duel again," Bailey said. He left a large sum of money to help Wigg back to health and fortune. Later on in life the incredible Bailey was converted at a frontier camp meeting, and enjoyed a pious, Scripture-filled old age. This was the story of one sojourner in eighteenth-century Virginia: a saga full of anxiety and abandon, hope and felicity, things which, in Robert Bailey's opinion, gave life its spice.

Many other people, of high and low estate, came to see or to settle in the Valley. A French nobleman, visiting a tavern, asked if he might be served privately. "Eat at the common table," the inn-keeper said, "or move on." The man destined to be Father of his Country surveyed the Valley in 1748. Young George Washington found one of the beds he slept in "nothing but a little straw matted together without sheets or anything else, but only one thread-bare blanket with double its weight of vermin such as lice, fleas, etc." Young Thomas Jefferson was so excited about the Natural Bridge he purchased from the Crown in 1767 for twenty shillings that he did not complain about accommodations. When Calvinistic Philip Fithian visited the Valley just before the Revolution, he was shocked to find much "drinking, horse-racing, hollowing, and carousing. They talk of supporting Freedom by meeting and practising Bacchanalian Revels." Later on a Hessian soldier who was taken as a prisoner of war to Augusta County complained to his friends in Germany: "We do not have good neighbors here, for there is hardly a *Gentleman* living within forty miles of Staunton."[5]

Gentlemen or no, the men of the Valley had imprinted their manners and character on it by the time of the Revolution. There would be more Indian trouble, privation, and dissent, but the worst was over. The Baptist circuit rider James Ireland, touring the Valley in 1760, found the people "living in a common state of sociability." By then there were about 20,000 whites and 1,000 Negroes in a Valley that was two hundred miles long and from ten to seventy miles wide.

There were numbers of indentured servants (some convicts, others who were working out passage money), free laborers, apprentices, and slaves. A laborer got about two and a half shillings a day, or two pounds a month, for ordinary labor. The chief money crop of this rural economy was hemp. A single county, Augusta, averaged over 100,000 pounds a year after 1770. Next in importance was wheat. Small industries, such as distilleries, gun factories, and iron works, prospered. Wills began to list such items as china cups, looking glasses, and silver spoons. Life was getting easier.

Homes like Jacob Hite's Hopewell, Isaac Zane's Marlboro, William Preston's Greenfield, and Andrew Moore's Cannicello were sturdy and spacious. They were few and far between. In the 1760's only half the Valley homes had kitchen utensils, a third beds, and a sixth chairs and tables. The people cooked Indian style, slept on the floor or in bunks, and sat on stools. As an old Valley song puts it:

> They raised them rough, they raised them well,
> When their feet were set in the paths of hell
> They put in their souls the fear of God
> And tanned their hides with a stiff ram-rod.

The fear of God was a by-product of the evangelical fervor which swept the frontier in the eighteenth-century. England's Toleration Acts, passed after the Glorious Revolution of 1688, gave such dissenting groups as the Presbyterians, Baptists, and Methodists new freedom. From 1745 to the end of the American Revolution, sixty Presbyterian churches were started from Winchester to the present Tennessee line. The Great Awakening made the Baptist Church a powerful force in Virginia, filling the frontier with religious enthusiasm. Because the Baptists insisted that the Church should be free of government control, they were opposed by the authorities in Williamsburg. Fifty Baptist preachers, including such spellbinders as Lewis Craig, James Childs, James Read, and William Marsh, were jailed in the 1760's as disturbers of the peace. The Methodist phase of the Great Awakening, which began in 1773 when Devereaux Jarratt welcomed Methodist preachers from the northern colonies to his Dinwiddie County church, also had a large Virginia following.

Still it would be wrong to say that the Valley was completely won over to piety. Front Royal deserved the nickname of Hell Town. Berryville brawled enough to be called Battletown. Old World feuds continued in the new. Scots paraded St. Michael with a sauerkraut necklace, while Germans caricatured St. Patrick. Ribaldry and split skulls resulted. Red men continued to do most of the skull damage.

Land-hungry settlers were reluctant to deal fairly with the aborigines, as surveyors' lines moved ever westward. White men, carrying European civilization into this rich and fertile outpost, prevailed.

No frontier area in colonial America surpassed the Valley in its revolutionary zeal. Valley soldiers marched wherever they were needed—north to join Washington, east to oust Dunmore, southwest to fight Cherokees, west to stalk Shawnees. They were at Trenton, Brandywine, Valley Forge, and Yorktown. Seven became Continental generals. General Andrew Lewis drove Dunmore from the colony and rid the Chesapeake of British domination. General Peter Muhlenberg, an ordained minister, preached his last sermon in the Valley on the text, "There is a time to every purpose; a time to war and a time to peace." He concluded by saying, "There is a time to fight, and that time has come now!" Throwing off his black robe, he stood in the blue and buff uniform of the Continental army.

Another of the Valley generals was Daniel Morgan. He should not be tucked away at the end of a chapter. Daniel Morgan was the kind of man who reached places first. The least we can do, having acknowledged this, is to let him open our chapter on the Revolution.

5 *Liberty or Death*

WE ARE AT THE END OF OUR TETHER, AND NOW OR
NEVER OUR DELIVERANCE MUST COME.
George Washington, April, 1781

Daniel Morgan was a born cusser. Cussing a British officer on the
frontier brought him five hundred lashes on his bare back. This
ribboned his flesh but did not improve his vocabulary. In Berryville, Daniel cussed Bill Davis and kicked the living hell out of him.
Bill's body proved unexpectedly resistant; Daniel broke his big toe.
It never would stay in place after that.

One bad toe didn't slow up Daniel Morgan. Before long he had
joined up to march with Braddock. In 1774 he went out to the Ohio
Valley, stopped a rifle ball with his neck, spit out the teeth on the
left side of his mouth, cussed intolerably, and kept going.

The Revolution came. Washington called for troops. Daniel recruited a regiment and marched from the Valley of Virginia to
Boston in three weeks. His men rested a spell, then pushed on to
Quebec. Daniel arrived first—by so much that he was cut off and
captured. The British offered him a commission, but Daniel cussed
so hard that they eventually released him. He joined Washington
again and formed Morgan's Rifles. Nothing scared the British so
thoroughly as this band. Next to shooting squirrels in the trees,
these mountain boys liked shooting redcoats in the field best.

They had their big chance in the fall of 1777 at Saratoga, where an entire English army, under "Gentleman Johnny" Burgoyne, surrendered to the Americans; and this in turn was instrumental in securing French recognition for American independence.

Morgan and his men moved down to South Carolina in time for the battle of Cowpens. Here the British under Colonel Banastre Tarleton were surrounded and almost destroyed in the fracas. When bad health forced Morgan to retire, he came back to Virginia and built a house named Saratoga to commemorate the British defeat he had helped bring about.

Comparable to Morgan was Virginia's George Rogers Clark, who more than any man was responsible for the final conquest of the Northwest Territory. He was a good cusser, too. The line of English forts extending down from Detroit to the old French settlements of Vincennes and Kaskaskia, gave him good cause.

His plan was to surprise the British and capture the Northwest Territory. Governor Patrick Henry approved, and gave Clark authority to enlist seven companies of fifty men each. Recruiting his little army from Virginia frontiersmen, Clark floated down the Ohio on rafts, marched to Kaskaskia, and on the Fourth of July (these were patriotic fellows) attacked and captured the fort.

When Colonel Henry Hamilton, British Governor of Canada, marched onto the scene, the fighting was tougher. In the bitter winter of 1778, Clark and his men plodded 180 miles across flooded Illinois prairies, often neck-deep in icy water, to capture Fort Vincennes and Colonel Hamilton. What George Rogers Clark did, with plenty of fortitude and a few hundred men, was to conquer the Northwest Territory. Put a price tag on Ohio, Illinois, Indiana, Michigan, and Wisconsin, and you will know how much the future Republic owed this band of frontier fighters.

Chroniclers of our Revolution have said much about its legal and political aspects, but little about its first-rate cussing. There was more blood and blasphemy in our Continental army than talk of Locke and Blackstone. Only when the words were made flesh did freedom come.

Towering above all the cussing and ignorance were the ideals—rational, enlightened, and very British. Not everyone comprehended them. But those who did, and who provided the necessary intellectual leadership, understood them very well. The American Revolution resulted from American opposition to strict Parliamentary control. Because they were inherently and belligerently British, the colonists refused to tolerate discriminatory treatment.

This was a moral conflict between the citadel and the caravan—those who stayed at home to accept the old, and those who left home to discover the new. It had been brewing for years; John Smith's "Rude Reply" of 1608 pointed up the essential dichotomy. The Americans tangled with the French before the English; they were moving west and the French south, making a collision unavoidable. Virginia's Governor Dinwiddie sent George Washington, then a young adjutant of the Virginia Militia, to warn the French to keep out of the Ohio country. The French answer was lacking in grace but strong in flavor. "It is our absolute design to take possession of the Ohio, and by God, we shall do it!"

Virginians understood the reply, but didn't like it. Dinwiddie sent a small force to build a fort at the junction of the Monongahela and Allegheny rivers. The French not only captured the advance party, but went on to build Fort Duquesne themselves.

The resulting French and Indian War was not a local skirmish, but one aspect of a world-wide struggle, the Seven Years' War (1756–63). Her brilliant victories gave Britain colonial supremacy over her archenemy, France. Virginians, who had fought hard for the Mother Country, gloried in the victory, but were stunned by the peace terms. The country west of the Alleghenies was closed to English settlement. In the next decade many issues involving taxes, privileges, maritime practices, and military policy arose and festered. But it was the muddled land question, more than any other, that brought on the American Revolution.

Virginia's Governor Fauquier warned London: "I much fear we shall not be able to live upon the same terms with the Indians as the French did, unless this enthusiasm of running backwards to hunt for fresh lands can be stopped."[1] The British replied that the western land would be the Indians' hunting ground. The order was as futile as Canute's when he commanded the waves to retreat. The settlers moved west. The Indians struck back, and a reign of terror set in.

Governor Dunmore took the offensive, authorizing two divisions of his Virginia militia to march west and destroy the Indian forces. He would command one, and Andrew Lewis—a tall, powerful figure at fifty, noted for his long hair and long knife—the other. Lewis and his force of about 1,100 men marched west for nineteen days, and camped at Point Pleasant to await word from Dunmore. Two soldiers who slipped off into the woods to hunt blundered upon

Cornstalk and his full war party. There was nothing to do now but fight.

Because he was an Indian, and opposed the western settlement, Cornstalk had not been accorded his rightful place in Virginia history. Majestic and princely, the Shawnee chief was considered a great orator by men who heard Patrick Henry and Richard Henry Lee. "For many years this was our land," he once said. "Then you came, and took it for your own. You plowed our field, so we could no longer burn the prairie every autumn to make good grazing for the buffalo and deer. You do not keep your word; still you ask us to keep the truce." Gradually he came to realize he had no defense except force. That night his braves crossed the Ohio and struck at dawn. Fighting continued throughout the day and into the dusk. Although two hundred whites were killed or wounded, the Indians retreated. Later on, while holding peace talks under a flag of truce, Cornstalk was treacherously killed. The most important Indian battle in Virginia's history—one which some scholars call the first battle of the American Revolution—had been won.

Two years later the gentlemen in Williamsburg and Philadelphia, better dressed but no better intentioned, would make speeches and render formal the break with Britain. Virginia's frontiersmen were ready for war. They had been fighting it for several years.

On April 20, 1775, Lord Dunmore, Virginia's last royal Governor, ordered the gunpowder stored in Williamsburg's public magazine moved to a warship. His moving to a British man-of-war practically dissolved the royal government. Declaring the colony to be in revolt, he proclaimed all Virginia slaves free and occupied Norfolk. He could not hold it and was driven back to his warship, where he shouted: "Good God, that ever I should come to this!" In July, 1776, His Lordship sailed out of the Chesapeake, never to return.[2]

Having declared the colony free and independent, the Fifth Virginia Convention went on to instruct her delegates in Congress to propose separation from Great Britain. This Richard Henry Lee did. Three days later the committee to draft a Declaration of Independence was appointed. On June 12, 1776, the Virginia Convention adopted George Mason's Bill of Rights; on June 29, it approved a constitution. The die was cast. When the Declaration of Independence (which was largely the work of Thomas Jefferson) was adopted on July 4, the United States of America was born.

In order to triumph, the revolting colonies would have to find friends and allies. France could be, and actually was, the key to victory. A critical economic struggle went with the establishing of a new nation. After 1776 the rebels offered equal rights of trade with any country which would sign a treaty-reciprocity clause. As belligerents, they extended legal protection to neutrals, and asserted that only instruments of contraband were instruments of war. In this, as in so many other actions, they reflected the thinking of the very nation they were rebelling against. Having been for generations well established in the British orbit, the colonies found their struggle for cultural and literary freedom the most difficult of all. Many patriots insisted on fighting this battle too. Instead of importing knowledge and foreign erudition, we should exercise our own talents. Americans should carry on the war of words as well as the war of guns.

Having said and done all this, the colonists were still confronted with this inevitable proposition: no bleeding, no independence. Rain would not bring forth blossoms on the tree of liberty; its roots would have to be watered with the blood of patriots. The state that provided many of the leaders also provided its share of followers. Of the four cavalry regiments authorized in 1777, two were Virginia's. Her sons fought from Quebec to Savannah, from Boston to Vincennes. In 1779 the British carried the war to Virginia soil. Sir George Collier took Portsmouth and set about raiding the surrounding countryside. Because the reinforcements he expected never arrived, Collier abandoned his campaign. Later on that year, General Alexander Leslie again occupied Portsmouth, but abandoned it to join Lord Cornwallis further south.

We think of our Revolutionary soldiers as blue-clad Continentals. Many were buckskin-clad woodsmen. The mountain men mixed their cornmeal with maple sugar and their patriotism with profanity. As the British found out to their sorrow, they were mean men in a row.

The British plan to destroy the lead mines near Fort Chiswell was entrusted to Tory sympathizers. Through the efforts of Colonel William Campbell of Aspenvale, Walter Crockett and William Preston of Montgomery County, and Charles Lynch of Bedford County, the Tories were captured and executed without official trial. (Because of Lynch's prominence in the affair, the term "lynch law" came into being.)

Rounding up his western Virginian mountain fighters, Campbell joined with riflemen from North Carolina and set out to destroy the British force under Major Patrick Ferguson. They caught up with the redcoats at Kings Mountain, on the border between North Carolina and South Carolina. There was fought one of the most celebrated battles of the war.

Ferguson took his position on top of the mountain, so that the Americans would have to charge up the steep mountainside to dislodge him. Campbell divided his force into two parts, one for each side of the mountain. One segment was to rush to the top, fire, and retire to load while the men on the opposite side attacked. This seesaw movement was so effective that most of the British, including Ferguson, were killed or captured. To the visitors went the spoils. Cleveland took Ferguson's white horse, Shelby his silver whistle, Sevier his silk sash, and Campbell his letters and papers.

The battle of Kings Mountain, fought on October 17, 1780, upset Cornwallis' plan for overrunning the Southern colonies and united the western counties in their fight against tyranny; it was, in fact, the turning point of the Revolution in the South.

Kings Mountain was good news for the patriots. But the best news of all came from Yorktown. By one of history's quirks, the American Revolution was destined to end only a few miles from the place where the first settlers had come ashore in 1607.

Even with France aiding the American cause, it looked as if the British might triumph; but they did not. No one battle or campaign drove them from the colonies. They lost because their repressive policies outran their ability to enforce them; because their pride overcame their flexibility.

Walking close to the brink of chaos, the patriots were forced to formulate ideas about the nature of society and government. The most important thing about the Revolution may be, as Charles Sydnor has suggested, that it drove many Americans to deep and sober thought. They pondered fundamental problems, such as the relationship of parts to the political whole, of the balance of liberty and authority, and of the responsibilities, as well as the privileges, which freedom brings.[3]

From these thoughts came the vision of a democracy set up and governed by and for its citizens. To this vision were coupled the ability of outstanding leaders and devotion of faithful fighters. The Revolution left marks on the souls, as well as the bodies of men.

Moving to more specific matters, one finds that a number of historical factors played their part in the American victory. Among these were Britain's involvement in Continental affairs; the tendency of her leaders to underestimate the Americans' strength and determination; difficulties among British commanders; shortages of man power, supplies, and equipment; poor communication between forces in the field; and a lack of direction on the broad strategy of repression. No single blunder or shortage, but rather a combination, finally allowed little David to bring Goliath to his knees.

It was the continuing American ability to wage war, and to find a symbol for that ability in the figure of Washington, that made military victory possible.[4]

Just as critical, in some ways, was the battle of words and ideas; for without this, the bloodshed would have been mere carnage. Four sharp bright Virginia minds marshaled the English language and hurled it at the English tyrants—Patrick Henry, George Mason, James Madison, and Thomas Jefferson. So successful were they that we tend to overlook the Blands, Wythes, Randolphs, and Pendletons who in other places or periods would have been first-rate. Never was the competition for a place in the sun keener. This, for Virginia, was the Great Generation.

In all Virginia's history, there never has been a half century to match, idea for idea, that which lapsed between the grasping of power by Patrick Henry and the relinquishing of power by Thomas Jefferson.

Born in Hanover County, Patrick Henry was considered lazy by his early teachers; but he was energetic later on. His fame, won in the Parsons' Case in 1763, burned brightly until the day of his death. In evaluating him, we should remember that until the Civil War the orator-politician was the leading heroic type in Virginia, Henry the best-known example of it. Jefferson might have been more profound, Mason more rational, Madison more incisive; but Patrick Henry best dramatized the revolutionary cause. To his and later generations, his assertion of March 20, 1775, at Richmond's St. John's Church was the Revolution's motto: "I know not what course others may take, but as for me, give me liberty or give me death!"

A generally held notion, fostered both by the urgency of the times and Henry's own sense of mission, holds that he "threw himself into a sentence, and trusted Almighty God to get him out." Conceding that he was a brilliant orator, one can hardly say that he practiced extemporaneous art. There is too much careful contrivance, too much system, for that. Patrick Henry was no extemporizing

orator, but a rigorous disciplinarian; student of the King James
version of the Bible, master of the monosyllable.

He did not spring to his feet unprepared when the Revolution
came. As a hard-working trial lawyer in Hanover County, he had
collected 1,185 fees during his first three years of practice. Before
coming to the Convention of Delegates at Williamsburg, Henry
established his reputation as a shrewd, forceful speaker. He made
every effort to find out what others were saying in this Age of
Oratory—Pitt, Burke, Chatham, Erskine, and Fox in England;
Randolph, Lee, Wythe, and Madison in Virginia.

Now that none of us can hear him roll out his mighty Anglo-
Saxon phrases, we can never fully appreciate his magnetism. We can
only wonder, when we know that so level-headed a person as Thomas
Jefferson said that he spoke as Homer wrote.

He used words like buckshot. Three of his best-known lines
illustrate it: "The next gale that sweeps from the north will bring to
our ears the clash of resounding arms!" Eighteen words—seventeen
monosyllables. "Is life so dear, or peace so sweet, as to be purchased
at the price of chains and slavery?" Nineteen words—seventeen
monosyllables. "We must fight! I repeat it sir, we must fight; an
appeal to arms and to the God of Hosts is all that is left to us!"
Twenty-seven words—twenty-five monosyllables. If this be accidental,
then Patrick Henry made the most of it. At his best, he sounded
like destiny speaking English.

George Mason was cut out of a different bolt of cloth. He was
no rabble-rouser. Lacking the stuff that makes popular idols, he was
well supplied with the stuff that makes unassailable merit. His life
was not well known, but well worth knowing; people who look
closely at Revolutionary times always "discover" Mason, and wonder
why he does not enjoy greater acclaim.

One reason is that he abhorred publicity and notoriety. He advised
his sons to "prefer the happiness and independence and a private
station to the troubles and vexations of public business." Not that he
shirked public commitments. The same man had this to say about
the Revolution: "I will risk the last penny of my fortune and last
drop of my blood upon the issue." Opposition to slavery was the
most consistent feature of his political life. The slave trade he found
"diabolical in itself and disgraceful to mankind." Believing in the
rule of right reason, he looked clearly and rationally at the issues
confronting him. In some ways he was like Voltaire, his counterpart
across the sea. Both had geometrical gardens (in which they paced

out their ideas), the same streak of humor, the same ability to formulate the political philosophy of revolutionary states in the making, even the same disease, gout. Both could lash out at taunters. "You are old, Mr. Mason, and the public notices you are losing your faculties," one of his enemies charged. "Sir, the public will never notice when you lose yours!" Mason thundered back.

In one regard, history was kinder to the Virginian than the Frenchman. Mason wrote his ideas directly into the constitution of his people during his lifetime. Voltaire had to wait until the Third Estate carried him to the Pantheon.[5]

On May 17, 1776, George Mason rode quietly into Williamsburg. Immediately he was added to the legislative committee empowered to draw up a declaration of rights and constitution. His outline of a working democracy was adopted on June 15 and used as a model for the other colonies. Mason's document asserted that:

All men are created equally free and independent, and have certain natural rights, of which they cannot, by any compact, deprive or divest their posterity; among which are the enjoyment of life and liberty, with the means of acquiring and possessing property, and pursuing and obtaining happiness and safety.

Mason's draft endorsed separation of powers, freedom of elections, and rotation in office. It enumerated such fundamental liberties as swift trials, moderate bail, judgment by one's peers, humane punishments, militia instead of standing army; adding others that were not yet fully secure in England—freedom of conscience, prohibition of general warrants, majority right to alter government, and freedom of the press. Dozens of the stock phrases of American statecraft may be found in this work, unquestionably drawn up by George Mason.

Noting that Mason regarded Washington as an upstart, some have called the writer of Virginia's constitution a snob. They should recall Mason's line painted into the mural of the Virginia State Library: "We came equals into this world and equals we shall go out of it." Mason never said we were equals while in it. He believed, along with Jefferson, in the rule of the *aristoi*—these talented by nature. He believed in style, tone, and intelligence. His own home, Gunston Hall, exemplifies these qualities.

Named for his grandfather, Gerald Fowke of Gunston Hall, Staffordshire, and built by William Buckland, it is snug, sensible, and serene. A story and a half high, it impresses us with proportion rather than size. Gunston Hall was the center of a world, in which slaves, carpenters, coopers, sawyers, blacksmiths, tanners, shoemakers, spinners, and weavers worked. Mason kept no steward or clerk, preferring to do all his bookkeeping and supervising himself. There were generally around five hundred people on his estate. From his own wharf he sent up to 23,000 bushels of wheat in a single shipment.

Small details of his life, such as the layout of his orchard, indicate what kind of man Mason was. On the north front of Gunston Hall he planted double ranges of blackheart cherry. They were raised from stone to assure uniformity of growth. Beginning at a spot two hundred feet from the house, they lined a road a thousand feet long. The trees were so aligned that the common center of the rows was exactly in the middle of the outer doorway of the manor house. Because of the careful planting and trimming, only the first four rows were visible from the porch.

Mason delighted in standing guests who had entered from the river side exactly in the middle of the porch and asking, "How many trees do you see?" Four. "Be good enough to move a few steps to either side," Mason would say, and the long rows of additional trees would appear. His trees, his thoughts, and his life were well ordered.

The master and mistress of Gunston Hall were revolutionaries, but not equalitarians. Visitors might find Mrs. Mason dressed in a crimson satin bodice trimmed with lace, a black tabby petticoat, silk hose, and shoes of gallooned leather. She frequently wore a string of matched pearls on her neck. The diamonds and rubies on her fingers made sparkling patterns as she moved her jeweled fan back and forth. Her husband, expecting guests, would be dressed in a coat and breeches of olive plush, trimmed in bright red broadcloth. He would also wear an embroidered waistcoat, elegant silk stockings, silver buttons and shoe buckles, and lace ruffles at his neck and wrists. They were one of the most handsome and attractive couples in colonial America; but it is for his mind, not his clothes, that we revere George Mason's memory.

James Madison may have matched him in brilliance, but not in stature. Washington Irving described Madison as "no bigger than half a piece of soap—poor Jeemy, withered little apple-john!" When Patrick Henry's tall sister wanted him to pray, she simply put her hand upon his head and pressed him to his knees.

But what a head she was pressing! In it, more than in any other, was the knowledge and vision which made the federal Constitution a reality. After the intoxicating prose of Tom Paine and Patrick

Henry had done its work, the sober, legalistic words of Madison added law to liberty.[6]

Author of the American Bill of Rights, Madison saw freedom of religion as the fundamental item on which other forms of civil liberty depended. When he was only twenty-five, he undertook his first legislative endeavor—the writing of a clause guaranteeing freedom of conscience for the 1776 Virginia Constitution. To him bigotry was "a monster that, feeding and thriving on its own venom, gradually swells to a size and strength overwhelming all laws divine and human." As a young boy defending jailed Baptist ministers, as a member of Congress drafting the national Bill of Rights, as a President enforcing it, and as an elder statesman retired to his Virginia farm, Madison made the insistence on freedom of religion one of his lifelong goals.[7]

This friend of freedom took up the study of law so as to have a profession which "depended as little as possible on the labour of slaves." Fascinated with natural history, he secured through Jefferson a set of the works of the great French naturalist, Buffon. He later sent his friend Jefferson detailed measurements and descriptions of moles, weasels, and other animals—at the same time confessing that he had "a little itch to gain a smattering of chymistry."

Madison's scientific interests were sidetracked by a stormy and energetic political career. So that he might be prepared in this area, he spent years studying the history of ancient and modern confederacies, to the great enhancement of the Constitutional Convention in which he figured so prominently. "Every person seems to acknowledge his greatness," wrote a fellow delegate of Madison. "He blends together the profound politician with the scholar. In the management of every question he evidently took the lead in the Convention." The Virginia Plan, which Madison helped to shape, was the basis on which the Constitution was written. When widespread opposition developed in his own state, Madison was instrumental in winning Virginia's ratification in June, 1788.

That victory, won on the floor of the new capitol at Richmond, was a memorable moment in an unforgettable age. An aged eagle, Patrick Henry, spread his wings for the last time. No man in American history had been so willing to refuse high honor and power as he. The offices of United States Senator (1794), Secretary of State (1795), Chief Justice of the Supreme Court (1795), Governor of Virginia (1796), and Ambassador to France (1799) could not lure him from his Virginia plantation. Nor could the arguments of his colleagues persuade him that the new Constitution did not take from Virginia some of the independence her sons had won. This was his last-ditch stand against adoption.

"Our own happiness alone is not affected by this event," he said in his Olympian voice. "All nations are interested in the determination. We have it in our power to secure the happiness of half the human race. Its adoption may involve the misery of other hemispheres. . . ."

What else did he say? Most of the audience never knew. His voice was submerged by the fury of a tremendous thunderstorm which ripped through the skies and turned the window panes opaque with pelting raindrops. Flashes of lightning illumined the pale, pinched features and frenzied eyes of the Great Orator—talking in vain against forces he could not master.

Two days later the Commonwealth of Virginia became a part of the United States of America. The Union was assured. The Virginia general who had led the colonies in war would lead the nation in peace. Well might the people rejoice.

6 *The Squire of Mount Vernon*

WASHINGTON'S MONUMENT IS STILL THERE.
Calvin Coolidge

In the American Revolution, patriotic Virginians were tried and, in the main, not found wanting. Some of their sacrifice and suffering is known and remembered. Much has been obscured or forgotten too quickly. Yet the general glow remains, illuminating the face and form of the Virginia squirearchy, and particularly that noblest Virginian of them all, the master of Mount Vernon plantation.

"He was a human angil in a three kornered hat and knee britches," wrote Artemus Ward. "He personally was ninety per cent of the force which made of the American Revolution a successful issue," claimed William Carlos Williams. "Know the intimate character of Washington himself, and you will know practically all there is to understand about the beginnings of the Revolution."

But who can know this marble demigod intimately? "Every American considers it his duty to have a likeness of Washington in his home, just as we have images of God's saints," Paul Svivin reported in 1815. "He had no nakedness, but was born with clothes on, and his hair powdered, and made a stately bow on his first appearance in the world," wrote Nathaniel Hawthorne.

All this would have surprised Washington, who was a man not of marble, but of fire. In him there burned a mad rage which, on the

64

few occasions when it was loosed, seared the souls of those who stood in the way. He demanded "news on the spur of speed," and had no sympathy with cowards who "ran like the wild bears of the mountains." He could boil and explode. What Washington told General Charles Lee at Monmouth raised goose-pimples on old sergeants' necks; when "the rascally Freneau" opposed his presidential policies, Washington wanted him ousted from his clerk's post in the State Department. There was hotter blood in his veins than ever the D.A.R. dreams.

If any American was molded by his Virginia environment, it was George Washington. He was a country boy, born in Westmoreland County where his great-grandfather had settled. Land was the continuing passion of his life. Very few people knew as much about Virginia—its human and physical dimensions—as did George Washington. While still a lad of sixteen he undertook an extensive surveying trip into the Shenandoah Valley for Lord Fairfax. He learned to run a line through the wilderness and to search out the frontier. He found out, just as had William Byrd before him, that the wilderness was in fact no fanciful garden. His diary entry for April 4, 1748, reads:

Men women & children attended us through y* Woods as we went showing there Antick tricks. I really think they seem to be as Ignorant a Set of People as the Indians. They never speak English but when spoken to they speak all Dutch. This day our Tent was blown down by y* Violentness of y* Wind.[1]

Douglas Southall Freeman has explained the importance of this venture: "It both marked his fartherest journey from home and brought his first contact with the new frontier about which there was constant talk among the elders."[2] Washington did the job so well that he was retained as Fairfax's surveyor for three years. Here was the foundation on which his later career was built, and of his continuing passion for land. "How much more delighted to an undebauched mind," Washington wrote to Arthur Young in 1788, "is the task of making improvements on the earth than all the vain glories which can be acquired from ravaging it." At his death, he owned more than 60,000 acres of Virginia.

While still a youth, Washington's countrymen marked him for greatness. In a 1755 sermon Samuel Davies, later president of Princeton, spoke of "that heroic youth, Colonel Washington, whom I cannot but hope providence has hitherto preserved in so signal a manner, for some important service to his country." During General Braddock's rout two horses were shot from under Washington and four bullets tore through his clothes. So exaggerated were reports of his fate that he wrote home "to deny a circumstantial account of my death and dying speech."

Back in Virginia, he turned his attention to the political responsibilities of the planter class—and to the methods of the election day. During a July election day in Frederick County in 1758, George Washington's agent supplied 160 gallons of liquor to 391 voters and "unnumbered hangers-on." The good citizens could exercise their choice not only of candidates but of spirits; for 28 gallons of rum, 50 gallons of rum punch, 34 gallons of wine, 46 gallons of beer, and 2 gallons of cider royal were on hand.[3]

So outstanding was Washington as a colonial soldier that in 1775 the Continental Congress unanimously chose him to command the American army and lead the Revolutionary forces. John Adams was impressed by a man who would leave "his delicious retirement, his family, and his friends, sacrificing his ease, and hazarding all in the cause of his country." So were most Americans. Legends about Washington grew. Had you heard that he offered to recruit a thousand soldiers at his own expense, and march them to Boston? Of course you had heard and believed. Like most patriots, you were looking for a living symbol of your revolt. In George Washington you found it.

So you joined in celebrating his birthday while he was still the harassed commander of a lank, losing army. For months the news from the front was anything but glorious. Had the wind not providentially held north in the August, 1776, fighting on Long Island, Sir William Howe might have captured Washington's whole army, and thus ended the revolt. By the end of that discouraging year, Washington's forces dwindled to five thousand men.

But Washington never lost faith. Doggedly, even despairingly sometimes, he hung on. Finally his faith communicated itself to enough people to keep the army and American liberty alive.

In 1777 General Howe decided to take Philadelphia, and in September did so despite Washington's gallant but unsuccessful attack at Germantown. The British settled down for a comfortable winter in America's leading city, the former seat of Congress. The American army spent the winter at Valley Forge. Lesser men would have given up—not Washington.

Then, miraculously, the tide turned. From the north came news of victory at Saratoga, which persuaded France to enter the war as America's ally. This improved the situation, but in no way guaranteed an American victory. Throughout the war Washington never had an adequate army, enough supplies, or suitable co-ordination. States refused to honor requisitions in kind. The Continental currency was so poor that, as Washington commented wryly, it took a wagonload of money to obtain a wagonload of supplies. In the winter of 1781 the Pennsylvania line regiment mutinied. Trusted men, of high and low rank, deserted to the British. Yet Washington continued to act as if an American victory was the only possible outcome of the struggle.

His big chance came in the summer of 1781. Washington was near New York City, the French General Rochambeau was in Rhode Island, and Lafayette was in Virginia. Lord Cornwallis had marched east from Richmond to the coast, where he expected to rendezvous with the British navy. The French Admiral de Grasse was headed for the Chesapeake Bay with a large French fleet. Perhaps the British army could be trapped.

"About noon," wrote General Heath on August 19, 1781, "His Excellency Gen. Washington left the army, setting his face towards his native State, in full confidence, to use his own words, 'with a common blessing,' of capturing Lord Cornwallis and his army."[4]

He had never made a more anxious journey. Had the French fleet really landed, and would the plan actually work? On September 5 he left Philadelphia for Head of Elk (near present-day Elkton, Maryland), remembering perhaps that his last march down this road had ended disastrously at the Brandywine. If the French fleet didn't arrive, this might be worse yet.

Three miles past Chester he met a horseman who delivered the news which gave Washington what must have been his happiest moment during the Revolution. Admiral de Grasse had arrived, with 28 ships and 3,000 troops. Washington moved forward so rapidly that the others in the party, most of them many years his junior, were astonished that the "old man" outstripped them in the saddle. Washington was anxious to force the issue. He had waited a long time for this battle.

The plan of operation against Cornwallis was worked out in detail. In the opinion of Douglas Freeman, Washington's feat of concentrating his force at Yorktown in so short a time was his finest military

achievement of the war. The ships and troops assumed their position.
On September 28 Washington gave the order for the general advance.

That night he slept with his men, only a mile from the enemy's
lines. Washington Irving said the General slept under a mulberry
tree, the root serving for a pillow. Douglas Freeman, less poetic but
more factual, located headquarters "on the present line between
York and Warwick Counties, about 1060 yards northwest of the
junction of Jones's and Great Run." In any case, the 16,000 American and French troops formed a semicircle around the English,
opened a bombardment with seventy cannon, and inexorably beat
Cornwallis' army into submission. On October 17 the British Lord
sat down and wrote the one sentence for which Washington had
long waited: "Sir, I propose a cessation of hostilities for twenty-four
hours, and that two officers may be appointed by each side, to meet
at Mr. Moore's house, to settle terms for the surrender of the posts
at York and Gloucester."

David had managed to deliver the pebble, at just the right time
and place. Goliath fell hard. When the British soldiers passed
through the American and French lines to stack arms, their band
played "The World Turn'd Upside Down." As they laid down their
arms, some of the British soldiers, in a last gesture of defiance, tried
to break their musket locks by dashing the weapons on the ground.[5]

In the ensuing years Washington was, if possible, more important
to the American democracy than he had been during the war. As
president of the 1787 Constitutional Convention he provided the
authority which made the gathering a success. He also formulated his
political creed for his countrymen: "My political creed is to be wise
in the choice of delegates, support them like gentlemen while they
are our representatives, give them competent powers for all federal
purposes, support them in the due exercise thereof, and lastly, com-
pel them to close attendance in Congress during their delegation."[6]

Inevitably he was chosen as the Republic's first President, though
he admitted to Henry Knox that he took the chair of government
"with feelings not unlike those of a culprit who is going to the
place of his execution." Always a man to put his duty before his
preference, Washington made a superb President, giving that office
a tone and vitality which it has had ever since. His workday
generally began at 4 A.M. Because he knew that everything he said
would be quoted, and everything he did imitated, he was meticulous
in every expression and action. He did not intend to have Europeans

scoff at the new nation. At his Tuesday afternoon receptions, they would be greeted by bows, not handshakes. Washington would customarily be dressed in a black velvet suit with silver knee and shoe buckles, yellow gloves, and a silver sword in a scabbard of polished white leather. In his hand was a cocked hat trimmed with a rosette. He was a figure of state, a figure to remember.

He was also a former soldier who remembered his old friends. Woodrow Wilson illustrated this in a story included in his biography of Washington. An old Revolutionary soldier, who had come in buckskin all the way from Kentucky to Philadelphia to see the President, had been told that Washington "had become puffed up with the importance of his station, and was too much of an aristocrat to welcome him in that garb." But the old fighter was not daunted, pressed on to see Washington, and told later how both the President and his lady recognized him from the window, and hurried to the door to draw him cordially in.

"I never was better treated," he said. "I hadn't believed a word against him. I found out that he was still 'Old Hoss.' "

Though George Washington was every inch a President, he couldn't keep his thoughts, and sometimes his steps, from going where his heart was—to Mount Vernon. He not only slipped off for many personal visits home, but even managed to invent and put into operation on the Dogue Run farm a famous sixteen-sided barn, sixty feet in diameter, with an inclined runway. In 1793 he wrote his carpenters that he planned to build "a large Barn, and sheds for Stables upon the plan of that of Dogue Run (if on trial it should be found to answer to the expectations which is formed of it) at River Farm." Such a barn, he estimated, would require 139,980 bricks. His mind was specific, methodical, admirable.

Over the years Washington undertook innumerable experiments with trees, grains, and grasses. His Virginia estate was divided into five farms, each with an overseer. One was a Negro slave named Davy. As his various letters to his managers prove, he wanted nothing wasted: "The hides of the dead cattle (though not good) should be tanned by the old man Jack, who usually attends to this business. The leather may serve for inner Soals and repairing Shoes. Something ought also to be done with the skins of the Sheep which have died."[7]

On September 17, 1796 he delivered his Farewell Address and prepared to return to Virginia. The ship of state was well launched; the Iron Captain stepped down. "Farmer Washington" moved to what he called "a more tranquil theatre" to live out his days.

"Mrs. Washington and myself will do tonight what I believe has not been done within the last twenty years by us—set down to dinner by ourselves," he wrote shortly afterward. The shift from President to planter pleased him, but did not dispel his patriotism. "Solicitude for the country's welfare cannot end," he wrote, "but with my life."

Visitors, both invited and uninvited, came constantly to Mount Vernon, so that its busy proprietor never knew what company would be there when he came in from the farms. Some guests insisted on seeking him during his inspection tours. To one such person Washington's step-grandson said: "You will meet with an old gentleman riding alone, in plain drab clothes, a broad-brimmed white hat, a hickory switch in his hand, and carrying an umbrella with a long staff. That is General Washington."

No matter who they were, or why they came, they were impressed with the figure they found at Mount Vernon. It is hard to find a man who did not admire Washington. One such person was Charles Lee, a vain blusterer who had crossed Washington on military matters and drawn his full anger. "He has long been in a state of divinity," the resentful Lee wrote in 1782. "In recent months the legality of his apotheosis begins to be called in question." Lee was right about the apotheosis, wrong about its legality. Never was an apotheosis so legal in the court of final appeal. The people's judgment was practically unanimous. Overnight Washington became one of the few men in history big enough to fill the vacuum when no symbol existed for a major revolution. His prestige after Cornwallis' surrender was even greater than that of the government of the United States. When he died in 1799, a symbol and a tradition, as well as a human body, were buried at Mount Vernon.

Washington's appeal did not come after time had minimized his bad traits and magnified his good ones. His own generation lionized him. Parson Weems confidently called him "our demigod" in 1800. In the same year a Pennsylvania German farmer wrote *Washingtons Ankunft in Elisium,* in which Washington strolled around heaven chatting with Brutus and Columbus. Though he led a successful rebellion against British authority, Englishmen praised him as extravagantly as the most uncritical Americans. Few men have aroused such high regard from those against whom they rebelled.

Did Washington pass over to Valhalla at any particular moment? Probably not; only Hollywood can simplify the historical process to that extent. But if Washington had a finest hour, it came in 1797 when he voluntarily left the Presidency. His conduct in war, as leader of the Revolution, won him fame; but his conduct in peace, as first President of the new Republic, won him immortality. In youth he craved war; in maturity he wisely avoided it. Rather than indulge in the popular practice of twisting the lion's tail, he sanctioned Jay's treaty with England, which won precious years of peace for the wobbly young democracy.

"I heard the bullets whistle, and believe me, there is something charming in the sound," Washington wrote his half brother after a skirmish at Great Meadow in 1754. But the Washington of 1790 rejected the pomp and power of warfare. He would rather be on his farm than be made emperor of the world.

Washington resisted the powers of peace, which as King or dictator he could have enjoyed in the vaguely united states. He not only wielded authority but relinquished it. Having the key to unlimited power challenged but did not corrupt him. Thomas Jefferson recorded an interesting remark of Washington's after a stormy Cabinet session in which Jefferson and Hamilton attacked each other with verbal daggers. Washington, Jefferson reported, "said he had never repented but once having slipped the moment of resigning his office, and that was every moment since; that by God he had rather be in his grave than in his present situation."

Such reluctance to revel in power is one of the several attributes which help explain why Washington was immortalized during his lifetime, and why his fame was held up over the generations. He was capable, aristocratic, commanding; he had the look and manner of greatness. He lived at a time, and participated in events, which aroused the heroic. His incredible patience and tenacity personified the colonies' noble but difficult cause. He would not accept dictatorial power but, like Cincinnatus of old, went back to his plowshare when the battle was won.

"Surely no one else has been so thoroughly venerated, and so completely frozen into legend," concluded a British historian, Marcus Cunliffe, in his 1958 biography.[8] Mr. Cunliffe believes that Washington has been made to play four roles: the Copybook Hero, the Father of His People, the Disinterested Patriot, and the Revolutionary Leader. Yet by the very nature of his life and legend, the portrait of Washington is still opaque. His personality is all the more baffling because there was no mystery and virtually no excess in it. By the middle of the Revolution the man had merged with his country, and the symbol had absorbed the man. In later years Washington gradually became a myth of suffocating dullness, the victim of civic elephantiasis.

No one was more responsible than Parson Weems, Virginia clergyman, bookseller, keeper of the public pulse, and fiddler extraordinary. The nineteenth son of a Scotch immigrant, Weems was our makeshift Plutarch. What he lacked in veracity he made up in daring. Though he himself had a rather hectic home life,[9] he concentrated on biographies which were, among other things, defenses of the American family. He wrote not only of Washington but also of Benjamin Franklin, William Penn, and Francis Marion. Studying great men made his "bosom heave with emotions unutterable, while the tear of delicious admiration swelled in my eyes." When he got to Washington, the tears became a torrent. His temperament and experience were highly susceptible. He took naturally to praising famous men fervently in his sermons and stump speeches. While he probably had met the General and had been a collector of Washington items, this hardly justified his conferring upon himself the rectorship of Mount Vernon Parish—particularly since there was none of that name. The Parson was not the type of man to be bound by the tyranny of facts, even when they were covered with clerical garb.

Anticipating Horatio Alger, Weems made Washington's life a pious success story. "Here was a proper rise for you!" he gloated when Washington snared the rich widow Custis. Perhaps Weems' critics have been unduly severe to this mixer of mythology, musket balls, and melodrama. Of course his Washington was different from the one born and reared in Virginia, but his readers wanted it so. They read with their hearts, and cried when they came to their hero's death scene: "Swift on angel's wings the brightening Saint ascended. Voices more than human were warbling through the happy region and hymning the great procession towards the gates of heaven. His glorious coming was seen from afar off. Myriads of mighty angels hastened forth with golden harps, to welcome the honoured stranger."

No attempt at subtlety lurks here. Weems' achievement can be put in three words. "He got across." The same cannot be said for the equally devoted but less compelling biography of Chief Justice John Marshall, whose five-volume work John Adams described as a mausoleum a hundred feet square at the base and two hundred feet high. Parson Weems thought of a better description—the Washingtoniad.

The vast literature of Washington adulation need not concern us. The over-all effect was to crystallize the priggish, aloof Washington partly formed by Parson Weems and John Marshall. The man was turned into marble. He had no vices; he had no temper, and he had very little color. The cryptic Gertrude Stein summed it up in *Four in America* when she wrote: "She is very sleepy, George Washington."

When debunking became the fad in the 1920's, Washington was one of the idols under fire. Books like William Woodward's *George Washington: The Image and the Man* portrayed a vain, ordinary, and undemocratic man. The attack was of no avail. President Calvin Coolidge, famous for his monosyllabic granite-block answers, was asked if Washington's reputation had been destroyed. He looked out of the White House window and said, "Washington's Monument is still there."

So was the admiration of the officials and people of the Republic, as the Bicentennial Celebration of 1932 amply demonstrated. Over 16,000 celebrations were held, involving over four million separate programs.[10] The official opening of the bicentennial occurred at Alexandria, Virginia, at Christ Church. Later on, the George Washington Masonic National Memorial was dedicated in the same town.

Hero-worship tends to obscure the real flesh-and-blood Washington. Our *pater patriae* would not have approved of this; he was a fun-loving man who lived every day fully, and enjoyed the company of "pretty little frisks." His jackass stories were decidedly Rabelaisian. When the fiddler struck up his tunes, Washington could never resist "High Betty Martin," "Leather the Strap," or "Pettycoate." Once he danced for three hours without a pause. We do him an injustice when we dehumanize him.

On December 8, 1799, the Squire took his usual morning ride into the fields. He was caught in a heavy, cold rain. Arriving back at the mansion just in time for his meal, he did not bother to change his clothes, although his greatcoat was soaking wet.

The cold that developed did not stop him from going out again the next day, in three inches of snow, to mark trees which were to be cut down between the portico and the river. The cold was worse that night, but he would take no medicine.

"Let it go as it came," he said. General Washington had made many right decisions; but this was a wrong one.

He awoke between two and three the next morning, and told his wife he felt quite unwell. Dr. Craik, who came as soon as he could, thought it a bad case of quinsy. Although Washington had been bled once already by a farm overseer, Dr. Craik bled him again. Then he had him inhale the fumes of tea and vinegar, and swallow some calomel and tartar emetic. After that, the doctor applied blisters of wheat bran to his legs and feet.

About ten o'clock Washington rallied. "I am just going," he said. "Have me decently buried, and do not let my body be put in the vault in less than three days after I am dead. Do you understand me?"

"Yes," replied Tobias Lear, who was nearby.

" 'Tis well," Washington said. Half an hour later he died, without a struggle or a sigh.

Jefferson said simply what most Americans felt: "Verily, a great man has fallen this day in Israel."

7 *The Sage of Monticello*

JEFFERSON STILL LIVES.—*John Adams*

He may have been the last of an old breed, the Renaissance man, or the first of a new one, the American agrarian-democrat. What is certain is that Thomas Jefferson led one of Virginia's memorable lives. He stood amid giants: frequently challenged, seldom surpassed. His critics—he had enough and to spare—admitted that he could argue a case, break a horse, calculate an eclipse, translate an ode, plan a university, play a violin, win an election, or cause a colony to revolt. He synthesized the enlightened thought of his age, molded it into a unified system, and tempered it with experience.

Jefferson belongs more with those who applied than with those who dreamed, with practical men like Locke or Lenin rather than with speculative thinkers like Hobbes or Marx. He strove to find practical solutions to tangible problems, by tempering book knowledge with horse sense. He never hesitated to borrow from other thinkers, such as Locke, Blackstone, or Palladio. The main quality of his thinking is its incredible lucidity. His mind was as clear and pure as spring water. The European with whom he best corresponds, basically, is René Descartes.

Born in Albemarle County in 1743, Thomas Jefferson's leisure was made possible by three generations of slaves. His father left

2,700 acres and many bondsmen. Aristocratic by birth and temper, his son stanchly denied all but the natural aristocracy of talent. When he was seventeen, Thomas entered the College of William and Mary. Rising at dawn, he would lay his own fire, turn to his classes and books, and study into the afternoon. At twilight he ran down the road to a certain stone, jogged back to his room, and resumed study. The lank, square-jawed, sandy-haired youth made an ideal student. At twenty-four he was admitted to the bar. Two years later he entered the House of Burgesses. That his life was largely devoted to politics was more a matter of accident than design. His lifelong ambition was to be a Virginia planter.

Before that could be, a Revolution must be planned and fought. The crisis found him in the prime of his life, able and ready to write a Declaration of Independence. He swore upon the altar of God eternal warfare against all tyranny over the human mind. "We are resolved to die free men," he told fellow Virginians who elected him wartime Governor, "rather than to live slaves." A courageous iconoclast, he was even more valuable in bringing order out of revolutionary chaos. The various "reforms" which he saw through the Virginia legislature were his most enduring contribution to the Old Dominion—bills dealing with the abolition of entail and primogeniture, slavery, criminal law, religious freedom, and education. Their enactment seemed so crucial to Jefferson that in 1776 he turned down an appointment in France to see them through the Assembly. All his ideas were not accepted. Nonetheless, he was able to accomplish, by democratic methods, a social revolution.

Believing that the only good government rested squarely on the will of the people, he was convinced that ignorance was the first enemy of any enlightened state. Citizens should be able "to read and understand what is going on in the world, and keep their part of it going on right: for nothing can keep it right but their own vigilant and distrustful superintendence." Hence one of his most important bills called for a public school system.

The state would be divided into districts five or six miles square. In each there would be an elementary school for instructing the young in reading, writing, and arithmetic. The ablest pupils from these schools would move on to a grammar school, or academy. There would be twenty of these, offering four years of training in Greek, Latin, and other subjects necessary for the educated man. The brightest students would move on to the College of William and Mary, which would be transformed into a state university.

Thus, the state would see to it that talent, as well as tobacco and corn, was cultivated. "The tax which will be paid for this purpose is not more than the thousandth part of what will be paid to kings, priests, and nobles," Jefferson argued during the ensuing debate.

The rich objected to being taxed to educate the poor, and the dissenters did not want the Anglican-dominated college in Williamsburg to be the capstone of state education. Banding together, they defeated the bill. It was Virginia, as well as Jefferson, that was the loser. Undaunted, Jefferson continued his fight against special privilege and political conservatism. Unable to endure the Federalists, he founded a party of his own, which in time became the Democratic party. He organized it so well that it dominated first his state, then the young nation; so well that he was elected the third President of the Republic.

Jefferson's presidential inauguration in 1801 expressed the deliberate, almost ceremonial, abhorrence of ceremony which grew from his deep-rooted democratic beliefs. As the first Chief Executive to be inaugurated in the newly built capital, he entered Washington under simple circumstances, dismounted to take the oath, tethered his horse with his own hands. His openness and generous spirit contrasted sharply with the haughty bitterness of his defeated rival, John Adams, who refused to welcome his successor at the White House and spent his last hours there feverishly appointing Federalists to public offices.

The most memorable act of Jefferson's administration was the Louisiana Purchase. Though usually a strict constructionist, Jefferson did not hesitate to interpret the Constitution broadly on this point in order to acquire a vast hinterland for his people—a typical Jeffersonian decision, proving that he would never let a theory stand in the way of right action.

No historic name other than that of Jefferson in our history is so intimately associated with the twofold theme of agrarianism and democracy. He believed in natural rights, in the cause of American independence, and in private property as a means to individual happiness. He felt that the gift of being simple made men free, and that a close relationship to the earth made them strong. The land he loved above all else. "I return to farming with an ardor which I scarcely knew in my youth," he wrote to John Adams in 1794. "I have often thought that if heaven had given me choice of position and calling, it would have been on a rich spot of earth, well-watered, and near a good market for the productions of the garden. No occupation is so delightful to me as the culture of the earth."

He thought persistently and profoundly about democracy. Having devoted months of serious study to the Greek and Latin classics, he moved on to the works of Hume, Locke, Bolingbroke, Montesquieu, Voltaire, Adam Smith, and many other savants. Almost as much at home in the intellectual circles of Europe as he was in his Albemarle wheat fields, Jefferson never lost his appetite for the printed word. He had a standing order with book dealers in Paris, Amsterdam, Frankfort, Madrid, and London for volumes dealing with America. From Paris he wrote to Mr. S. H. Smith: "I devote every afternoon I am disengaged in examining all the principal book stores, turning over every book with my own hands, and putting by everything which relates to America and indeed whatever is rare and valuable in every science." No wonder that this man's books became the nucleus of the Library of Congress.

If there was much in the past that delighted Jefferson, there was much in the present that disgusted him. Some of his fellow planters seemed to him obstructionists and "cyphers of aristocracy." His mind was a relentless machine which crushed proud-standing Old World prejudices. He, if anyone, was America's *revolutionnaire*. Kings did not faze him. "This, Sire," he wrote to George III, "is our last, our determined resolution."

Some men deserve high honor because they tear down. Jefferson was not content merely to destroy. With words, ideas, and stones, he built up what he and others had torn down.

Just as his Declaration of Independence helped to liberate us from English political control, his architecture aided in releasing us from English aesthetic domination. His bricks and his words set us free. The first American to view architecture objectively within the framework of eighteenth-century thought, he found "natural" principles on which distinctively American architecture could rest. Discovered by the ancients, revived by Palladio, they crossed the ocean with him. Working with men like Latrobe, Bulfinch, Thornton, Mills, and Hallet, Jefferson brought a school of American architects into being. Never one to send others where he had not been, he was himself the best practicing architect of the lot, crowning the river bluffs and hilltops from the Chesapeake to the Blue Ridge with red brick houses which seemed always to have belonged on their sites —ordered, calm, and serene.

While still in his twenties, Jefferson drew big plans for his little mountain (in Italian, "Monticello"). Getting away from the Georgian, "the most wretched style I ever saw," was one of his obsessions. In the year of his marriage, 1772, he constructed a one-room cottage to receive his bride, and commenced planning the house which would supply him with most of his architectural education. His first design made use of a square mass with two rectangular wings. How he modified that design to closer conformity with the Palladian, built and rebuilt the house, ever returning to the problem that wars, crises, and high offices interrupted, is well told in architectural histories. Monticello was thought out, both an architectural and an intellectual achievement. It opened a new epoch in American architecture and design.

Jefferson's public buildings made clear just how far-reaching his new ideas were. In 1785 he drew up plans for the Virginia State Capitol at Richmond. Obviously this was "a favorable opportunity to introduce into the state an example of architecture in the classic style of antiquity." The building, called by an English architectural historian the "first case in the world where it was attempted to give an administrative building the external character, undeviatingly, of a classical temple,"[1] was of inestimable importance to the American aesthetic. It stands today, the most significant public building in Virginia.

Still, the very best that Jefferson would build would be erected closer to home, where the old man could sit on his front porch at Monticello and watch through his spyglass as the bricks were put into place.

Having retired from many years of public service, he learned in 1817 that his plans for a state university had been approved, and that two hundred acres west of Charlottesville had been purchased. The land, Jefferson noted enthusiastically, was "high, dry, open, furnished with good water, and with nothing in its vicinity which could threaten the health of students." The University of Virginia provided the greatest architectural and educational opportunity of his life. He made the most of it, accepting three fundamental principles as his guides: to strive for an architectural democracy by constructing distinct yet blended, independent yet affiliated, units; to conform to the laws of art so that public taste might be educated; and to create an academic village around a central square, where men might mingle in intellectual companionship.

There would be a central axis or lawn, formed by the construction of two parallel rows of professors' pavilions with connecting student quarters, and a great circular Library or Rotunda closing the upper end. Paralleling this lawn and its pavilions, three hundred feet to the rear along either side, would be smaller ranges or student quarters, with connecting quarters for student dining. From February to October, 1819, the seventy-seven-year-old Sage of Monticello worked on the plans. Such buildings as the Pantheon, Diocletian's Baths, the Theater of Marcellus, and the Temple of Cori were his models; they were reduced and modified, adapted to the rolling Albemarle hills, designed tastefully and solidly according to the nature of the material to be used. "We had," Jefferson wrote in his report to the Literary Board, "no supplementary guide but our own judgments." Posterity has considered these judgments sound.

In October, 1822, Jefferson reported that ten pavilions with gardens, six hotels, and 109 dormitories were completed "except for some garden walls, a little plaistering, some of the capitals, and part of the grounds." These deficiences were soon remedied. The Rotunda was erected, to tower over the academic village and provide the whole university with a pivot. The master plan had been translated from Jefferson's brain to the Virginia landscape. Thoughts had been metamorphosed into bricks.

Though his mind ranged over many fields, and his excellence illuminated them all, Jefferson remained throughout his entire career pre-eminently a farmer, striving to engraft the doctrines of the French physiocrats on his own plantation tradition. Three of his chief aides were John Taylor, Edmund Ruffin, and Cyrus McCormick, a quartet of American agrarians unmatched in perception and influence.

John Taylor was born in Caroline County in 1753, reared by his kinsman Edmund Pendleton, and educated at William and Mary. Articulate, honest, and brilliant, he eventually owned several plantations and became a leading philosopher of agrarianism. "He belonged," says Thomas H. Benton in his *Thirty Years' View,* "to that constellation of great men which shone so brightly in Virginia of his day, and the light of which was not limited to Virginia, or our America, but spread through the bounds of the civilized world."

Taylor, like Jefferson, was convinced that the farmer was the only true producer, and land the only true wealth. More concerned with realities than appearances, he was not awed by the "petty paper kingdoms" the Federalists were erecting. Expanded and contracted at the will of speculators, paper money subjected the country's business to the exploitation of money brokers. He was convinced that agrarianism and capitalism were incompatible. Sooner or later, America would have to choose between them.

In accordance with his premises, Taylor opposed governmental promotion of manufacturing, protective tariffs, and corporations. He defended the Louisiana Purchase on the grounds that it would encourage the westward expansion of agriculture, and argued that freedom of property was a natural right which should not be tampered with by the state. The policies of the Federalists, under Hamilton and Adams, seemed to him to be centralizing power in the national government at the expense of the states. Banking laws should be repealed, he said, and paper money prohibited. Only the educated should be allowed to vote; judicial review should be opposed because it made the federal government judge of its own powers. The landed interest is the only basis of democracy—a defense against communism on the one hand and capitalistic exploitation on the other. A nation made up of free and equal farmers would avoid factionalism, tyranny, and misery. To ensure such a state, Taylor demanded expropriation of the exploiters and a deliberate division of power.[2]

Though his writings were neglected in the latter half of the nineteenth century, Taylor appealed strongly to such twentieth-century historians as Charles Beard, V. L. Parrington, and A. Whitney Griswold. One of the most interesting groups of political and economic theorists that has sprung up in the twentieth century, the Nashville Agrarians, has paid him special homage.

As to the extent of Jefferson's agreement with the ideas of John Taylor of Caroline, there is no question: "Colonel Taylor and myself have rarely, if ever, differed in any political principle of importance. Every act of his life, and every word he ever wrote, satisfied me of this," he wrote in 1810.

Edmund Ruffin, born in Prince George County in 1794, also attended the College of William and Mary. After serving in the War of 1812 he married and settled down on Coggins Point Farm, which he gradually turned into an agricultural experimental station. His interest ran toward the more practical and pressing agricultural problems, such as soil depletion and fertilization. An alarming amount of Piedmont and Tidewater land was being misused by planters seeking quick profits. On worn-out fields, Ruffin observed, sorrel and pine always grew, and there was an insufficient quantity of calcareous earth. Eventually he proved that marl, a marine deposit rich in calcareous material, would cure worn-out acid soils. In the fall of 1818, while Jefferson was making plans for his university, Ruffin presented his findings to the Prince George Agricultural Society. He favored the growing of the southern cow pea, and the adoption of crop rotation. Although these ideas encountered opposition at first, they gradually took hold. First through the pages of *The American Farmer* and then through his own journal, *Farmers' Register,* Ruffin spread his program. As corresponding secretary of the Virginia State Board of Agriculture, and president of the Virginia State Agricultural Society, he was instrumental in bringing about the increase in the state's grain and fodder crops in the first half of the nineteenth century.[3]

In the year Thomas Jefferson was leaving the White House, another Virginian was born not many miles west of Monticello. The child would be smaller in intellect but greater in material success than Jefferson. He would supplement the thinking of Jefferson, Taylor, and Ruffin with a mechanical device that would revolutionize farming. Having tried unsuccessfully to sell it in Virginia, he would push on westward, the way history was going. Cyrus McCormick's reaper adds the inevitable coda to the Jeffersonian agrarian dream.

The world in which young McCormick grew up was simple, solid, and sweaty. His Scotch-Irish grandfather had migrated south from Pennsylvania and, halfway down the Valley of Virginia, had bought 450 acres near Steele's Tavern. Because he opposed the introduction of hymns into the Presbyterian service, the elder Robert helped erect the Old Providence Meeting House. His son Robert, hard-working and able, acquired 1,800 acres, ran saw and flour mills, and became a man of affairs. By Valley standards, the McCormicks were well-to-do.

This did not mean that their children were pampered. They worked hard on the land, picking up what "book learning" they could from the hearth and old field school. Cyrus studied Webster's *Speller,* Adams' *Geography,* and the Bible. Close to the land, he learned from nature, too; learned of the mystery, the wonder, the symmetry of things.

On late summer days he watched the ripe grain blow in the wind; saw his father and the men harvest it by hand. As he watched, he wondered. Robert had always said there should be a machine to do this job. Inside his son's mind, wheels began to turn.

Cyrus was thirteen when his father built a new home for his growing family. He got the stone from his own fields, the lumber from his trees, and the lime from his kilns. On top of sturdy foundations he erected a red brick house with a broad hallway and eight rectangular rooms on two floors. There were hand-carved mantels, broad fireplaces, and a porch on which Robert could sit and look out over his land. The house stands today, just as Robert McCormick built it.

Cyrus spent hours tinkering about the blacksmith's shop. He made a light cradle out of locust wood to ease the work at harvest, and a terrestrial globe on which he depicted the seas and continents. At night he liked to play the fiddle. When he went to church on Sundays, he noticed the neighborhood girls, as did all the other young men in the Valley. On October 31, 1831, he wrote to a friend: "Mr. Hart has two fine daughters, rite pretty, very smart, and as rich probably as you could wish; but alas! I have other business to attend to and can devote but a small proportion of my time to society."

The "other business" would carry the name McCormick around the world. That business was the perfecting of a reaper, the first to include all the basic parts of the modern grain cutter—the straight reciprocating knife, guards, reel, platform, main wheel, side-moving cutter, and divider at the outer end of the cutter bar.

Cyrus' machine was first demonstrated on John Steele's grain field in 1831. It touched one of man's basic needs, and took much of the drudgery out of a necessary chore. He opened the door for a new era in agriculture by finding a way to replace muscle power with mechanical power on a job that had to be done. He saw to it that the multitudes were fed.

No easy task, this. Inventing the reaper was only part of it. Afterward he had to invent the reaper business. The hilly country of Virginia was not nearly as well suited to his purposes as the western prairies, where the man shortage led to increased demands for labor-saving devices. Cyrus traveled thousands of miles before he established his factory. The town he chose was one of America's youngest, ugliest, and least prosperous. Exhausted by mud, droughts, debt, and panics, it did not look like the site of a future metropolis. It had no railroad, gas, sewer, or stockyard. Only one short block of its streets had been paved when Cyrus first went there. Even the name was unpromising: Chicago.

Virginian Cyrus McCormick had the vision to see what Chicago could become. The town's first big manufacturer, he built a large factory and grew with Chicago. He, as much as any one man, helped to make it the principal wheat center of the world.

The reaper was introduced to Europe at the 1851 London World's Fair. At first the London *Times* called the machine "a cross between an Astley chariot, a wheelbarrow, and a flying machine." But when the Englishmen saw what McCormick's machine could do, they hailed it as the revolutionary instrument it was.

Many of the Americans who toasted and praised Cyrus McCormick had nothing good to say about the master of Monticello. When the first reaper was tested, Jefferson had already been five years in his grave. The Jeffersonian years were over—and many Virginians were glad of it. Few leaders have been so bitterly attacked as he who championed the abolition of primogeniture and entails, breaking up "the hereditary and high-handed aristocracy which, by accumulating immense masses of property, divides our country into nobles and plebeians."[4] Jefferson's insistence on favoring the *aristoi* rather than the aristocracy brought the theory of social control into conformity with the revolutionary situation. Many Virginians never accepted his ideas. Some never will.

One way of judging the impact of Jefferson's ideas is to note the stature of the men who debated and opposed them—John Adams, Alexander Hamilton, John Jay, even his own cousin, John Marshall. Marshall's father was a pioneer settler of the same type as Jefferson's, and it was during Jefferson's Presidency that Marshall began his monumental work as Chief Justice of the Supreme Court. Any evaluation of Marshall's decisions should take into account the dreadful winter he spent at Valley Forge, watching patriots suffer and starve because the government was too weak to supply and feed them. He held that the Supreme Court should decide whether or not the Constitution was being violated, and that the national law was superior to any state law. He championed unity as vigorously as Jefferson championed diversity, and both of them shaped the destiny of the Republic.

Throughout his life Jefferson fought and argued hard, despite the opposition. When he was elected President, Yale's president, Timothy Dwight, warned the New Haven ladies to stay off the streets, lest they be subjected to a fate worse than death. Rumor had it that the infidel Jefferson would confiscate all Bibles. Jefferson's enemies solemnly warned that he would destroy capitalism, culture, and Christianity. So strong were his enemies, even in the Louisiana territory he acquired, that newly formed states flatly refused to be named Jefferson. At the convention which named Louisiana, a delegate threatened to blow up the building if the name were debated on the floor. The Jefferson faction fared no better at the conventions that named Colorado and Idaho. His ideas were genuinely and widely disliked. Few kind allusions were made to the chief architect of American democracy by Republican spokesmen from Grant to Hoover.

Such neglect is all the more remarkable when one notes that Jefferson was the intellectual father of the American advance to the Pacific. While in Paris, he had worked out a plan with John Ledyard, who would go eastward through Siberia to the Pacific Northwest, then overland across the continent to Virginia. The Russian Empress Catherine blocked that trip; but no one halted the Louisiana Purchase, or the Jefferson-sanctioned trip of Lewis and Clark to the Pacific Northwest. This expedition, as Henry Nash Smith has noted, "lay on the level of imagination: it was drama, it was the enactment of a myth that embodied the future."[5] Once more Jefferson leaped ahead of his time; history is only now catching up with him.

The last seventeen years of his life were spent at home. The Sage of Monticello wrote his letters, received innumerable guests and visitors, and built his University. He never abandoned a principle, a plan, or a friend. He worked hard, thought earnestly, and died poor. Buried on his little mountain, he rests under a stone on which were engraved words he himself composed:

> Here was buried
> Thomas Jefferson
> Author of the
> Declaration
> of
> American Independence
> of the
> Statute of Virginia
> for
> Religious Freedom
> and Father of the
> University of Virginia

Had someone else written the epitaph, there are many achievements he might have added, and virtues he might have praised. A century later Jefferson's pivotal place in American thought would be acknowledged. A likeness of his face would be carved on Mount Rushmore, engraved on the nickel, and printed on the three-cent stamp. Europeans, in re-evaluating the contributions of a nation suddenly thrust into world leadership, have found few Americans so worthy of study and analysis as the master of Monticello. In the dark days of World War II the United States chose him as the symbol of their endangered democracy, and drew again from his faith and vision. The national government gave him a marble shrine not far from those of America's two earlier ones. All three of these tributes to our demigods were designed more wisely than many politicians knew.[6]

The Washington Monument is the earliest and loftiest, the most abstract and Olympian. There is no human resemblance, only the white marble shaft soaring upward.

The Lincoln Memorial is the most dramatic and popular. Inside sits the figure of a tall brooding man. His face is wrinkled from trying to solve problems for which there are no solutions. Patiently he waits, day and night, for the sound of battle and rebellion to subside.

The Jefferson Memorial is dome-shaped and classical, symmetrical and deceptively simple. April surrounds it with green grass and pink cherry blossoms. Inside stands the erect figure of a bold uncompromising man, alertly watching lest some new tyranny over the human mind go unnoticed.

8 *Bountiful Harvests and Bad Seeds*

FAT BEANS, GRAPES SWEETER THAN MUSCADINE
ROT ON THE VINE: IN THAT LAND WERE WE BORN.
Allen Tate

In the spring of 1807 an immigrant wagon, pulled by a five-horse team, started west from Timber Ridge, Virginia. The man of the family had died. Elizabeth Paxton Houston, straight and strong-faced at fifty, must take her brood of nine children into the wilderness without him.

Her fifth son, a sturdy fourteen-year-old, was named Sam Houston after his father. Later on the eyes of Texas—and indeed the whole nation—would be on him. It was in Virginia's soil that this oak tree of a man, and many other western heroes, was firmly rooted. The power and the glory were moving to the other side of the mountains.

Still, the state the Houstons were leaving was not yet past her prime. Though Kentucky had been severed from her, Virginia was still the Union's largest, wealthiest, and most powerful state. One of her sons, George Washington, had set the course of the ship of state. Another, Thomas Jefferson, was at the helm; his neighbors James Madison and James Monroe would succeed him, and men would talk of the Virginia Dynasty.

Their years would be marred by the War of 1812. Begun with discontent, continued with indifference, and concluded without victory, the war did set respect for American writing and thinking to soaring. The struggle reinstated the national feeling which the Revolution had given. "The people are more Americans, feeling and acting as a nation," Albert Gallatin observed in the decade after the fighting.

If posterity viewed the War of 1812 as less than triumphant, few then living took so dim a view. We had shown England we would not be bullied. Old Hickory had trounced the British regulars at New Orleans. With the signing of the Treaty of Ghent in 1815, Americans for the first time ceased to doubt the path they were to follow. "Not only was the unity of their nation established, but its probable divergence from older societies was also well defined," wrote Henry Adams.[1]

The bundle of years following is called the Era of Good Feeling. James Monroe was re-elected President in 1820 with only one dissenting electoral vote—cast so he would not duplicate Washington's unanimous victory. His 1823 Monroe Doctrine, feasible because of the strength of the same British navy which Americans had fought in 1812, announced that the New World was no longer open to European colonization. Well might the nationalists rejoice.

National optimism and chauvinism were clearly reflected in Virginia. New enterprises flourished from the seaboard to the Kanawha River. Horse paths gave way to turnpikes as urban population jumped 158 per cent from 1790 to 1810. Plows bit deep into the virgin land, changing forests into grain and tobacco fields. Merchants whose fathers had stocked a few necessary items advertised duffel and rose blankets, callimanicoes, ladies' fashionable hats, and ribbons of newest taste.

Summer spas and watering places catered to people with new leisure and income. As early as 1791, Captain Ferdinand Bayard of Paris found Bath gay with a troupe of Irish comedians, billiards, and such active gambling tables that planters who arrived with a carriage and attendants sometimes left with only a horse. White Sulphur Springs, Hot Springs, Warm Springs, and Rockbridge Alum Springs had gay seasons. Medicos swore that the water would make barren wives fertile, to say nothing of curing consumption, dropsical spleens, and king's evil. The plagues which beset coastal towns did not spread to the mountains. Life and love at the waters made a romantic chapter in the story of nineteenth-century Virginia.[2]

The Revolutionary generation had planted seeds of liberty, pretention, and prosperity. The early decades of the nineteenth century took in the bountiful harvest.

To tie her vast western territory to the east, Virginia needed canals. When George Washington traveled beyond the Alleghenies in 1784, he inspected the falls of the western rivers and made a prediction. "But smooth the road and make easy the way for Western settlers," he wrote to Virginia's Governor Benjamin Harrison from Mount Vernon, "and see how amply we shall be compensated for any trouble and expense we may encounter to effect it."

The next year two companies were formed. The Potomac Company was to build a waterway which would ultimately connect that river with the Ohio. The James River Company proposed to link the James and Kanawha rivers by a canal over the Allegheny Mountains, thus providing an all-water route to the Ohio Valley.

Their reach exceeded their grasp. Having constructed four short canals between the City of Washington and a point above Harpers Ferry, the impoverished Potomac Company transferred its charter to the Chesapeake and Ohio in 1828. Aided by the federal government, as well as Maryland and Virginia, this larger company managed to push the canal as far as Cumberland, Virginia, by 1850. By that time the Erie Canal had been opened for twenty-five years, giving the Hudson River and New York a priority in western traffic. And only two years later the Baltimore and Ohio Railroad reached Wheeling, funneling off western traffic to the port of Baltimore.

Why was Virginia outstripped by her northern neighbors? One major reason is that instead of concentrating on the Potomac, she wasted millions of dollars trying to build a second Western waterway. The James River and Kanawha Canal cost Virginia not only much treasure and time but also her greatest commercial opportunity.

This was not apparent in the early years of the century. Small flat-bottomed boats could by 1805 carry as much as a hundred tons between Richmond and Lynchburg. Coal, iron, and wheat came east; flour, tobacco, and manufactured goods went west. Rugged men like Corny Comes, Dug Dovel, Sharp Good, and Columbus Kite manned the barges or "gundalows." River towns were as sinful as short stay-overs would allow. Old-timers still retell grandfathers' tales with twinkling eyes. To announce its arrival, the barge lookout blew on an eight-foot tin horn. The sound carried for five miles, splitting the air on cold clear mornings. There is nothing on today's railroads or highways to match it.

The state's goal was to extend the canal westward over the Alleghenies, so Washington's vision might become a reality. By 1851 the canal had reached Buchanan, 196 miles west of Richmond. But there was no more money, and no practical scheme for getting a canal over the Alleghenies. A short-range success, the canal was a long-range failure. The Yorkers had the plum, with their Erie Canal. The only recourse for Virginia was to expand her railroads.

Once again she did not act quickly or boldly enough. The horse-drawn Chesterfield Railway succeeded in carrying coal a few miles from Chesterfield County mines to Richmond. The Petersburg Railroad ran steam locomotives from Weldon to Portsmouth by 1837. Richmond saw that she might become a manufacturing and transportation center; but two other cities, Baltimore and Charleston, South Carolina, became the real railroad capitals. The Richmond, Fredericksburg, and Potomac Railroad, chartered in 1834, did not reach Washington until 1872. In 1844, the nine independent Virginia railroad companies were operating a combined total of only two hundred miles of track. Beyond the Valley, most of the western mountains of Virginia were serviced by the rails from Baltimore.

In the matter of ocean trade, too, Virginia fell behind her competitors. Although she had at Norfolk one of the world's best harbors, flanked by a network of inland waterways, the state watched maritime traffic dwindle to less than that of Boston, New York, Philadelphia, or Baltimore. In *Norfolk, Historic Southern Port,* Thomas J. Wertenbaker illustrates how for all of Virginia, but especially for Norfolk, this was a time of wasted opportunities and bitter disappointment. "The proud Old Dominion, once the undisputed leader in the Union," writes Dr. Wertenbaker, "saw one state after another pass her in all that makes for influence and power."[3] The high promise of the first quarter of the century was not fulfilled in the second. Audacity gave way to complacency, and nationalism to sectionalism. A new generation planted bad seeds, and the following generation would reap in tears.

The most important fact about the wedding of Jeffersonian ideals and state politics is that it ended in a divorce. Virginia turned her back on her Revolutionary leaders and ideas, and built up an aristocratic social order quite like the one the Jeffersonians had overthrown. Often presumed to be an continuation of the old aristocracy, the new gentry was nothing of the kind. "In whose hands now are the once proud seats of Westover, Cerles, Maycocks,

Shirley, and others in Virginia?" asked Henry Clay in 1833. "They have passed into other and stranger hands." The small farmers and overseers who bought up the decaying plantations were not the match of their predecessors. Generally unaware of the driving forces shaping the fast-moving nineteenth century, they sowed the bad seeds.

Contrast the three Virginia Presidents in the first quarter of the century (Jefferson, Madison, and Monroe) with the three in the second (Harrison, Tyler, and Taylor). Although it is hard to generalize about individuals as different as these six men, one can assert that while the first three were looking toward the future, the second trio were looking toward the past. The Jeffersonians drove the country forward. Their Virginia successors, by vetoing measures to establish a Bank of the United States and to use federal funds for internal improvements, tried vainly to hold it back. The way in which Thomas Jefferson and John Tyler used their years after retirement makes another sharp, and not insignificant, contrast. At Monticello, Jefferson continued to study, invent, and keep in touch with Europe. He planned, founded, and built a University. At Sherwood Forest, his plantation, John Tyler was chiefly concerned with teas, balls, and visits among prominent Tidewater neighbors. He and his beautiful young wife plied the James River in a bright blue boat with rich satin damask cushions. The oarsmen, picked slaves, wore blue-trimmed uniforms, white linen trousers, and black patent leather belts. Their shirts were embroidered with a bow and arrow, since their master came from Sherwood Forest. Their straw hats were sky-blue, with the boat's name, *Pocahontas*, emblazoned on them. Here was the pomp and pretense Thomas Jefferson had despised.

Before his death in 1826 Jefferson observed the trend away from toleration and intellectual freedom. His appointing Thomas Cooper to the faculty of the University of Virginia brought strong protests from zealous religionists. Cooper asked Jefferson if he should resign. Jefferson urged him to stay on, admitting the state's ministers were "violent, ambitious of power, and want nothing but license from the laws to kindle again the fires."

Cooper's reply of July 1, 1820, was both perceptive and prophetic: "The reign of ignorance, bigotry, and intolerance is fast approaching. It will pass away, but not in my time."

Various accounts of the ensuing religious spirit bear out Cooper's observation. There is, for example, Jesse Burton Harrison's letter from Lynchburg. Writing to a German professor, Dr. Floriep, he reported that the town was "over-run with a fanatical religious spirit that employs all thoughts, interrupts all business, forbids all social parties, and treats all dancing as the greatest of crimes."[4]

The sectionalism of the time was no less fanatical. Judge Beverley Tucker's 1836 novel, *The Partisan Leader,* not only foretold the Civil War, but gloried in its coming. Tucker's own speech at the Nashville Convention in 1850 showed how completely the rational and cosmopolitan tone of the eighteenth century had evaporated: "What Virginia says, I am ever ready to vindicate; what Virginia does, I, at all hazards and to the last extremity, will maintain."

Jefferson's insistence that Virginia adopt a thoroughgoing free-school system for all qualified students was forgotten in the next generation. Education remained a luxury in the Commonwealth until the Civil War. Here Virginians lost their greatest opportunity. Their failure to maintain leadership of the Union was largely due to the scarcity of well-educated minds.[5]

Statistics document the sad story. In 1840 there were almost 60,000 white illiterates in Virginia; one out of twelve whites could not read or write. At the same time the ratio was one to 164 in Massachusetts, and one to 300 in New Hampshire. In that year Virginia had 35,321 pupils in primary schools, less than a third of them at public charge.

Ten years later, there were only 52,000 students enrolled in all Virginia's public and private schools. The proportion of native whites in school was 12 per cent, the lowest in the Union except for Florida and California, then frontier states. When the Civil War came, Virginia had a population of a million and a quarter, but only 67,000 were attending schools. Of that number, 31,000 were pauper children. No semblance of a free public school system existed.

Consequently the state was lacking in well-informed and urbane leaders at a time when they were desperately needed. Long before the secession crisis, Virginia was confronted with two internal revolutions. Her inability to find adequate solutions for these made her decline inevitable. In a sense, the Civil War did not wreck Virginia. She wrecked herself in the preceding generation; the war was the unnecessary, bloody coda.

One of the internal revolutions was political, the other social. For generations western Virginia had chafed under Tidewater domination. In 1771 a group of leaders west of the Blue Ridge petitioned the Crown for a separate government. The Revolution halted negotiations, and the dissident west was included in the new Commonwealth of Virginia. Nearly all government buildings were in the east. To them went the bulk of state funds. Representation in the state legislature was patently unfair. For example, Warwick County with 614 white population and Berkeley County with 17,832 had the same number of representatives in the Assembly. Since there were few slaves in the west, and slaves were taxed at a lower rate than beasts of the field, the system of taxation worked against western Virginians. As people west of the Ridge increased in numbers and power, so did their demands. They hated the highhanded aristocrats of the lowlands. They were Virginians, too, and would have a fair share in the government.

When demands made at the 1816 Staunton Convention were not heeded, the dispute became so bitter that veteran leaders expected to see the state split asunder during their lifetimes. The 1829 Constitutional Convention was in effect a major effort to keep Virginia intact.

To the convention came three patriarchs, in the evening of their glory—James Madison, James Monroe, and John Marshall. They were voices and faces out of the past, faint and anachronistic. Madison, who had begun his political career in the 1776 Virginia Convention, was seventy-eight years old now, too weak of voice to make himself easily heard and too frightened when on his feet to enjoy speaking publicly. Monroe, at seventy-one the youngest of the trio, was chosen to preside over affairs. Marshall, seventy-five, was as careless about his appearance as he had been in 1782 when he entered the House of Delegates. Undoubtedly the presence of these three venerable figures and their insistence on sectional harmony helped to make the work of the Convention acceptable to a majority of the state's voters.

Though passed, the new constitution was not successful. It was essentially a compromise and, like many compromises, not really satisfactory to either side. The seats in the House of Delegates were reapportioned. The western gains were confined to the Valley. The trans-Allegheny area actually suffered a slight decrease in its proportion of the seats. Delegates from the trans-Allegheny counties voted to a man against the final arrangement, but could not defeat it.

The new document did not allow all white men to vote; did not give the western counties a fair share of representation and internal improvements; did not further the cause of democracy. Worst of all, the compromise was frozen into a rigid constitution, with no procedure for amending its provisions. Politically speaking, the state continued to move toward crisis and fragmentation. In the 1860's the western and not the northern portion of Virginia broke off from Virginia and sided with the Union.

The social revolution was inherent in the system of chattel slavery. Jefferson had consistently opposed it; Madison had called it a dreadful calamity; Monroe had acted to repatriate Negroes in Africa. Yet Dixie's agricultural economy was built upon slave labor. Federal laws forbade the importation of slaves; many a Virginian profited from slave breeding. Cotton was king in the deep South, and high prices paid for surplus slaves might restore a portion of Virginia's earlier prosperity. Slavery, which for half a century had been a moribund institution without apologists, came back into its own. Two Virginians, George Fitzhugh and Thomas Dew, were among its loudest defenders. The Old Dominion was in the unenviable position of the man holding a highly charged electric wire. She wanted to let go, but couldn't.

One year after the 1829 political convention which exposed the internal tension, a slave revolt in Tidewater dramatized the racial tension and crystallized sentiment for and against abolition.

The man who led it was Nat Turner, whom the other slaves called "the Prophet." Born in 1800, not far from Dred Scott's birthplace, Nat had on his head and breast marks which he interpreted as signs from the Lord. Because his work was not especially hard on the plantation of Joseph Travis in Southhampton County, Nat had time to fast, pray, and read the Bible. He lived in a mystical world, and communed with the Spirit. In 1825 he ran away from home, but the Spirit told him to return. Like Moses in the Old Testament, he was to set his people free.

Nat saw drops on the corn and blood on the leaves. In the spring of 1828 the Spirit told him that the Serpent was loosed. The time would soon come when the first would be last. Nat listened, believed, and watched for a sign. It came in the form of a solar eclipse on February 12, 1831. Sick that day, Nat delayed the uprising. On a hot August day six months later the sun turned greenish-blue. Nat struck.

Placing a ladder against the chimney, he entered the Travis house, went downstairs, and unbarred the door. Travis, his wife, and three children were killed with axes. Throughout the night Nat Turner's band increased and the slaughter continued. Next morning Mrs. Waller and ten children who gathered at her home for school were murdered. Within twenty-four hours, fifty-seven whites had been butchered. Bands of farmers, local militia, and federal troops converged upon the district, murdering at least 120 slaves. For weeks afterward voluntary patrols roamed the countryside, torturing and maiming Negroes suspected of taking part in the uprising. Turner himself eluded his pursuers for over two months. He was finally captured, sentenced to death, and hanged on November 11.[6]

The insurrection had profound repercussions throughout the South. In nearby Fayetteville hundreds of women and children fled to the swamps, to emerge muddy and starved two days later. Troops poured into Virginia from neighboring states and from United States ships of war. The horrible nightmare of every Southerner was becoming a reality—the Negro was fighting back.

The Southern states adopted drastic measures to curb possible rebellion. The movement of free Negroes was restricted, and stringent curfew laws for Negroes were enacted, Slave codes were made harsher. After 1831, Virginia and other Southern states adopted an attitude much more belligerent and intolerant than that of former days. Both the pro- and antislavery factions became even more inflexible and incapable of understanding the opposing points of view. Both sides were caught in a polemical trap. Reason deserted the field; emotionalism took over.

A hatred of the abolitionists was easily transferred to the northern states which harbored the most vociferous. In some ways the outstanding Virginian of the period was John Randolph. Judge the shift from national to sectional thinking by pondering his often-quoted remark: "When I speak of my nation, I mean the Commonwealth of Virginia."

The speeches, newspapers, textbooks, and novels of the mid-nineteenth century documented the intellectual blockade. Neither side had a corner on dogmatism. Three years after its publication in 1852, *Uncle Tom's Cabin* had elicited fourteen fictional "replies" from Southern authors. Gone forever were the casual and sentimental portraits of novelists like Kennedy, Cooke, and Simms. Portraiture of Negroes descended from caricature to libel.

Tensions and unsolved problems mounted. A small, smug Richmond clique was running the state. Education was for the privileged few. Fanaticism was replacing toleration in religion. Sectionalism was driving cosmopolitan thought underground. Slavery was being defended by men who a generation earlier would have opposed it. Though it had cost him his life, Nat Turner's vision had been valid. His people would be set free. There would be blood—a very great deal of blood—on the leaves.

9 *Lean Men and Long Rifles*

LAY DOWN, BOYS, TAKE A LITTLE NAP,
WE'RE ALL GOING DOWN TO CUMBERLAND GAP.
Folk song

Anyone could sense that there was going to be right smart helling. The whole neighborhood, and especially the young people, were all riled up. Eyes sparkled. Horses pawed the ground as if they wanted to feel the wild wind in their manes. Grandpa, who had been counted on to die ten years ago, let out a war whoop that put you in mind of a Huron spotting a Mohawk.

"What's brewin', neighbor?"

"Pot licker and a spring weddin'!"

The east was all right, but America began the far side of the Valley. Mountain weddings were enough to prove it. They were the drinkin'est, hog-killin'est, chair-flingin'est time of the year.

Preparation started long before marrying day. For miles around women prepared the vittles: pork, beef, turkey, fowl, bear meat, and shucky-beans in wooden bowls and pewter dishes. To inaugurate the occasion, the men played a game called "Run for the Bottle" —a dash on horseback toward a dangling bottle. The more logs, brush, and obstacles, the better. The start was announced with a yell. Horses leaped forward, the devil took the hindmost, and the winner claimed the bottle.

Guests started moving before daybreak, since the ceremony took place at noon. There was no store, tailor, or dressmaker close by; but somehow everyone managed to have a little extra color for the big day. There was plenty of red and green around.

Right after the ceremony, which only took a few minutes, they ate dinner, which took hours. The table, a large slab of wood hewed out with a broadax, was supported by branches set in auger holes. There were gourds and hard-shelled squashes to drink out of. Horn-handled table knives might not cut too well. But scalping knives were sharp as razors, and hardly a man around was without one.

So they ate up the infare—bones and all—and got ready for the shivaree.

After dinner, dancing, which might last several days, commencing with three- and four-handed reels and square sets. Pretty soon the young 'uns would be jigging and cutting out, as the fiddlers ripped through "Hell Amongst the Yearlings," "Frog Mouth," "Nigger in the Woodpile," "Bear Creek," and "Rats in the Meal Barrel." If, after four or five hours, anybody tried to slip off for a cat nap, he was hunted out, dragged back, and paraded on the floor while the fiddler played "Hang Out Till Morning." When chairs ran out, the boys held the girls on their laps.

About midnight somebody would ask, coyly: "Wonder how the bride and groom are doing?" Loud guffaws. "They must need a little refreshment by now. Where's Black Betty?" The bottle so named would be sent up to the loft where the couple were bedded. Beef, port, and cabbage went with it. Dancing would stop momentarily while some one proposed a toast:

"Here's health to the groom, not forgetting myself, and health to the bride, thumping luck, and big children!"

Sooner or later the folks would be reconciled to going home and waiting till the next wedding. There they would weave and spin, despair and dream, rock the young and bury the dead.

Frederick Jackson Turner, noted historian of the frontier, compiled a list of traits which life on the cutting edge of civilization engendered: a coarseness and strength combined with acuteness and inquisitiveness; a masterful grasp of material things; a restless nervous energy; a dominant individualism, working for good and for evil; a buoyancy and exuberance which come from freedom. Let it stand as the communal epitaph for the lean men who manned Virginia's eighteenth-century frontier.

A livelier, perkier bunch of people than these early back-country pioneers you never hoped to see. Even the five-year-olds could out-mock mockingbirds, catch Juney bugs, and call doodlebugs out of their holes. Boys who could hardly tote a rifle knew that if a white pigeon settles on the chimney, or an owl screeches with a hoarse voice, calamity is near. They knew you can't catch a weasel asleep, and that toads never open up their mouths in dog days. They could show you the place in the swine's forefoot where the devil came out.

The little girls were mountain-wise too. They kept an eye out for ravens. King Arthur was turned into a raven, and in the springtime came to circle over Virginny. Raven once snow-white, a tattle-tale, now he is black. Robin plucked a thorn from Christ's temple, now his breast is red. If a bird gets into your house, there's sure to be a death in the family. If you bite the head of a butterfly, you'll get a dress the color of that butterfly. But try not to tear it the first time you wear it. If you do, somebody will tell a lie about you before sunset.

The old women who appeared to cut loose the newborn and bury the dead could cure anything. They used pipsissewa for dropsy and snakeroot for headache. Jerusalem-oak tea was good for worms. A spider in an old quilt, hung around the neck, cured ague. Sass tea a spring tonic, tansy tea too. Pokeweed leaves made a good poultice for sores. Peppermint tea did wonders for indigestion and the blood of a black cat cured St. Anthony's disease. For strange and ornery complaints, it was best to get help from the seventh child of a seventh child.

West of the Shenandoah Valley the geography changes. Instead of peaceful meadows and green countryside, there are ancient blue mountains, underseamed with coal and massive resistance. Ridges and valleys form a jigsaw of compartments; every ridge and valley is different from the rest. The steep slopes have shallow and stony soils. From them spring red honeysuckle, lavender lilacs, snowballs, and many kinds of lilies. Standing on top of these hills, the first settlers looked out at an ocean of leaves, moving like waves in the spring breezes. They saw elms with slim weeping branches, sturdier plumper maples, gnarled stubby-fingered oaks, broad leafy lindens. Here and there a pine pierced the horizon, dwarfing all the other trees in their royal silences.

There are different versions of reports as to the first white man to move into the Alleghenies. Certainly Thomas Batts and Robert Fallam had crossed the Valley and pushed on to a Totero Indian village near present-day Roanoke by 1671. Two years later James

Needham and Gabriel Arthur got as far as Tennessee. They were trailblazers rather than settlers. In 1748 the first major survey of the area was conducted under Colonel James Patton. He had a grant from the Crown for 120,000 acres, to be located west of the Alleghenies and north of the North Carolina line. The next year Dr. Thomas Walker organized the Loyal Company and petitioned Virginia's royal Governor for a grant. He and his associates were authorized to take up and survey 800,000 acres. When Walker and his party pushed west to do so, they came upon the cabin of an Indian trader named Samuel Stalnaker, near future Abingdon. Stalnaker, at that time the westernmost white settler in Virginia, told them about the wilderness beyond, and the "Cave Gap" which passed through the Allegheny wall. Three weeks later Walker found the narrow, six-mile long canyon, and guessed that many other people would follow him through it in the future. The name was later changed to Cumberland Gap. On the other end was dark and bloody ground which had to be won and settled.

At this time "western Virginia" meant the same as "western America." Orange County, established in 1734, stretched to the Mississippi River. Kentucky, a Virginia county, was not permitted to call a convention to organize a state government until 1786. The Wilderness Road was for many years a Virginia road.

Draper's Meadow was founded at present-day Blacksburg in 1750. The Shawnees, encouraged by the failure of Washington's expedition in 1754 and remembering past grievances, attacked and pillaged the western village. Instead of improving, conditions were deteriorating. "Our situation at present is very different from what it was when we had the pleasure of your company," Colonel William Preston wrote George Washington on July 26, 1763. "All the valleys of Roanoke River and along the waters of the Mississippi are depopulated, except Captain English with a few families on New River, who have built a fort."[1] The Indians, encouraged by their French allies, enjoyed a short-lived supremacy. The treaty of Paris in 1763 marked Britain's rise and France's decline. Five years later, at Fort Stanwix, the white men persuaded the Iroquois to relinquish claims to land between the Alleghenies and the Ohio River. The "shakeguts" could roll west.

What an incredible ragamuffin procession it was: landless and often penniless pilgrims, "passing large rivers without shoes or stockings," Moses Austin noted, "and barely as many raggs as covers their nakedness." What they lacked in comfort they made up in faith. Few were as eloquent as an eighteenth-century Piedmont farmer, Thomas Jefferson. But many of them believed as fervently in the land as did the master of Monticello, who wrote: "Those who labour in the earth are the chosen people of God, if ever he had a chosen people."

The mountains these settlers faced were man-sized; tough to walk over, let alone to conquer. Talk about wilderness—there was nothing like this back in Tidewater. Out here the grass was crotch-high on a nine-foot Indian.

Call up the hogs, pack the pony, spit on the fire, and get moving! It was a rough-and-tumble life. Only the hardiest survived. Eye gougings and nose bitings were so common that the Virginia state legislature passed a law making it a misdemeanor "to disable the tongue, or eye, or slit or bite the nose, lip, or ear of another." The names on the land told the story: Poverty Hollow, Scuffle Ridge, Scrabbletown, Purgatory Creek. West of the Valley, men had to fight the devil and give him an underhold.

They were going out back of civilization as a shock absorber; their job was to take it:

> I came to this country in seventeen-forty-nine
> I saw many a true love, but I never saw mine
> I looked all around me and found I was alone—
> And me a poor stranger, and a long way from home.

There wasn't a chance of conquering this type of country, only sickness, toil, and danger to look forward to. But there would be another land, later on; it was this one the settlers sang about when things looked bad:

> I'm just a poor wayfaring stranger
> A-trav'ling through this world of woe;
> But there's no sickness, toil nor danger
> In that bright world to which I go.
>
> I'm going there to see my daddy,
> I'm going there no more to roam;
> I'm just a-going over Jordan
> I'm just a-going over home.

There was almost as much Calvinism as coal in the hills. Most of these people were Scotch-Irish or Roundhead English, with some Germans and French Huguenots. They had little use for ritual and endless respect for the Word found in the Old and New Testament.

They believed it, literally and thoroughly. Not to believe that troubles and disasters were the direct expression of God's wrath was the rankest of heresy; to die out of church was to die out of grace. By 1800 there were at least 138 congregations of Presbyterians established in the mountains.[2]

Religion, cut off from the main sources of ideas and change by the mountains, sometimes evolved into superstition. The Virginia mountains were, and still are, full of Gothic tales of witchery, superstition, and charms. Fear hung over daily life as clouds hovered over mountain peaks. Witches soured dough, caused cows to go dry, killed hogs, and created maggots in cream. A sharp-edged instrument under the bed relieved the pains of childbirth. Most houses had ghosts who wailed in the long lonesome nights.

Things came hard in the hills. Crops didn't do well on the sides of hills, especially when the rain started washing away the topsoil. The only plows were forked saplings with one iron-covered prong. This ground was tough to break. The horse, if there was one, had a grapevine or a rawhide harness. If there wasn't any horse, the old woman or one of the boys would have to pull. If the corn wasn't in the ground when the oak leaves were the size of squirrel's ears, somebody was like to go hungry.

Travelers might notice a cloud of dust up ahead, and see as they moved closer a gnarled figure emerge, beating the particles from his homespun pants. "What happened?" the newcomer might say. The question would give the farmer a chance to do a little legpulling, as well as complaining. "Third time I've fell out of that damned cornfield today," he might say, "and I've still got ten rows to grub!"

The men who broke this ground rose before dawn and toiled into the darkness, with their wives or children holding a pine torch for them to see by. Aided by neighbors, they piled the trunks of trees into heaps and burned them, grubbed up the stumps, hacked away the underbrush, clubbed the snakes. Every day the sun was in the sky, and many nights when the moon was out they drove plows and hopes into the earth, with uptorn roots and briars bruising limbs every step of the way.[3]

Animals had a hard time, too, frequently dying from injuries, snakebite, and exposure. Pigs did best; they were too tough for rattlesnakes. Before long, hog and hominy were standard frontier fare. Families which were better settled, and blessed with a cow, dined off mush and milk. Vegetables were scarce. Game bagged by the long rifle provided the only real variety on the table.

Calendars were all right, but upcountry the four seasons were plantin' time, hoein' time, fodder-pullin', and cold. In between they could set around, sing love songs and hymns, and think about heaven. Heaven was the place where grandpa expected to have spareribs every meal.

What did best on the Virginia frontier was not the crops or the animals, but the men. They raised them tough all the way through. Their mas started them out with mountain dew, and kept on till they had milk teeth. Then they might move to cracklin' bread and squirrel stew, with maybe a little barbecued shoat for good measure. Pretty soon the young'n would be bellowing for persimmon beer, honey in the honeycomb, and dewberries picked in springtime. First thing you knew, you'd have a mountain man on your hands.

A man like "Rimfire" Hanrick of Webster Springs. He is one of the innumerable local folk heroes who made the study of any American area fascinating—a hunter who got with words what he couldn't get with shot. One Rimfire story has to do with his dilemma when fronting thirteen wild turkeys, with only one shot left. This is the way Rimfire handled it:

"Well, I noticed the whole thirteen of 'em was perched on a limb no bigger'n a man's wrist. That gives me an idear. Loadin' my bar'l about a quarter way full o' powder and rammin' the last bullet down on hit, I tuk aim at the limb of the tree an' fired. The bullet split the limb and let them there turkeys' toes drop down in the crack. Before they had time to fly off, the split closed up an' ketched their toes. I clumb up the tree, cut off the limb with my pocket knife, and packed the whole dang flock home just as I'd ketched 'em."

Or a man like Daniel Boone, patron saint of western Virginia and the states she spawned. The Boones wandered about like Indians. Almost everybody liked Shenandoah Valley country, where, with their hands their only company, men could work all day listening for the screech of a soaring bird or the gush of water going over limestone ledges. Not the Boones. They were always answering the call of something that manages to stay just over the next ridge.

They left Virginia and headed for Carolina. The kids and dogs trailed behind. The fifteen-year-old boy was already strong as a man, and could knock the eye out of a weasel running the other way at a hundred yards. The Boone boy was named Daniel.

Daniel didn't forget the Valley. How could he, when he married a girl with good Virginia blood; married her, and almost shot her?

Fire-hunting for deer one night, Daniel saw two eyes gleaming in the night. As he prepared to shoot, he heard a little cry. That cry saved Rebecca—the girl Daniel took to wife.

The young couple moved back to Virginia when the Cherokees went on the warpath, and settled in Culpeper County. Daniel hauled tobacco to Fredericksburg, but he didn't like the job. The Boones joined up with six families and forty men who had Kentucky fever. At Cumberland Gap the Indians struck, and among those killed was Boone's son, James.

In 1774 Boone was sent by Virginia's Governor to warn the surveyors in the Kentucky territory of an impending Indian uprising nearby. Boone was accompanied by "Big Mike" Stone, who shared with him some amusing and thrilling adventures. They covered a distance of eight hundred miles in sixty-two days, going as far as the Falls of the Ohio. Boone was then placed in command of Moore's Fort in the Clinch River Valley. In 1775, he was commissioned by Colonel Richard Henderson of the Transylvania Company to carve out the Wilderness Road to Boonesborough. There he built a fort. He returned for his family and brought them to Boonesborough. At a meeting in Sycamore Hollow, Boone sponsored the last three of the nine laws which were adopted for the infant colony in which the seaboard states of Virginia and North Carolina were interested:

For establishing courts of jurisdiction and regulating the practice thereof; for regulating a militia; for the punishment of criminals; to prevent profane swearing and Sabbath breaking; for writs of attachment; for ascertaining clerks' and sheriffs' fees; to preserve the range; for improving the breed of horses; for preserving the game.[4]

In 1776, Daniel and his companions fought off several Indian attacks on Fort Boone; during this same year he was the leader in the famous rescue of his daughter, Jemima, and the Calloway girls, who had been kidnapped by the Indians.

After resisting a British-inspired Indian attack on Boonesborough, Boone was captured by Indians at Blue Licks and adopted as a son by the Shawnee chief, Blackfish. He received the tribal name "Big Turtle," then escaped in time to warn his comrades at Fort Boone of an Indian attack.

When the Virginia legislature appointed a land claims commission in 1779, Boone went to Richmond on foot to plead his case. He was robbed of his money en route, and received no satisfaction for his case. Two years later he made the trip to Richmond again, this time as an elected representative to the assembly from newly formed

Fayette County. When the state legislature was dispersed by the British in 1781, Boone was taken prisoner, and later paroled.

Not as a legislator, but a pathfinder, did he capture the imagination of his neighbors. In 1785, Mrs. Francis Scott, who described herself as "An Inhabitant of Washington County, Virginia; who after the murder of her husband and children by the Indians, was taken prisoner by them," published *The Adventures of Colonel Daniel Boone*. It was a romantic tribute, though no match for a long epic poem by Daniel Bryan of Rockingham County. Bryan's work, published in 1813, bore the title *The Mountain Muse, Comprising the Adventures of Daniel Boone; and the Power of Virtuous and Refined Beauty*. This ambitious effort is the first account in which Boone achieves a legendary status, and cavorts with the fates. His mission is plainly superhuman:

> O'er all the mazy complicated chain
> Of objects, which are link'd to the grand theme
> That with sublime sensation swell the soul;
> Boone now in all its forceful influence felt.[5]

All the forces of evil confront Boone, but the "sinewy sons of Enterprise" will not be denied. They push on into the "rude featured Wilderness." When Boone finally reaches the Mississippi, he looks ahead to a time when the mighty valley will prosper:

> With the products of a thousand farms
> And riches of Mercantile Kingdoms fraught
> With Freedom's Cities and Republics too
> And Happiness and Heavenly Virtue cheered.[6]

In his later life Boone's chief concern was contesting the loss of land which he had improperly entered. Ejectment suits deprived him of his holdings. Dismayed, the old hunter left the area that later considered him its special saint, and moved west. Eventually he reached what is now Missouri, where his son Daniel lived, and became magistrate of the district. Once again his holding was voided, this time by the United States land commissioner; but Congress finally confirmed his claim. Boone traveled back to Kentucky to pay off his debts and (says tradition) ended up with fifty cents. He stayed only long enough to transact his business, then headed west again. Admirers traveling into the wilderness to see the frontier sage wondered why he preferred to live his life out on the cutting edge of the frontier. His answer was in keeping with his legend. "It was too crowded back East. I had to have more elbow-room."

Boone's uneventful later years did not dull his earlier achievements. James Audubon recorded after interviewing him: "The stature and general appearance of this wanderer of the western forests approached the gigantic. The very motion of his lips brought the impression that whatever he uttered could not be otherwise than strictly true." This is all the more remarkable when we note that Boone was only five feet eight inches tall. Audubon viewed Boone as more than a historical figure. The component parts of his myth were recognizable even then: a Promised Land beyond the mountains; land-hungry families who considered it a new Eden; a lone wanderer guiding his generation on a God-sanctioned mission.

So they named towns and mountains and children after Daniel Boone. Many others who came, as self-sacrificing and perhaps as heroic as Boone, were not so honored. Their homes were rude log cabins, and their lives were case studies in loneliness. These are the ones who have no memorial. They worked, hunted, gave birth, and died young because they plum give out. They kept the fire going, so that a thing wisp of smoke could go through their wide-throated stone chimneys and tie them to heaven. They held on.

There were at least 30,000 people in trans-Allegheny Virginia when, far to the east, the patriots in Williamsburg decided to seek independence from England. In the west, the Revolution was largely an Indian war, with British-led armies making three major invasions. Significantly, the Indian raids were confined to land west of the Alleghenies—proof of the strength of the pioneers on the frontier.

Long after the redcoats had gone home, the redskins continued to harry western Virginia. Even after "Mad Anthony" Wayne's decisive 1794 victory at Fallen Timbers, there were bloody incidents. There was still a lot of unoccupied land. "From the pint [Point Pleasant] to Elke [Elk River] no inhabitance," Daniel Boone reported in 1791. "From Elke to the Bote yards [Kelly's Creek] 20 miles all inhabited." The old scout saw that elbowroom was getting scarcer; so in 1795 he and his family headed west.

As they left, other families came. In one generation they tamed the Virginia frontier, and replaced squat log cabins with noble Greek Revival houses. They built bridges, mills, and iron furnaces. When he looked at their struggles and achievements, Ralph Waldo Emerson said, "America begins west of the Appalachians."

The philosopher's statement is convincingly supported when we focus attention on one life, such as John Jordan's. Born in Tidewater Virginia in 1777, he brought his bride to the Rockbridge County frontier just at the turn of the century. The county seat, Lexington, was growing up along the Great Path, over which the pioneers drove their "shakeguts" and "mountain ships." No bridge spanned the North River on the edge of town, so John Jordan got busy and built one. Then he erected a "new flouring mill" and a blacksmith shop. Here wagons were made and ironed as families stopped at Jordan's Point before starting over roadless mountains. When the War of 1812 came, John Jordan beat himself a sword out of metal tempered with twenty silver dollars and went to fight the British. He returned with the rank of colonel and a passion for the neoclassic architecture which was just making itself felt in the more settled coastal areas. The series of buildings he erected during the rest of his life made him one of the notable self-trained architects of his generation.[7]

The houses he built embodied elegance achieved through imaginative and bold use of materials. His was a refreshingly naïve architecture; both American and classical, free from the slavish imitation and pomposity of the "temples on the hill" built in other parts of the state and region. In 1821 Jordan built the central building for Washington College. There were six slim Doric columns, two-story wings with Doric pilaster, and porticoes of square-paneled antae. The cupola was topped by a wooden statue of Washington, carved by a local craftsman and ex-Revolutionary soldier named Matthew Kahle. "No more impressive expression of the ideals of the time could be imagined than this classic group," Talbot Hamlin wrote. "Its pediment and orders are seen through embowering trees, over swelling lawns, its cupola crowned with the image of the Pater Patriae."[8]

Proud that the new nine-thousand-dollar Washington Hall was an architectural masterpiece, the townspeople set about celebrating its completion. The public was invited, and came. "Jocky" Robinson, famous for his love of learning and Irish whisky, donated a forty-gallon barrel of fifteen-year brew. The donor himself tapped the barrel. For a time, courtesy in the order of approach was observed. Then politeness disappeared.

The crowd attacked the barrel, a witness recorded, "with tin cups, pitchers, basins, buckets, and a variety of dippers, some of them more handy than nice." Next followed "a glorious exhibition of what free whiskey can do for the noble creature made in the image of God." The Presbyterian minister arrived to find his flock rolling on the ground like swine. Finally two gentlemen upset the barrel, and the ancient brew was absorbed by the thirsty earth. "Still," said the minister, "enough had been consumed to make College Hill look like a battlefield after a hard fight." The building, builders, and visitors all survived.

Later on John Jordan built the barracks for the new Virginia Military Institute, and portions of the James River Canal. The James River Company hoped to connect the west with the Atlantic. Western communities were urged to build additional links with the help of state funds. John Jordan completed his Balcony Falls section in record time, but the whole job was never finished.

Iron smelting became Jordan's chief interest in the 1830's. Eventually he and his sons operated a score of furnaces. One of them, the Lucy Selina in Allegheny County, produced over 50,000 tons of fine pig iron from 1828 to 1865. Many unskilled and semiskilled men were used in the charcoal burning pits, ore mines, and loading areas. Chopping wood, digging ore, feeding furnaces, and handling pig iron were jobs generally assigned to slaves. The size of the operation involved may be estimated by noting that the inventory book for the Bath Iron Works in 1830 lists on hand in the kitchen 27,000 pounds of pork and 6,000 pounds of beef.

As a corollary to iron manufacturing, the Jordans were road builders. John Jordan, untrained in engineering, built the road over North Mountain so well that it was used for seventy-five years as the only means of travel from Lexington to the west. Men and mules constituted his total working force. Winter rains washed out the dirt roads as fast as men could replace them. Rocks were expensive to crush, and funds were inadequate for the first steps of dirt scraping and erecting green-pole waterbreaks. Knowing all this, John Jordan appeared before the county officials and said, "Give me the men and the mules and I will build the road."

This was the soil, and these were the men, from which Jacksonian democracy could and would spring.

Back in the Old World, a Scottish writer and philosopher observed and admired. His name was Thomas Carlyle. "How beautiful to think of lean tough settlers, tough as guttapercha, with most occult unsubduable fire in their belly, steering over the Western Mountains, to annihilate the jungle, and bring bacon for the Posterity of Adam," Carlyle wrote. "There is no *myth* of Athene or Herakles equal to this *fact.*"

10 *Eden, in Fiction*

EVERY GOOSE A SWAN, LAD,
AND EVERY LASS A QUEEN.

The New World bred strange birds, strange beasts, strange afflictions. No one knew just what to expect next. In Virginia, for example, almost everybody got the Sir Walter disease.

Mark Twain, who thought Sir Walter Scott had "set the world in love with dreams and phantoms," went too far in asserting that the Highland Bard "had so large a hand in making Southern character as it existed before the war, that he is in great measure responsible for the war." But even those who have disagreed with Twain have admitted he was right in stressing Scott's profound influence.[1]

Scott spent much of his life (1771–1832) reading, preserving, and writing romance. Everything he touched seemed to turn into moonbeams. Why, he asked, should not he do for ancient Border chivalry what Goethe had done for Rhenish feudalism? He should, could, and did. Achieving early success in 1805 with *The Lay of the Last Minstrel,* Scott wrote historical novels and tales of high adventure at a rapid rate. Not that they were thoughtlessly done; for it was this man, as George Trevelyan pointed out, who "showed us how not only clothes and weapons, but thoughts and morals vary according to the period, the province, the class, the man."[2] Scott

109

knew that history is exciting because it is dominated by human beings; in this, he found the basic patent for successful historical fiction.

Sir Walter's technique was to bring figures out of the past and into the present by reproducing "all those minute circumstances belonging to private life and domestic character, all that gives versimilitude to a narrative and individuality to the persons introduced." Completely unaware of the relativism that was later to come into vogue, Scott posited men and morals that were immutable. He could depend on his heroes, just as his readers could depend on him. The nineteenth century found this a satisfactory arrangement. From it many American writers learned the formula which shaped their fiction.

Make no mistake about it: Scott's books, and those of his American imitators, *did* have a real effect on American life and character in general, and Virginia's in particular. So many historians (William E. Dodd, Charles Beard, W. J. Cash, William B. Hesseltine, Francis Simkins, and James Truslow Adams among them) have asserted this that there is no originality left in the claim. No originality, but a good deal of truth.

What did Scott teach? Mrs. T. P. O'Conner answered the question as well as has anyone in *My Beloved South:* "He taught loyalty and self-sacrifice, a sense of obligation to your kinsfolk, chivalry, tenderness, and protection to women, honour and truth to your neighbor, courage and valour in battle, open-handed hospitality, and a sense of responsibility towards those dependent on you." Here were lessons Virginians could endorse and engender.

The Waverly Novels were our first best sellers. Over five million copies came off American presses between 1813 and 1823; no one knows how many more were imported. The whole set could be obtained in 1845 for five dollars. If that was too much, you could buy the set on the installment plan for a quarter a week. Men would saddle their horses and gallop to town when a new Scott novel was expected. They felt it indispensable for any Southern gentleman worth his steed.

In Scott's romances Southerners found fictional values which helped justify their plantation economy, caste system, and feudal psychology. In the novels from *Waverly* to *The Fair Maid of Perth,* they saw the mirror held up to their life and ideals. Read for pleasure, the tales soon became dogma. "It was good form," William E. Dodd tells us, "for Southern gentlemen to place Sir Walter Scott's novels on their library shelves, and for all Southern boys and girls to read these books as the great models of life and good breeding."

Dozens of diaries and accounts confirm it. Mrs. Roger Pryor, in *Reminiscenses of a Long Life,* remembered that parents offered a Scott novel as a reward to studious children. Most Confederate leaders, including Jeff Davis, made public their admiration for Scott. If you had tiptoed into General Lee's living room in the evening, you might have heard the South's military idol "repeating from memory line after line of 'Lady of the Lake.' "[3]

One bond which connected Sir Walter and his many Virginia admirers was a common body of folklore and folk songs, shared by Scotland and the Old Dominion. His *Minstrelsy of the Scottish Border* was made up of songs and tales earlier generations had brought across the ocean with them. A keen appreciator of folklore, Scott had a natural talent for absorbing it. In one instance, his biographer tells us, Sir Walter recited from memory an eighty-eight-stanza ballad which he had heard only once, three years earlier.[4]

His influence permeates Virginia literature. The planter replaced the British aristocrat, the indentured servant and Negro the vassal and serf, the Indian the outlaw. It is not much of an exaggeration to say that colonial Virginia is essentially part of the background of British historical romance.

In architecture Virginians began to favor the eccentricities of Gothic form and mock medieval designs. In their homes they read Scott's novels. In their fields they re-enacted his tournaments. No one knows just how the tournament vogue was started. Willard Thorp thinks that the famous shindig which Lord Eglinton staged at his Scottish castle in 1839, to which many Americans came, was instrumental. The idea of reviving "medieval" tests of skill quickly spread throughout Dixie, where a long-standing interest in horses and horsemanship provided a ready-made backdrop.[5] Such tournaments offered the ideal occasion to glorify the female sex and to stage pageants. "Knights" were addressed. "Grand Marshals" oversaw the contests. Riding at full gallop, the horsemen tried to spear rings with the tips of their lances. The winner obtained the privilege of crowning the "Queen of Love and Beauty." If speeches in praise of Southern womanhood and Southern politics were thrown in, so much the better.

Here occurred a blending of the past and the present, of illusion and reality. John M. Turner has preserved for us the actual words of a Grand Marshal:

"Fair ladies and gallant knights: let us consider for a moment the significance of the ceremony which we are about to witness. Designed, as it is, to commemorate the days when knighthood was in flower, in it we see the first attempts of bravery to pay some tribute to beauty, to show what appreciation of that inspiration which has lifted man from the depths of early savagery and placed him on the high pinnacle of civilization. We are taught that woman was, in the beginning, the indirect instrument of the fall; but how nobly has she striven to make amends, and we have but to look about us today to see with what success these efforts have been crowned."[6]

The Knights of Snowden, Marmion, Ivanhoe, and Glen Arvon took to Virginia's fields—and, amazingly enough, still do. Bold knights have ridden and tilted for fair ladies at such fashionable places as White Sulphur Springs, Capon Springs, Warrenton, and Mount Solon; in the Tidewater counties of Accomac, Nansemond, Northampton, Warwick, Gloucester, Dinwiddie, and Isle of Wight. The Noble Ashby, colorful Confederate whose early death created a legend of gallantry, often rode in tournaments as the Knight of the Black Prince. Prancing steeds, lances, heralds, and damsels, in varying degrees of distress, have always been in fashion in Virginia, no matter how dark the hour or bleak the prospects. In the last grim months of the Civil War, when the Yankees were bragging that even a crow couldn't fly across the Valley without carrying rations, a splendid equestrian tournament was held on the grounds of Jefferson's Monticello.

Who could help cheering when a skillful rider captured a ring, or gasping when another fell from his steed trying too daring a maneuver? Who could doubt, when he read the list of entries, that blood would tell? Who could deny the regality of the Queen of Love and Beauty, crowned victoriously at the Coronation Ball? Who (except a pathetic Yankee stuck away in the bowels of some cotton mill) could assert that the South was poor, when it had all these treasures?

More cautious and research-minded historians remind us that Scott had strong influence on many other parts of the world (including Scotland). They remind us that other nineteenth-century writers like Byron, Moore, Bulwer-Lytton, G. P. R. James, Dickens, and Thackeray also won Virginia's heart. True; but none were loved like Scott, as birth certificates, final documentation of hero worship, show. On many a Virginia family tree you will find a Walter Scott, Ellen Douglas, Flora MacIvor, Rowena. Whence do you suppose came the name of the 1831 valedictorian at William and Mary, Richard Ivanhoe Cocke? And for what novelist, except Scott, would Virginia newspapers have embellished the edition carrying a novelist's death notices with a black border? Nor was there in all the city a man with soul so dead as to protest it.

As important as Scott's influence was on Southern thinking and acting, he was only one of a number of ante-bellum writers, politicians, and historians who shaped the plantation tradition. An offshoot of the English romantic movement, this tradition first took form in the Old Dominion, assuming its salient features in the hands of George Tucker, John Pendleton Kennedy, and William Alexander Caruthers. Beginning in the late 1820's, sentiment blossomed into romance, and pleasantry into exuberance. A new generation, deeply indebted to Sir Walter Scott, undertook the pleasant task of showing the familiar plantation life in glowing colors, and investing it with romantic charm.[7]

These novelists told of a bucolic society, the most idyllic and picturesque in the nation. Plantation life was free of the drab routine and skimpy meanness of the Yankee farm, the coarseness and roughness of the frontier, and the sordidness of the middle-class towns. Virginians did not have to sail to Spain or England, as did Washington Irving, to find suitable romantic material. All they had to do was look outside their windows.

The novel proved to be the best means of stating their case. While the historian does his canvas by checking meticulously every individual brush stroke, novelists using bold brush and bright colors, capture with a few strokes the whole feeling and motivation of an age.

As in so many ventures, Virginians received inspiration from a skillful Yankee, James Fenimore Cooper, who wrote his first novel on a bet. He won, and so did America. Vigorous and readable, it marked the beginning of an important literary career. Next came *The Spy*, rich in dramatic incident and vivid description. Several leading characters (Captain Jack Lawton, Major Dunwoodie, and Mr. Harper, a thinly disguised George Washington) are Virginians. The Negro house servant, Caesar, is fresh from the plantation garden. Cooper went on to write the Leatherstocking Tales, one of the most popular series of American novels. The heroic woodsman was modeled on Daniel Boone, idol of frontier Virginia, and he looked and dressed like the real Boone: tall, leathery, and solemn, with a coonskin hat sitting casually on his noble head. Cooper specifically acknowledged his debt to the Boone stories, and based part of *The Last of the Mohicans* on Daniel's rescue of the white girls from the Cherokees.[8] William Thackeray thought Leatherstocking a better fictional figure than any invented by Scott. So did many Americans.

After Scott and Cooper came Virginia writers who succeeded in establishing the Cavalier Eden—very different from the land William Byrd had seen and described with such ruthless realism. In this the novelists were helped by the historians, politicians, and folklorists. Virginia's first native historian, Robert Beverley, noted the presence of some of the King's old supporters. John Daly Burk found the Cavaliers provided a convenient escape from certain knotty historical problems. History may not repeat itself, but historians have a habit of repeating one another. Once the Cavalier stories were in print, they were part of Virginia's accepted history, legends of the founding fathers.

In studying these legends, Wesley Craven has noted that in Virginia both Tory and Republican politicians molded and adopted them to their own purposes.[9] Men like Hugh Blair Grigsby wanted to "strip every jack daw of his borrowed plumes." These fact-seekers did not prevail, and were not able to control the development of popular tradition.

The prevailing Virginia sentiment was summed up in 1837 when the editor of Richmond's *Southern Literary Messenger* wrote: "New England is descended from Puritans, Virginia from Cavaliers, 'the enemies and persecutors of those old Puritans.' Naturally, then, good Virginians keep something of an hereditary and historic antipathy against the children for their father's sake."

George Tucker's *Valley of the Shenandoah* appeared in 1824, only three years after *The Spy*. Of aristocratic vintage, Tucker graduated from William and Mary in 1797, and married Mary Byrd Farley, a granddaughter of William Byrd. For a while he practiced law in Richmond. The social life and cardplaying there bored him. So he moved out to Woodbridge Plantation, where he could have more time for his own thinking and writing. In 1824 Tucker finished a novel which he hoped "presented a faithful picture of Virginia manners and habits." Cooper's publisher, Charles Wiley, brought it out, and 1828 editions appeared in London and Germany.

Sandwiched in between the seduction, renunciation, and suicide of Tucker's conventional plot are delightful vignettes of Virginia plantations, barbecues, and court days on both sides of the Blue Ridge. Tucker planned a second novel. When his friend James Madison helped to arrange a faculty position at the new University of Virginia, he accepted and curtailed his writing plans. But he never abandoned the notion that Virginia must have a vigorous literature. "We have written fewer (and perhaps worse) books and contributed less to the advancement of the arts, ornamental and useful, in Virginia, than in any country on earth equally civilized," Tucker wrote in the *Virginia Literary Museum* for November 4, 1829. "The time has arrived in Virginia when the minds of our youth should expand to a nobler emulation than the mere scuffle after a law-suit or a case of bilious fever." His own novel had been written to hasten the time, to show a "distinctively Virginian" flavor in its use of landscape and character. From this, other and better books would spring.

One such book was John Pendleton Kennedy's *Swallow Barn,* which merged the streams of charm and verisimilitude in a broad meadow of episode. In Kennedy himself two other streams met— the Scotch-Irish merchant and the Virginia planter. A gentleman-writer whose primary occupations were law and politics, he passed the evening by writing a little fiction. Though he knew the stylistic principles of Edgar Allan Poe, he preferred the meandering grace of Washington Irving. "Nowhere else," says Vernon L. Parrington, "does the plantation life of the Old Dominion in the days before its decline appear so vividly as in his discursive pages."

Swallow Barn was the name of a fictional Virginia plantation, which Kennedy might have modeled on Westover, Shirley, or Carter's Grove: "an aristocratic old edifice which sits, like a brooding hen, on the Southern bank of the James River. It is built with thick brick walls and surmounted by a double-faced or hipped roof. The hall door, an ancient piece of walnut, is shaded by a narrow porch, with a carved pediment upheld by massive columns of wood. Between the gate and the house a large willow spreads its arched and pendent drapery over the grass."

The story meanders on and the reader basks in the mellow luxuriance of rural Virginia society. The overflowing hospitality knew no ebb. The places and people of the book became stock scenes and characters later on. But these plantation feasts, court days, fox hunts, and romantic walks through the countryside were among the first to be recorded. We have encountered the chivalric master, the faithful mistress, and the lovable old Negro so many times that we can hardly believe that Kennedy is inventing these types. The style and pace are so easy that we do not notice how skillfully he is weaving his spell, idealizing those days of quiet but perennial mirth which made an Arcadia of what was really not a very idyllic countryside.[10]

The will to believe is strong; social and economic values described in *Swallow Barn* and similar stories came to be taken as axiomatic. Young writers who had not known the plantation world nevertheless defended it. Their words, like the speeches of politicians and bedtime tales of nurses, reinforced what Richmond Croom Beatty has labeled "the grand Virginia Tradition."[11] Social lines between the aristocracy, the poor whites, and the Negroes were sharper in fiction than in reality. Unpleasant details were ignored. The plantation was viewed as a special world, and the Old Dominion as a planetary system.

Here good taste, good breeding, lighthearted parties, and fascinating visitors prevailed. The Manor House was not merely a conglomeration of sticks and stones but also a storehouse of memory and tradition. The state was, quite simply, a school for gentlemen. Virginia life was superior to life anywhere else—less material, less frantic, less prosaically equalitarian, "richer in picturesqueness, festivity, in realized pleasure that reeked of hope or fear or unrejoicing labor."[12] We like the Cavalier Eden for the same reason that we like fairy tales. Here we find a world of enchantment.

The role of the court jester in this world—that is, the humorous and kindly slave—was important. Full of song and rhythm, spontaneously happy, the Negro became indispensable to the fairyland. So did a stock characterization of the Happy Darky, Rousseau's "natural man" in dark hue. Thus it was that that T. D. Rice "jumped Jim Crow," the banjo-picking, heel-flinging jack; gave America a sterotype which would persist for a century, and whose name would be associated with segregation laws throughout Dixie.

Another Virginian who helped create the legendary Garden was William Caruthers. *The Cavaliers of Virginia* chronicled "that generous, fox-hunting, wine-drinking, duelling and reckless race of men which gives so distinct a character to Virginians wherever they may be found." Born in Lexington, Virginia, Caruthers studied at Washington College, then went to the University of Pennsylvania to study medicine. He himself had a severe case of the Sir Walter disease. "We thank God," he wrote, "that we have lived in the days when those tales of romance were sent from Abbotsford, to cheer the desponding hearts of thousands, and tens of thousands." He wanted to do for Virginia what Scott had done for the Highlands. It was too big a job, but Caruthers did the best he could.

After an epistolary novel, *The Kentuckian in New-York,* Caruthers published his most influential book, *The Cavaliers of Virginia, An Historical Romance of the Old Dominion.* Nathaniel Bacon is depicted as a forerunner of George Washington and independence. Equally heroic is the fictional Gideon Fairfax, who comes as close as anybody to being the beau ideal of the Virginia school of fiction:

> He was one of that remarkable race of men which has so powerfully influenced the destinies of the Ancient Dominion from that day to the present. . . . There was a sparkling of boyish vivacity in his eyes, and a cheerful expression always hovering about his mouth, which instantly dispelled anything like formality in his intercourse with others. Yet withal there was a bold, reckless daring in his look, together with an open-hearted sincerity which served to give a manly dignity to the lighter expressions.

Caruthers, like the other writers of this school, was not so concerned with utilizing historical fact as with forwarding fanciful tradition. At his best, he did both. *The Knights of the Horse-Shoe* told Governor Alexander Spotswood's story, and so dramatized his trip to the top of the Blue Ridge that this eventually became the best-known scene in the drama of early westward movement.[13] His descriptions, like the horseshoes Spotswood gave as souvenirs, were golden. Caruthers continued to make his living from medicine, practicing first in New York City and then in the low country of Georgia. A strenuous work schedule hastened his death, depriving the South of one of her best stylists.

Because of the success of these nineteenth-century novelists, the fame of Virginia life and hospitality spread to other states and countries. More than one Yankee had to admit that in comparison to the Southland, their land and life left much to be desired. "I blush for my own people when I compare the selfish prudence of a Yankee with the generous confidence of a Virginian," William Ellery Channing wrote. "There is one single trait which attaches me to the people more than all the virtues of New England. They love money less than we do. Their patriotism is not tied to their purse strings."

This is how the tradition began to take shape and the way in which key authors added to it. William Byrd's *Land of Eden,* plagued with ignorance, misery, and disease, was transformed into a garden of love and delight, full of aristocrats, faithful servants, and Eves bedecked in crinoline. Where there had been darkness, now there was light. Growing in the Garden was a good deal of tobacco and cotton—but no apples.

In general, the pendulum swung from bitter truth to sweet fancy. Yet it is no fairer to say that the new version was entirely false than it is to say that the old one was entirely true. History has in it blacks and whites; but the predominating color is gray.

The desire to reconcile the real and the romantic has been one of the chief motives of Virginians, and most Southerners. The resulting tradition cannot be discredited merely by counting the number of model plantations, announcing triumphantly that there were only a few dozen, and throwing out all later literary and historical embellishment. The point is not how many but how important the existing ones were. Big houses and big men were models as well as entities. Nineteenth-century Southern society was far from closed; mobility was its redeeming grace. The plantation, not the town, was the *ne plus ultra,* and the planters were the men who called the tricks at Williamsburg. Everybody wasn't a great planter —but almost everybody wanted to be.

Most plantation reminiscences resemble a patchwork of bright pieces joined with black squares. The black squares weren't pretty, but they were necessary. To women like Letitia Burwell, who in the mid-nineteenth century represented the ninth generation of the rural aristocracy, the world was "one vast plantation bounded by negro quarters. Rows of white cabins with gardens attached; negro men in the fields, women working, children dancing, romping. . . ."[14]

The special flavor of the plantation world was attested to by countless northern and foreign visitors. Henry Barnard, a young New Englander and Yale graduate, toured Virginia in 1833, and wrote to his sister Betty: "You would delight in this region, merely to observe the difference of manners and habits, and to experience the princely hospitality of the gentle-born families." The Yankee went on to describe in detail the dinner of the preceding evening:

Mrs. C. is at one end of the table with a large dish of rich soup, and Mr. C. at the other, with a saddle of fine mutton; scattered round the table you may choose for yourself—ham, beef, turkey, ducks, eggs with greens, potatoes, beets, hominy, etc. etc. On the second table cloth is the dessert, consisting of fine plum pudding, tarts, etc. etc. After this comes ice cream, West India preserves, peaches in brandy, etc. Off goes the second table cloth. Upon the mahogany table is set the figs, raisins, and almonds, not to mention the various wines.[15]

Here is substance to the legend of hospitality. Not without reason did Virginia's writers (in the words of an English visitor, Arthur Granville Bradley) "unconsciously conspire to over-idealize Virginia."

In so doing, they did away with the "second families" and modest dwellings. The unromantic 1860 census reminds us that only 114 of Virginia's million white inhabitants owned as many as a hundred slaves. The writers did more than distort—they obscured what was very likely the chief charm of the greatest plantations: their homespun simplicity. "The planter was a cultivated and leisurely farmer, but he was no baron," Jay Hubbell reminds us. "His estate of two or three thousand acres was no principality, and his house no baronial mansion. His luxury consisted in the numerous ragged and inefficient servants who attended him and in the abundance of homegrown provisions. His life was a simple and monotonous one, varied chiefly by guests and changes which the seasons bring upon the farm."[16]

The idyllic story, as promulgated in Virginia fiction, was farthest from the truth in the economic sphere. Actually, only a few of the great plantations were self-sufficient. William Byrd was hard-pressed by debts. When the English merchants faded out of the picture, the Yankees took over. As one of the Virginia planters put it: "From the rattle with which the nurse tickles the ear of the infant, to the shroud which covers the cold form of the dead, everything comes to us from the north."[17]

The fictional picture was closest to the truth in the social realm. This was indeed a latter-day feudalism, complete with social brilliance, *noblesse oblige,* and outgoing hospitality. There was a genuine self-forgetfulness which marked plantation entertainment, a warmness that permeated all who went there. Nor was the planter-politician a straw man. The Virginia Dynasty really ruled.

As a check of recent books on the plantation world indicates, nostalgia for the Good Old Days is far from dead. Typical volumes are Armstrong's *Old Massa's People,* Christy's *Plantation Melodies,* Johnson's *Shadow of the Plantation,* Kane's *Plantation Parade,* Peterkin's *Roll, Jordan, Roll,* and Rutledge's *God's Children.* In a democratic century, Southerners have defended the aristocratic. Just what the South which emerges in the literature we have reviewed really did imply is difficult to explain. Stark Young admits, in his essay published in *I'll Take My Stand,* that it was one of those things half of whose mysterious virtue lies in their arbitrariness. He continues: "The aristocratic implied with us a certain long responsibility for others; a habit of domination; a certain arbitrariness; certain ideas of personal honor, with varying degrees of ethis, and the fantastic. . . . Good system or not, from this Southern conception of aristocracy certain ideas arose."[18]

Such statements as this, not uncommon in contemporary Southern writing, show plainly that Virginia and the South are not defensive in the current meaning of the word. There is no tacit admission of guilt or inferiority here. These are defense-minded writers, defending something that is to them very dear and grievously misunderstood. One recalls how a noble Greek may have explained his country's greatness to a conquering Roman, or a Roman, in turn, to a Visigoth.

Because they first adopted this attitude, the early Virginia novelists, creators of a fictional Eden, were important figures. As novelists, they were limited. They did not have a large following in their own day, and they are seldom read now. Yet their region pays them the greatest possible compliment—it understands and believes them without reading them. Their monument exists not on dusty library shelves, but in the living, pulsating life of thousands of human beings who have been touched by them without knowing it.

11 *Washington to Richmond, Via Air*

ALL QUIET ALONG THE POTOMAC.
Civil War song

Loud-speaking voices and louder-speaking propellers battle it out. "Flight 312 for Richmond, Charleston, and Atlanta, now loading at gate 20. Please have your tickets ready." Bag in hand, I walk through the gate toward the stubby-nosed plane. The well-tailored young lady at the gate asks, "Where to, sir?"

"Richmond."

"Straight ahead. Take your seat. We're scheduled to leave in eight minutes."

We take off and soar into fluffy white clouds. The man across the aisle reads a magazine, but I stare out and down. The pompous white-columned buildings are toy-sized now. The largest, a pentagon, has leaped the river and dug in on the Virginia side. It would startle Washington, Grant, or Wilson. We cross the big brown serpent sprawling across the land and enter Virginia. I am home.

Rivers no longer make good boundaries. Chain stores, television, and automation do not respect geography. Technology has become a state of mind, and New York is everywhere. The invasion is complete; we have little left to defend. Perhaps Virginia's tragedy lies not in the battles she lost, but in those she never waged.

Yet she is still very much herself: proud, cohesive, and occasion-

121

ally belligerent. One such occasion was the 1850's; in the 1950's we have reached another. Recalling the tragic developments between 1855 and 1865, and observing the widening breach between 1955 and 1965, we cannot help but ponder.

Virginia is compounded of white supremacy, *noblesse oblige,* greatness, meanness, ancestor worship, and the spell of a gloriously remembered past. The Civil War of 1860, fought so furiously on land I fly over so effortlessly, destroyed Virginia's political and social leadership, while accentuating and inflating memories of better days.

Down below are neat rows of box houses, lined up like bottles on a vast pharmaceutical shelf. Suburbia.

Americans, and in their corner of it Virginians, have always wanted to keep up with the Joneses. In surburbia they are the Joneses. Homogenization takes command. The problem, to get cohesion without conformity, is no newer than Plato's *Republic,* and no closer to solution now than in 400 B.C. But it's easier to *think* we have solved it. By insulating our attics and our lives—

"Your dinner, sir," the efficient stewardess says, in a voice tempering attraction with authority.

"So soon?"

"We're due in Richmond in thirty minutes. So we have to start serving now to finish up."

Half an hour. The decompression of time.

"Sure. Thank you." I balance the tray on my knees, but am not eager to eat the well-balanced meal in the aluminum pockets. I prefer to look out at Virginia, and think of those who spent not minutes but years going from Washington to Richmond—on foot.

This land, dotted now with undramatic sumac, scrub pine, and brambles, once teemed with marching armies—young men, ambitious men, bone-tired men, lonely men, bleeding men. One America died, and another was born, in these fields. I take Allen Tate's suggestion:

> Turn your eyes to the inscrutable infantry rising
> Demons out of the earth—they will not last.

Nor will my view or reverie; but I cannot help looking and thinking. Almost a century ago a hard-mouthed man full of pent-up passion came to a sleepy Virginia town. When that passion erupted, the United States was rent asunder.

The man was John Brown. The town was Harpers Ferry. Osawatomie John, avenging angel, swept down with his little army of twenty-two, to free all Negroes. The first man killed was a freed Negro, Heywood Shepherd.

John Brown's soul may or may not go marching on, depending on your point of view. Certainly his capture, execution, and canonization set inexorable wheels in motion. The American Juggernaut began to roll.

Why? Scholars spend their lives on the why, the when, the how. They find fragments of the answer. Psychologically, the South was defending her minority status. She tried a dozen tricks which might preserve economic and political equality before resorting to arms. To the end she considered her most potent weapon not explosives but cotton. Europe needed it desperately, and would support the Confederacy to secure it. Politically, the secessionists drew not only from the thought of Calhoun, but of Jackson, Jefferson, and Washington. Their thought was built on the sovereignty of the states, with the federal Constitution as model. They kept George Washington on the Confederate seal because Confederates considered themselves more, not less, American than their enemies.

Culturally, two "ways of life" collided. Northeast fought southeast over tariff, northwest fought southeast over the extension of slavery. Dixie refused to submit to such hardships as the protective tariff, commercial strategy which put Southern wealth into Northern pockets, and abolitionist demands which created constant tension and bloodshed.

For many Virginians, the dilemma was moral rather than political. For years the state's leaders had questioned the validity of slavery and nullification. What they were willing to defend were freedom and justice and—most of all—honor. As E. A. Pollard put it: "The glory of history is indifferent to events—it is simply honor. The name of Virginia in this war is historically and absolutely more important to us than any other element of the contest."

Firebrands squared off against fire-eaters. Congress, which should have been a cooling-off place, became a tinderbox. Arsonists spouted inflammatory speeches. Naturally there was a fire. It burned out the Old South, almost the whole Republic. What was left, in the charred ruins, was the bootless glory of battle, and a handful of precious memories.

Ashes and memories, mixed well, make a powerful medicine.

There were honest differences between the sections, and genuine contempt each felt for the ideals of the other. The sectionalism was egocentric. "All we have," Rhett Butler says in *Gone With the Wind,* "is cotton and slaves and arrogance."

No one can say Virginia bled four years for either cotton or slaves. For what, then? It is hard to say; and what has been said does not hold up well under logical scrutiny. Poets and writers, as Sir Philip Sidney observed, are least liars. Let a writer say. In one of her early novels, *The Battleground,* Ellen Glasgow had an ignorant private admit: "I didn't see how I was goin' to fire my musket, till all of a jiffy a thought jest jumped into my head and sent me bangin' down that hill. 'Them folks have set thar feet on ole Virginny,' was what I thought. 'They've set thar feet on ole Virginny, and they've got to take 'em off damn quick!' "

For whatever sufficient or insufficient reason, the Commonwealth of Virginia did secede from the Union, not with the deep-South states, but only when in her opinion certain acts of the Union left her no choice. On April 4, 1861, the Richmond convention rejected secession by a two-to-one vote. But when Lincoln called for Virginia troops to coerce the other Southern states, the Old Dominion seceded. Once committed, she fought with a fury born of determination and sustained by desperation.

Some strange and intangible thing makes men and women sacrifice, struggle, and, if needs be, die. This thing was at work in the South and in the North, too. As Stephen Vincent Benét wrote:

> If the heart within your breast must burst
> Like a cracked crucible and pour its steel
> White-hot before the white heat of the wheel,
> Strive to recast once more . . .*

I look out the plane at patchworked green fields and quiet stone bridges. That crooked creek boarded with oak-and-rail fences might be Bull Run, where the first major battle was fought. It started with a festive air. Senators in spats and ladies with parasols came out to see the United States Army put down a rebellion. Yankee boys, three months trained, were anxious to squelch the rebellion. They wanted to scare the Rebs, stack their rifles, and return to their jobs before the first frost.

They returned, on the double, many without rifles. Not that the Southerners were better trained or braver; only that they had ridden more horses, shot more squirrels, and camped outdoors more nights.

---

* From *John Brown's Body* (Rinehart & Co.). Copyright 1927, 1928 by Stephen Vincent Benét; copyright renewed 1955, 1956 by Rosemary Carr Benét.

McDowell versus Beauregard: two West Point classmates, neither one of whom had ever commanded more than a regiment before. The bloody game was on. The stakes were going to be high.

Down there, maybe over where the barn is now, a stubborn, incredible Presbyterian eccentric named Thomas Jonathan Jackson, stood like a stone wall on that hot, bloody afternoon.

The next August, when the troops met again at Bull Run, it was a different matter. They had hardened up by then. Both armies knew they had a long fight on their hands. Statistics indicated clearly that the North would win. There were 23 million Northerners and only 5 million white Southerners; most of the industrial capacity of the country was in the North. The Rebels at second Bull Run fought under Lee, and the Northern boys under Pope. The Yankees headed back for Washington again, on the double. It might have been better for everybody had Pope won, and ended the matter in 1862. But tragedies usually have five full acts.

"Is there something wrong with your food, sir?" the stewardess asks.

"Oh—no. Just looking out at the scenery. Pretty country, isn't it?"

"Yes sir; but there's not much time, so if you're getting off in Richmond . . ."

"Of course. I understand." Perhaps I don't understand as I push aside the preplanned meal and look out again at the Virginia meadows. Who really understands why they fought on, the young and the not young, for those four useless awful years? Or why the cadets of the Virginia Military Institute, ranging in age from fourteen to eighteen, marched through seas of mud as the Confederate band played "Rockabye Baby," then kept going into the mouths of Yankee cannon at New Market? Why?

Yankee armies kept coming, under McDowell, McClellan, Burnside, Hooker, Pope. Always between them and Richmond were the Johnny Rebs, mean as hell, their uniforms torn and patched with clumsy hands, their bruised feet firmly upon the ground. They were devoted fighters, in a way not unlike Cromwell's Old Ironsides two centuries before; just as Jackson, with his narrow Presbyterian rectitude, was a reincarnation of the Puritan general. Above Jackson was Lee, whom Jackson said he would follow into battle blindfolded; Lee who was defiant and proud to the end, proposing as late as March, 1864, to capture Washington if two weeks' rations could be provided.

Then it was that President Lincoln, after many futile tries, found a general. Grant's critics thought he drank too much. Lincoln said he would like to know what kind of liquor Grant drank—it made him win battles.

"Unconditional Surrender" Grant destroyed the Confederacy. He stuck it out all summer. Here in Virginia he methodically pounded the Southern illusion to pieces.

The battles to the west and south might have been more decisive in the long run. Virginians know this, but continue to view the war as the personal property of the Army of Northern Virginia: a raggle-taggle bunch, singing, cussing, bragging, hating Yankees, bellowing blood-curdling yells that penetrated like buckshot—a band of wild brothers rather than a disciplined army. Once an officer walked up to a lank Confederate sentry and found him cleaning his gun. "Are you the sentry here?" he snapped.

"Well, a sort of sentry, I reckon."

"Well then, I'm a sort of officer of the day!"

"Is that so, now? Well sir, jest hold on till I slip this gun back together and I'll give you a sort of salute!"

They are gone now—those rawboned, unmachined, bloodhoundy men who smelled out enemy soldiers and didn't have sense enough to surrender. Some trudged home to die. Some sleep below me, under plain white crosses. Some have no memorial.

It is quiet now in Virginia's fields. But as I look, the Rebels seem still to be talking and cussing above the propeller's whir. A starving Georgia boy moans, "This heah campaign is austerity b'iled down." A veteran of the Texas wars says, "Fellers, if I ever love another country again, well damn my fool hide!" A foot soldier from the Valley explains how Jackson operated. "We cotched 'em in the rear and harried hell out of 'em." Talking and jesting, laughing so they will not cry.

I hear a lot about Old Jack, who liked to play hide-and-seek with Yankee armies and keep his plans inside his own head. "If my coat knew what I intended to do," he said, "I'd take it off and throw it away." He moved so fast that when sentries saw something scurrying through the underbrush, they yelled: "What's that? A rabbit or Jackson?"

If you had looked at his battle plan on paper, you might have thought that Thomas Jonathan Jackson was crazy. If he was crazy, it sure is a shame he didn't haul off and bite some other generals and infect them with the same kind of lunacy.

In the South, we remember his soldiering. In thirty-two days, with less than 15,000 men, he marched 400 miles, skirmished almost daily, fought five major battles, routed two armies completely, defeated a third, took 4,000 prisoners and immense stores—all this with the loss of less than 1,000 men killed, wounded, or missing.

"Why Old Jack likes to suck on a lemon, damned if I know. Lessen it's a Yankee lemon he captured. He likes to suck the guts right out of everything Yankee. . . ."

"Look at him, standing over there cool as the center seed of a cucumber, just starin' out with killer eyes, and thinkin'. Afore God, Old Jack is a born killer. I'd hate to be on the other end of what he's thinkin'."

That's what the men said about Jackson, who sent money to a Negro Sunday school, carried his Bible into battle, and prayed before attacks. He was a twice-a-Sunday churchgoer, an iceberg, cold, quiet, ready to rip; most of him was under water.

Once, when he was on the V.M.I. faculty, the Superintendent ordered Jackson to sit down and wait in his outer office until he called him. The Superintendent became engrossed in another matter, and left by the rear door. The next morning he found Jackson still sitting in the outer office. He had received no order to change position.

His battle uniform was a dingy yellow, and you would not have noticed him riding along on Old Sorrel. Yankees would hardly have wasted a special bullet on a man that looked so ordinary. He might be anywhere when the fighting came—riding in between the guns, up front with the snipers, always enjoying the drama as though he was in a playhouse instead of a deathtrap.

"Yep, I was close by when Old Jack rode up, easy going, and said to young Pendleton just like he was givin' the time of day: 'If the enemy is still standing at sunset, press them with the bayonet.' Dag-goned if that's not what he said." This prosaic, eccentric professor turned out to be the "desert fox" of the Civil War.

Stonewall had a favorite himself—young Turner Ashby, all muscle, bone, and nerve. Ashby slept under his dead brother's elk skin by night and fought Yankees by day. At Bolivar Heights, with 400 troops, he attacked Geary's 1,500 and took the breastworks without losing a man. At Kernstown, he held off an army with a handful of men until Jackson arrived. Around Edinburgh he engaged the enemy twenty-eight times in thirty days, always with the same instructions: "Drive 'em boys, drive 'em!"

Once a Yankee cavalryman fired five shots at him point-blank.

Ashby thought that was giving him a sporting chance, so he let the Yank taste a Confederate saber.

Turner Ashby fell in 1863, on a warm spring evening, in a field of budding wheat. Old Jack, a mighty hard man to wring a compliment out of, grimaced when the news came. "His powers of endurance were incredible," Jackson said, "his tone of character heroic."

Men liked Ashby and women liked "Jeb" Stuart, who jangled and glittered when he walked—ostrich feathers, gold spurs, white horses, red-lined capes, and pure effrontery. He was hard-riding, reckless, and devoid of a capacity for despair. He blinded and befuddled Yankees. Close behind him rode Joe Sweeney, his personal banjo player, so that any time, day or night, the General could burst into song:

> If you want to have a good time
> Jine the cavalry,
> Bully boys hey!

The ladies looked out the window and watched him ride by. What they thought they saw was Virginia on horseback.

They knew what this man was, and how he thought, by the names of his horses: Skylark, Lady Margaret, Lily of the Valley, Star of the East. They knew because he bedecked his mount of the day with fresh flowers. Not that Jeb Stuart had what might be called horse sense. If so, he wouldn't have risked his neck at Verdiersville just to capture General Pope's dress uniform coat. Or set out on a June morning with 1,200 men, riding right around McClellan's whole army, losing only one man.

Jeb pushed his luck too far. Like Ashby and Jackson and the society he defended, he was cut off in his prime. Young and golden, he fell in the dust of Yellow Tavern, a place too small to last more than a few seconds under my plane's wing. Virginia could have spared a better man—had there been one.

Major Chatham Roberdeau Wheat, leader of the tough Louisiana Tigers, lacked Stuart's courtliness, but not his devotion. On the morning of the battle of Gaines' Mill, which would claim his life, Wheat sat with a glass of whisky in one hand and his mother's prayer book in the other, partaking deeply of each.

Perhaps such reports as these are part fact and part fancy, better to tickle Southern pride than to tell documentary truth. What no documents can tell is how the battles and the defeats cemented an army and a people together. Eventually, these soldiers knew how to speak to one another, to arrive at a tacit understanding. Their attitudes toward life were alike. When they faced death it was in the same way. This makes for integrity, and belonging. It fills life and death with meaning.

Many stories illustrate this. A fifth-grade teacher told one to our class and she was a truth-bearing teacher. I remember it long after having forgotten all the stories in the textbooks from Columbia Teachers College. The story was about her grandfather.

After a bloody and foolish attack of the kind the Confederates seemed to specialize in after 1863, her grandfather, a colonel of cavalry, was carried into a rude field hospital. Orderlies stumbled over amputated arms and legs. Obviously his shattered, bloody right arm would have to be added to the pile. The doctor took a quick look, shook his head, and reached for a bottle of chloroform.

"No chloroform, Doctor," the Colonel said.

"We have some here, sir."

"I forbid its use."

"Forbid it? But why, Colonel?"

"Someone will need it worse."

No wonder men followed such officers. Followed, crawled, cursed, died. Along these smooth, black-topped roads I see below, once so muddy and furrowed, the Johnny Rebs dragged on: "Let's get this straight, you Georgia Cracker, I don't give a damn what Jeff Davis says. This is my last war!"

Jeff Davis—a proud and stubborn man who insisted on being both right and president, utterly devoted and well meaning. The Confederacy's strength, as well as its weaknesses, show in his life and career. His dignity was great, but his intelligence limited. The quality in which he seemed to be utterly lacking was humility.

What Southerners usually forget, when reviewing the glory of their war, is its cruelty and suffering. More men were killed by sickness and disease than by bullets. Hospital gangrene, fatigue, depression, exposure, combined with dysentery and scurvy to create conditions never featured in technicolor movies. Many times doctors had nothing but old tent cloth to bind up wounds. Soldiers were so exhausted that they didn't awake during operations. Operations were conducted on the tail gate of a wagon, the communion table of a church, or a door laid over barrels. John Claiborne found in a field hospital near Appomattox an open anatomy from which a surgeon had been refreshing himself during the work of mutilation. Emily

Mason recalled writing down the dying words of a young Rebel while he coolly surveyed the instruments, the surgeons with bared arms, and the great tub prepared to catch his blood.

Down below the landscape becomes more desolate, the clay redder. We must be near the Wilderness, where Grant made his first major thrust at Lee. The fire was so heavy that Minié balls from rifles severed tree trunks fourteen inches in diameter. Not far away, at Chancellorsville, the Rebels had high and low moments on the same day. High because the offensive fury unleashed was the full expression of their daring and courage; low because the man who was the center of that fury fell by the bullet of one of his own soldiers. What did the sentry who shot Jackson say later on? Maybe, "Sweet Jesus, I should 'a shot me!"

Why did we have to lose Jackson and the war? More important, why did we have to fight it?

Few answers are better than Douglas Southall Freeman's in *The South to Posterity*. There *was* historical logic to the right of secession; the right was maintained with conviction; the South fought its war gallantly and, so far as war ever permits, with fairness and integrity. Virginia, and her sister states, endured hardship with fortitude; achieved recovery through uncomplaining toil; gave to America the inspiration of personalities, humble and exalted, who met a supreme test and did not falter.

What kept the Confederacy going was some blind glory of the human soul which lashed out at the inevitable darkness. What wrecked the South, and threatens to wreck it again, is pride. Jefferson said it best: "Pride costs us more than hunger, thirst, and cold."

Whatever the reasons, and however foolish they now appear, the same disaster that made Virginia the Flanders of America also gave her a powerful tradition. Out of this antique courage came a fortitude and cohesion more precious than military victory. A tradition built on tragedy is apt to endure. This is the compensation.

> And while the prophets shudder or adore
> Before the flame, hoping it will give ear,
> If you must have a word to say,
> Say neither, in their way,
> "It is a deadly magic and accursed,"
> Nor "It is blest," but only "It is here."

"We're here," says the stewardess. "Please fasten your safety belts." To add authority to the request, a little red light comes on in the front of the cabin, illuminating the same order.

I am willing to fasten the belt, but not to admit that I have
traversed the distance between the two cities, the two sections, the two
worlds, in so few minutes. Greenness and brownness, toy soldier
panoramas, the slight uneasiness in the pit of my stomach, the un-
groundedness, the sound of space being devoured by power—all
these, yes; but not Washington to Richmond in thirty fleeting
minutes.

"Richmond, Virginia. Through passengers please keep their
seats."

What I could not explain to the men of those Civil War armies,
or to their horse-bound generals, is that since their day we hyphen-
ated space and time into space-time, and curved the straight hyphen
so that it matches the contours of heaven. They could understand
the murder of Lincoln; but what would they say if they were told
that we have murdered infinity, leaving only sounds in pursuit of
silence and frustration in pursuit of peace?

I step on earth. It is hard and firm and inviting, even under a con-
crete shell.

"Byrd Airport," the young lady says. I would not show my naïve
disbelief, so I look at her and smile. She, meanwhile, is glancing
down at her watch and scowling. "Just as I expected," she says. "Two
twelve. We're almost five minutes late."[1]

12 *The Man in the Crimson Field*

THERE WAS NOT A MAN IN THE CONFEDERACY WHOSE INFLUENCE
WITH THE WHOLE PEOPLE WAS AS GREAT AS HIS.

Ulysses S. Grant

He stood in the center of a crimson field, but there was no blood on
his hands.

After Jackson and Ashby and Stuart and all hope were gone,
Robert E. Lee stayed on. No reputation is harder to explain than
his; none is built more on intangible qualities. His people think
of him more as a saint than a slayer. I once stood at the bed of a
Virginia lady who was about to die. "I'm not afraid," she whispered.
"I believe I'll see heaven. Then I can see the three I've loved all
my life, Jesus, my husband, and General Lee."

A remarkable library of Lee adulation exists in the South. The
Honorable Henry Wickham added to it with his imaginary reconstruction of Lee's death: "Some devout clergymen have, with the
utmost reverence, likened Lee's last words 'Strike the tent' to the
last words of the Savior upon the cross of Calvary, 'It is finished.'
I believe when Lee uttered those words that a vision of glory appeared before his closing eyes; a vision of the progress of a pilgrim.
He heard a trumpet sound and lo! A troop cometh, and encompassed
by a cloud of witnesses a veteran pilgrim essayeth the flood."[1]

In an essay taking the form of an open letter, James Branch
Cabell assured Lee that if his career reveals any mistakes or short-

132

comings, "we stand ready to revere them also, for in remembering you, we believe, with a loyalty which we do not accord to any other person, that the man who had done the best of which we had knowledge could leave the rest to God. Nor in the event of an unfavorable decision, is it with Jehovah, Sir, that your people would be siding."[2]

Yankees as well as rebels have studied and admired Lee. By the middle of the twentieth century, the rebel leader who almost destroyed the Union was one of America's major heroes.

Unlike Abraham Lincoln, the heroic figure against whom he contended, Lee was no self-made man. Instead of going from rags to riches, he went from riches to poverty. His birthplace was not a log cabin, but a Georgian manor house. One of his ancestors, Thomas Lee, had been the colony's royal Governor. Long before that, the Lees had been known on both sides of the Atlantic as leaders and patriots. When the Lee mansion, Stratford Hall, burned in the eighteenth century, the English Queen gave money from the privy purse to help rebuild it. In a family-dominated state, his was the leading family.

After graduating from West Point in 1829, Robert E. Lee served as an army engineer, an officer in the Mexican War, and the superintendent of West Point. When John Brown's raid on Harpers Ferry occurred, Lee was the officer who suppressed it. Although he was opposed to slavery and hoped for a successful compromise, Lee was determined not to fight against his native state. He was a Virginian first, an American second. "There is no such thing as citizenship of the Nation," Thomas Dixon, Jr., has Lee say in *The Man in Gray.* "We are yet a Union of sovereign states." Thus, he declined Lincoln's offer of the field command of the Union Army, resigned his commission, and offered his services to Virginia. Fully aware of the consequences, the futility, of secession, he felt he had no choice but to defend his family, home, and heritage. For this reason his career is a monument to principle, a monument to reverence for law. Unterrified Virginia entered the Union; unterrified she left it. Lee, like Washington, did what he had to do. He was caught in the pincers of a historical situation.

Not all historians think he did the right, or the intelligent, thing. They say that here he revealed his greatest shortcoming: in the major decision of his life, he was wrong. He lacked the quality of prophecy, and the ability to see the shape of history. Believing that secession was wrong, he walked with the secessionists. Having freed his slaves, he led the slaveowner's army. There is no logic here. But how typical this decision is of Lee, and of the state which he put above the Union.

Having decided, he acted. When he offered his services to the Confederacy, he was made military adviser to President Jefferson Davis. The struggle between the two, undeclared and unending, was one of Lee's heaviest burdens. "Mr. Davis can be very sharp," he wrote to Mrs. Lee; that, and no more. But in retrospect we see that Lee fought two wars—one on the battlefield against Yankees, the other in Richmond against bureaucrats.

For months he moved back and forth between the war office and President Davis' office, a glorified clerk. The stray Yankee bullet that hit General Joseph Johnston gave Lee a field command in June, 1862. Disaster was in the air. Kentucky and much of Tennessee had been lost, the Northern blockade was working, and King Cotton diplomacy was failing. Nonetheless, the country soon saw what kind of soldier the soft-spoken, aristocratic Lee was. Underneath the look of repose was lightning. A tiger in battle, he never defended when he could attack. Only his incredible success defended him against the charge of recklessness—only the swift-leaping, brilliant fire.

Having defeated General McClellan and relieved the pressure on Richmond, he hurried on without rest to engage General Pope. His victory at Manassas produced a near panic in Washington. On Lee moved to Maryland, where the accidental discovery of his battle plans enabled the Yankees to stop his advance at Antietam. Back to Virginia he came, the Union army trailing after him. General Burnside prepared to launch what was to be the grand and final assault against the Rebels. Having shelled Fredericksburg in mid-December, Burnside crossed the Rappahannock and attacked Lee and Jackson on the south side. The Confederate infantry hid behind a sunken wall. Soon Yankees lay dead in piles, and Burnside was routed. Next came General Hooker. He too crossed the Rappahannock, ten miles above Fredericksburg. His plan was to envelop the less numerous Confederate forces in a pincer movement. Making one of his characteristic and desperate gambles, General Lee sent Jackson off at four in the morning of May 2 to attack Hooker's flank. The Yankees, taken completely by surprise, rolled back in defeat, and soon General Hooker too was taking the well-worn path back to the capital.

In bright and blossoming June, Lee invaded Pennsylvania. A panic-stricken North and a prayer-filled South waited. The armies met, by chance, at Gettysburg. For whatever reasons, and for whatever is beyond mere reason, the battle ended in a Northern victory. Lee's army, having made one last desperate lunge, recrossed the Potomac.

The closing phase of the war began in the spring of 1864, when General Grant, fresh from victories in the west, was placed in command of all Union armies. Of one thing the new general was certain: he did not intend to retreat. He, with his superior numbers and supplies, would fight it out if it took all summer. The cost might be heavy, but the outcome would be inevitable.

The triphammer blows began.

Sherman was to cut off the deep South; Sigel was to take the Valley of Virginia; Butler was to advance from Fort Monroe toward Richmond, while Grant and Meade were to crush Lee. Sherman burned his way through, but Sigel and Butler were stopped. Grant and Meade crossed the Rapidan on May 4, 1864. The names of terrible, bloody battles began to fill the papers: the Wilderness, Spotsylvania, North Anna River, Totopotomoy Creek, and Cold Harbor. Lee would not give way, no matter how great the force hurled against him. At Cold Harbor the trenches still stand to mark the lines of defense against which Grant lost 13,000 men in a single morning. Grant, crippled by more than 60,000 casualties, moved South to Petersburg, where he tried to cut off Richmond.

If Lee could not be defeated, he could be starved out. During the nine months' siege of Petersburg, the overtaxed, undersupplied, bone-tired Confederacy collapsed around Lee. By the time of the Union's final push, in the spring of 1865, only the ghost of what had been the Army of Northern Virginia remained.

Gathering his remnant around him, Lee retreated westward from Petersburg. He reached Appomattox Courthouse, twenty-two miles east of Lynchburg, but his troops were practically surrounded by Grant's Army of the Potomac. Appomattox was not a battle: only the crossroads where, as Clifford Dowdey put it, "the exhausted tatterdemalions were overtaken."

Just before the surrender, one of Lee's junior officers said to him: "You are the country to these men. They have fought for *you*. They have shivered through a long winter for *you*. Without pay or clothes, or care of any sort, their devotion to you and faith in you have been the only things which have held this army together."[3]

Such sentiments show that Virginians came to think of Lee not only as a good general but a godly man—a flawless knight, without reproach. Yet as a field commander, he had a serious flaw—it was his inability to shape opposing minds to his purpose.[4] Not once, but three times, did he yield to General Longstreet's obstinacy, seeking victory through what he believed was the second-best plan. Robert E. Lee was too much of a gentleman (one is tempted to say figurine) to be a man of battle to rank finally beside a Napoleon, a Rommel, or perhaps (touching the fringes of heresy) a Grant.

His excessive consideration for the feelings of others became a detriment in battle. The place of his undoing was Gettysburg. There, general of the greatest army ever under his leadership, he was beaten by the smallest force Lincoln had at his disposal since McDowell had met Beauregard in 1861.

Lee himself recognized the flaw and the failing; he tended his resignation to President Davis en route back to Virginia. Ordered to fight on, he did, until there was no advantage in continuing. Defeat merely confirmed in his own mind his military incapacity. "Life is indeed gliding away," he wrote when he arrived in Lexington in 1866, "and I have nothing of good to show for mine that is past. I pray I may be spared to accomplish something for the benefit of mankind, and the honor of God." His greatness sprang from his recognition of his inadequacy; it is the man, not the general, that we love.

At one o'clock on April 9, 1865, Lee surrendered. The man confronting his conquerors was flawless in build and personality, with well-shaped feet and small, tender hands. He had none of the small vices—smoking, drinking, chewing, swearing—and even his enemies seldom accused him of the greater ones. On that day he dressed in a new uniform. At his side was the jeweled sword Virginia had given him. Grant was dressed in a private's uniform with boots and mud-spattered breeches. Only his three-starred shoulder straps indicated his rank.

On order from Grant, victory salutes were silenced. "No man could have behaved better than General Grant did under the circumstances," Lee said. Having signed the necessary document, he made his last ride down the lines, and said to his army: "Men, we have fought through the war together. I have done my best for you; my heart is too full to say more."

He was a moralist, and the force that ruled his life was a moral force. He was a passionate man, but his was an unselfish passion of the sort which purifies men and armies. Lee fought for a section, but he was not sectionalized by his struggle. Surely no military historian could ever deny that this was a man who knew how to win, even though a final victory had been, from the first, an impossibility. Lee had taken the assignment and done the best he could, being content to leave the rest to God.

There is a second, milder, and even greater Robert E. Lee—the man who knew how to lose. This is the solitary, noble figure who was as humble and conciliatory in peace as he had been audacious and irreconcilable in war. He opposed removing Confederate bodies from Northern graves, on the grounds that this would increase antipathy. He did not approve of Matthew Fontaine Maury's setting up a Southern colony in Mexico, because this would only add to the bitterness. Whenever he appeared in postwar parades, he was careful to march out of step that he might not seem militaristic.

Many offers of lucrative jobs and honors came, but Lee was not willing to sell his name. "I have a self-imposed task which I must accomplish," he explained. "I have led the young men of the South in battle. I have seen many of them die on the field. I shall devote my remaining energies to training young men to do their duty in life."

Clad in a gray uniform from which all the Confederate buttons had been removed, he went to a ravaged Virginia village to become president of obscure, poverty-stricken Washington College. With the pen, in the five years before his death, he won a type of victory he had never been able to win with the gun.

As college president, Lee urged a young sophomore to better his study habits, so he might stay in college. "We do not want you to fail," said Lee. "But sir, you failed," the youth answered, with a brashness characteristic of sophomores everywhere. "I hope you may be more fortunate than I," Lee replied.

Meanwhile, Lee turned to the rejuvenation of Washington College. In 1859 there had been ninety-five students, all but one from Virginia. By 1867, the college was not only functioning again, but instructing 410 students from twenty-six states. A "School of Law and Equity" was established through an alliance with the privately owned Lexington Law School. In 1869 Lee reported that both a School of Commerce and of Journalism had been opened, pioneering in these fields. He had plans for expansion in other areas, such as agriculture, which were cut short by his death.

His success as an educator only added to his enemies' exasperation. Lee, the Radical Republicans insisted, was an archtraitor. The March 31, 1866, Baltimore *American* printed a purported interview with one of his ex-slaves, who, it was claimed, had been cruelly treated. A month later the *Weekly Morning Herald* announced: "Facts are being developed which prove that Washington College, of which General R. E. Lee is president, is one of the most violent rebel institutions in the land—a school for the propagation of hatred to the government and its loyal people. From the principal down to the humblest tutor, the faculty are thoroughly rebel."[5]

Eventually, however, more and more Northerners came to see that Lee's actions and attitudes after 1865 had been instrumental in healing the rift in the Union. No one argued this point with greater fervor than the Yankee aristocrat, Charles Francis Adams. Though his brother Henry had not been able to tolerate Rooney Lee at Harvard, Charles Francis not only tolerated, but even openly admired, Rooney's father. In truth, he defended the General despite the fact that he had faced the Confederates at Gettysburg, and had come from the fighting a physical wreck. He was nonetheless convinced that by prohibiting guerrilla warfare and preaching reconciliation, Lee had saved the North and South untold misery. This he explained in a paper read to the American Antiquarian Society in 1901, entitled "The Confederacy and the Transvaal: A People's Obligation to Robert E. Lee." He developed the idea in later articles; but his finest hour came when he was invited to make the Lee Centennial Address at Washington and Lee University in 1907. "The situation," Adams told the large audience, "is to a degree dramatic."

In that speech Adams placed Lee among the greatest Americans, not for his triumphs in battle, but those in his own mind. If Lee-the-soldier had been unable to save the Confederacy, Lee-the-citizen had helped save the United States; to overestimate this service would be difficult. Adams concluded with a quotation from Thomas Carlyle: "Whom shall we consecrate and set apart as one of our sacred men? Whom do you wish to resemble? Him you set on a high column, that all men looking at it may be continually appraised of the duty you expect from them."

Other Yankees seconded this view. The Massachusetts writer Gamaliel Bradford wrote a biography entitle *Lee, the American.* No Southerner could have handled the Virginian with greater sympathy. Lee no longer belonged exclusively to Virginia, or even to the Confederacy. He had become a hero of the entire nation.

In the 1920's, authors as varied as Woodrow Wilson, Edgar Lee Masters, John Drinkwater, Ellen Glasgow, and Stephen Vincent

Benét contributed to the growing literature about Lee. Wilson's *Robert E. Lee, An Interpretation,* is a sensitive study, making much of Lee's devotion to duty. Masters in America, and Drinkwater in England, found in him the qualities of a great leader. Lee is the Olympian hero of Glasgow's *The Battleground,* a man so magnetic as to be able to hold an army together solely by his personality. Benét's descriptive passages in *John Brown's Body** are the best poetical description of the Virginian yet done. To Benét, as to the others, this was a triumphant, not a tragic, life:

> But there is nothing ruined in his face,
> And nothing beaten in those steady eyes.
> If he's grown old, it isn't like a man,
> It's more the way a river might grow old.

The poet recognized the enigmatic aspect of General Lee's life and career:

> And a long challenge blew an anger through it
> That was more dread for being musical
> First, last, and to the end. Again he said
> A curious thing to life.
> "I'm always wanting something."

Just what that "something" was, no one can be quite sure.

In the middle of the Great Depression, Lee's admirers in all parts of the Union contributed a quarter of a million dollars to purchase and restore Stratford Hall and set it apart as a public shrine. Lee's reputation had survived both the sentimentality of his friends and the slander of his enemies. In the perspective of time, his life had assumed a classic simplicity and directness.

The product of an agrarian civilization, Lee stood all his life in awe of nature. When he came back to Virginia from the west, he "greeted every flower with a name." Like Washington, who was his hero, he preferred farming to fighting.

The God that Robert E. Lee venerated was the Old Testament Jehovah; before Him, Lee was humble all his life. He believed literally in the Scriptures and in God's intervention in human affairs. Lee knew to whom he must turn for aid. "God is our only refuge and strength," he said in a message to his troops. "Let us humble ourselves before Him."

Next to God came the family and the Commonwealth, and Lee

gave them unfailing devotion. Once Virginia seceded, he never for a moment doubted that he must follow her. Not only his immediate family but also his many relatives delighted him, and the General never tired of visits and reunions. At parties he preferred the company of women to men, and of daughters to mothers. In poetry his taste ran toward Sir Walter Scott. Like Lord Chesterfield, he believed so much in the world around him that his acts not only followed the style; they set it.

Dr. Edwin Alderman, president of the University of Virginia, saw in Lee a synthesis of desirable qualities. "Lee is a type and an embodiment of all the best of our state," said Alderman in 1909. "Its triumphs, its defeats, its joys, its sufferings, its rebirths, its pride, its patience center in him. In that regnant figure of quiet strength may be discerned the complete drama of a great stock."[6]

Although Virginia has shared this man with the nation, she has kept for herself certain local shrines and memories—Arlington, Stratford Hall, and the Lee House in Richmond. There are the battlefields, bridges, and historic spots where he said or did heroic things. There are, too, tender little stories, like that of the young mother who brought her baby to him to be blessed. The father, Lee remembered, had died in some bloody, chivalric, impossible attack. "What shall I teach him?" the mother asked. Lee took the infant in his arms, looked sadly at him and the mother, and said: "Teach him he must deny himself."

Finally, there is the Chapel at Lexington which Lee himself planned, and in which he and his ancestors are buried. On the floor above him, in the mausoleum, rests Edward Valentine's statue of Lee asleep on the field of battle. On either side stand Confederate battle flags. Whenever cadets from nearby Virginia Military Institute pass, they cease talking and salute the commander of the Army of Northern Virginia.

But even this Chapel is not Lee's sanctuary. The real shrine is the hearts and minds of the people. To them Lee is the hero defending his homeland with the last ounce of his strength. To the historian, he is a major figure helping to shape the national destiny. To the philosopher, he is the unmachined man, who trusted in an earthliness which has been all but forgotten in an age of whirring wheels. To the poet, Lee is the silent enigma, who said little but did much. To the educator, Lee is the college president whose innovations revitalized Southern education. To the churchman, he is the undeviating Christian, whose trust in Jehovah never faltered. To the genealogist, he is the flower of a great family, final proof that blood will tell. To the soldier, he is the most skillful American general, who said that duty is the sublimest word in the English language.

Every schoolboy knows the tribute of Light-Horse Harry Lee to Washington: "First in war, first in peace, first in the hearts of his countrymen." In Virginia the accolade applies not only to Washington, who made the most of victory, but to Light-Horse Harry's son, who made the most of defeat.

13 *Reconstruction*

After final defeat came ultimate humiliation. Victors have always
expected, and collected, the spoils. After such a struggle as that of
the 1860's, and such a display of pride, Virginians could expect to
be humbled. They could be certain that many tangible and intangible things would be taken away. But there were those who
thought that the conquerors would at least leave the Old Dominion
her name.

They did not. What had been Virginia became Military District
Number One.

Long-standing economic, social, and political customs disappeared as General John M. Schofield came south to administer his
District. Newly enfranchised Negroes and carpetbaggers took over
the tasks formerly performed by the "rich, wise, and well-born." The
last were to be first, and the bottom rail was to be on top.

Not all the Northerners were exploiters, of course. Some came to
rebuild, to teach, to heal the open wounds. Others observed and
reported back to Congress. Whitelaw Reid, New York journalist and
editor, wrote: "Abandoned fields alternated with pine forests,
destroyed depots, and ruined villages. Along the road a pile of
smoky brick and mortar seemed a regularly recognizable sign of

142

what had once been a depot; not a platform or water-tank had been left. Young pines covered the fields. Rebel soldiers and Negroes worked side by side. 'I tell you, sir,' said a Yankee to a Virginian who didn't approve of this social equality, 'a white man has got just the same right a nigger has—to starve if he won't work.' "[1]

An Englishman named A. G. Bradley told the same story. "Everywhere one sees the dismal skeleton of the past," he wrote. "Life flickers feeble still upon the old estates. Here and there a surviving scion of some old family may be found struggling with the briars. Miserable drudges, scarred by collar and tracechain, toil in these unprofitable furrows, or drag the crazy half-loaded wagon along the old rock road."[2]

"The collapse of the old order, the humiliation of defeat, the bereavement and bankruptcy involved, represented with its obscure miseries and tragedies a social revolution," wrote Henry James when he visited Richmond, "the most unrecorded and undepicted in proportion to its magnitude that ever was; so that this reversion of the starved spirit to the things of the heroic age is a definite soothing salve." Collapse, humiliation, revolution— these are the appropriate words for Reconstruction Virginia.

And brown was the dominant color. A long series of storms and rains had destroyed the sense of summer. The war shook the leaves from the trees and the boys from the homes, leaving only stripped trunks and families behind.

As Lewis Mumford says in *The Brown Decades*, there were browns everywhere: mediocre drabs, scorched brown earth, sooty browns, sober autumnal colors. Brown is the color of renounced ambitions and defeated hopes. The nation looked darker and sadder than it had ever looked before.[3]

Dead men were everywhere. Their portraits hung in parlors, their death masks in public places, their words and dying speeches on politicians' lips. They seemed to be concealed in the widows' weeds that turned the brownness into blackness. Soon they would be carved in marble blocks and displayed on courthouse squares.

If the dead seemed heroic, the living were cynical and disillusioned. The very methods and conditions of war had destroyed the ideals and goals for which it was waged. Greed and rancor were piled up behind the bodies of dead heroes.

There is no more chance of finding heroism in a postwar generation than there is in finding a high sense of tragedy in an undertaker. Facing death is one thing. Disposing of corpses is another.

After Lee's surrender, the state was without civil or military government. Cities, industries, and farms were ruined. Men had no deeds, tools, stock, or money. Warehouses, courthouses, and churches were heaps of ashes. The state's 700,000 whites and 500,000 Negroes, awed and bewildered, hardly knew where to turn. Newcomers were quick to offer suggestions. "The white men have houses and lands," said the Reverend James W. Hunnicutt, addressing Virginia's Negroes. "Some of you are old and feeble and cannot carry the musket; but you can apply the torch to the dwellings of your enemies. There are none too young—the boy of ten and the girl of twelve can apply the torch."[4]

With the breaking off of West Virginia in 1863, Virginia lost a third of her land, a quarter of her population, and most of her mineral resources. The percentage of Negroes in the state increased sharply, since there were few in the seceded western counties; so did the state debt, none of which West Virginia would assume. The political situation in Richmond was so corrupt that Union General Schofield, reported on April 18, 1868 to General Grant:

"The same baneful influence that secured the election of a majority of ignorant blacks and equally ignorant or unprincipled whites has proved sufficient to hold them firmly to their original purpose. They could only hope to obtain office by disqualifying everybody in the state who is capable of discharging official duties, and all else to them was of comparatively slight importance."[5]

Could any last straw be found to add to the backbreaking load? Yes, one. Harvard's President Hill made a speech which was meant to sweeten, but which actually soured, the taste of defeat. "The task for the North," he said, "is to spread knowledge and culture over the regions that sit in darkness."

"Go home and light the torches there!" Eustace Gibson advised the carpetbaggers from the floor of the 1867 Constitutional Convention. "Tell Congress to light the torch in its own land and clear away its own darkness. Then perhaps, while that bright illumination spreads all over the great Northern States, we who are benighted in the South may see the way that you would have us go."

This patronizing Yankee air, following in the wake of the mailed fist, caused a strong revulsion against the Union. All over Dixie people sang a song written by Inness Randolph, a Virginia major who served with Jeb Stuart's cavalry. "I'm a Good Old Rebel" was a red rag to enrage the occupying troops:

Three hundred thousand Yankees
Is stiff in Southern dust;
We got three hundred thousand
Before they conquered us;
They died of Southern fever,
And Southern steel and shot,
I wish it was three million
Instead of what we got!

I can't take up my musket
And fight 'em now no more;
But I ain't a-goin' to love 'em,
Now that is certain sure.
And I don't want no pardon
For what I was and am;
I won't be reconstructed,
And I don't give a damn.

People had many defiant schemes. Matthew Fontaine Maury wanted to set up a Confederacy-in-exile south of the border. Others favored guerrilla war and enlisted under the banner of the Invisible Empire of the Ku Klux Klan. A few, like Albert T. Bledsoe, classmate of Robert E. Lee and Jefferson Davis at West Point, continued to argue the legality and moral rightness of the South's position. Bledsoe founded *The Southern Review* in Baltimore, and warned his beloved homeland that it was in danger of being destroyed by Northern industry and science. He died at Alexandria, Virginia, in 1877, exhausted by ten years of controversy.

Meanwhile, a constitution had to be drawn up and a civil government formed. In the interim General Schofield appointed Henry H. Wells, carpetbagger and confiscationist from New York, as Governor. Wells was removed from office by General Stoneman, reinstated by General Webb, and succeeded by General Canby's appointee, Gilbert C. Walker. The 1867 Constitutional Convention which met in Richmond was dominated by Judge John C. Underwood and the radical Republicans. The proposed Underwood Constitution would have disfranchised about 95 per cent of the whites, and disqualified them from holding office. Because of the large number of Negroes and mulattoes involved in the work, this was referred to as the "Black and Tan Constitution." Only by understanding how far the pendulum swung to the left can we explain the later Thermidorian reaction when the conservatives reassumed control.

To accept such a constitution seemed to most white Virginians unthinkable; to reject it might bring even worse consequences. So argued Alexander Stuart of Staunton, who as chairman of the Committee of Nine played a major role in its adoption. A prostrate people must accept Negro suffrage, he argued, no matter how repugnant. In return for this peaceful acceptance, perhaps they could bargain with the federal authorities and get other clauses repealed. This is just what happened. When petitioned, President Grant allowed Military District Number One to vote on the constitution, the test oath, and the white disfranchisement clause separately.

On this basis the Underwood Constitution, the most democratic the state ever had, passed by an overwhelming majority of 210,585 to 9,136. The test oath and white disfranchisement clause were rejected, by smaller majorities. Congress was willing to accept this compromise, did so, and seated the duly elected representatives in Washington on January 26, 1870. Virginia was back in the Union she had been instrumental in founding.

As a shaky equilibrium was attained, a new type of political leader came into prominence—men like William Mahone, son of tavern keeper, and Thomas Martin, son of a former dirt farmer. Gone were aristocratic restriction and ante-bellum prerogatives. Votes from the Negroes and funds from the corporations were new keys to power. Baffling, and sometimes insoluble, problems arose. The methods used in the political area were often as unsavory as the problems confronted.

A typical example was the fraudulent use of the Negro's ballot. By placing a piece of paper over the ticket, officials made the ignorant Negroes (some of whom brought bags into town to get their franchise) mark the paper instead of the ballot. Afterward the election officials could remove the paper and recast the ballot. Voting dead or absentee Negroes was a common practice. Negro ministers were bribed to lead their flocks to the polls to vote the "right way." Railroads moved work gangs out of home precincts on election day so as to prohibit their voting. Intimidation and outright deception were not unknown.[6]

The race and debt problems dominated all others. The first became perennial. The second evolved into an all-out fight between advocates of the last-dollar-payment policy and those of forcible readjustment.

Meanwhile Virginia's credit, in James Kemper's words, "sank to the level of that of Santo Domingo." By 1871 the state debt surpassed $45 million. Bondholders were unwilling to share war losses with other property holders, and insisted that the full debt be paid. They were called Funders. Tradesmen and small farmers were anxious to scale down the debt. The man who could combine their votes with those of the Republicans and Negroes could take over political control of Virginia. That man was William Mahone.

Billy Mahone, as he was generally called, was born in Southampton County. He carried the mail between Courtland and Emporia when he was a youth, and managed to raise enough money to study engineering at the Virginia Military Institute. Small of stature and shrill of voice, he had a straggling beard, a sharp eye, and a belligerent spirit. In an age of railroad building, he distinguished himself by laying the tracks that connected Norfolk and Petersburg. When his state seceded, he served gallantly with the Confederate army, winning the rank of brigadier general after the second battle of Manassas, and major general after the battles of the Wilderness and of the Crater. But his most important battles were to be fought during Reconstruction, in the political arena.

He was the mastermind behind the Readjuster-Republican party. His insistence on reducing the debt brought Radicals, carpetbaggers, Negroes, and even some conservative Virginians to his side. He was able to gain control of the state Assembly, and to have himself elected to the United States Senate. In Washington he broke a tie by voting with the Republicans. For this he was rewarded with the control of state patronage and a sizable slice of Republican campaign funds. By putting this money to work in the right places, he and his various supporters swept the 1881 election. They argued for forcible debt reduction and widened social services. By wooing the Negro he won his election, but also the condemnation of the white supremacists. The debt was re-estimated at about $23 million, the poll tax was repealed, and Mahone became political boss of Virginia.[7] The scaling down of the debt meant that war losses were spread to creditors as well as those who lost physical property and possessions. Although the Funders insisted that the scheme was being forced upon the honest by the dishonest, the Supreme Court upheld the action, and the debt was revised downward.

The Readjusters sent Harrison Riddleberger to the United States Senate and, in 1882, captured five of the nine congressional seats. Their victory was to be short-lived. A firm believer in the Jacksonian spoils system, Mahone ousted Democrats from all possible offices, including the state schools and hospitals. As he exhibited increasingly highhanded and demagogic tendencies, more and more people deserted him and his "Black Republicans."

If the Democrats could regroup their forces and sound the trumpet note of white supremacy, they might beat Mahone. The obvious man to rejuvenate the Democrats was John S. Barbour, descendant of a family long prominent in state politics and Mahone's bitterest enemy in the railroad consolidation wars. "If General Mahone is an organizer of unsurpassed ability, Mr. Barbour is a tactician who can beat Mahone at his own game," commented *The New York Times*. When the Conservatives (who chose after this to be known as the Democrats) met in Lynchburg in July, 1883, they made Barbour the chairman of their state executive committee. He organized their platform, obtained railroad support, and piloted them to victory.

Getting party unity was in itself a major undertaking. As the pro-Mahone Richmond *Weekly-Whig* pointed out, there were at Lynchburg, in addition to Know-Nothings, Greenbackers, and Funders, "Withers and Conservative Democrats; Holliday and Veto Democrats; Daniel and School Torch Democrats; Walker and Liberal Democrats; Koiner and Funder Democrats; Tucker and Bourbon Democrats; Fulkerson and Readjustor Democrats; Goode and Tissue Ballot Democrats—every kind but Jeffersonian Democrats!"[8]

Despite all this, the Democrats were ready for the caustic and critical election of 1883. On the surface, it was hard to tell the major differences between the two parties. Both supported debt adjustment; favored progress and industrial expansion; sought the Negro vote. One factor which swung the scales was the insistance that loyal white men vote Democratic. Unfortunately for the Republicans, William Simms, one of their candidates for the state Senate, made an incendiary speech against the whites before a Danville audience of over 500 Negroes. A riot followed, in which both whites and Negroes lost their lives. The Democrats spread the story throughout the state. Negroes were openly challenging white men's rights, and killing those who fought back. Out with the Black Republicans!

Election tactics were nothing for either party to brag about. In order to beat Billy Mahone, who had used state offices for partisan and personal ends, and to overcome the Negroes and carpetbaggers, the Democrats ignored custom and conscience. "Not only did they use nearly every trick and method of the General," Allen Moger reports, "but they discovered new and clever methods of their own. Anything was considered justifiable in this 'fight between intelligence, virtue, religion, and our material interests on the one hand, and vice, venality, corruption, and unscrupulous rapacity on the other.' "[9] When the votes were finally counted, the Democrats had 145,000 to Mahone's 127,000. The inauguration of a national Democratic administration in 1885 insured the state Democrats of federal backing and patronage. Since that day, no Negro has been elected to any important state office, and no party save the Democratic has ever been in command.

Riddleberger was replaced by John Barbour, organizer of victory, in the United States Senate. Everyone, including Barbour, expected that he would live out his political career as state boss. Everyone, that is, except Thomas Martin.

Martin was the Horatio Alger of Reconstruction politics. Born on an Albermarle County farm in 1842, the oldest of eleven children, he served as a cadet at the Virginia Military Institute, fought with the Corps as a lad of sixteen, studied briefly at the University of Virginia, and returned home in 1867 when his father died. By studying borrowed law books at night, he learned enough to qualify as an attorney at the Palmyra court. His shingle, hung out in front of his second-story office in Scottsville, didn't attract many customers during his first years of practice. Sometimes, he later recalled, the biggest decision of the day was who was going to eat the evening meal—himself or his horse.

In the 1880's his fortune improved. Named local attorney for the Chesapeake and Ohio Railroad, he was singled out as a bright young man by John Barbour, and put on advisory committees of the Democratic party. Martin not only won the confidence of Barbour but of the Young Turks, a group of politicians dedicated to wresting control from the hands of their seniors. The Turks decided to support John Daniel of Lynchburg for the Senate against Barbour. Martin was chosen to direct the Daniel campaign.

Daniel won. Senior party members wondered what had happened; only gradually did they realize that a youth movement was beginning to take over the party. The new era of the corporation machine was beginning. The undisputed head of that party, and that machine, would be Thomas Martin.

Martin continued to work quietly but ceaselessly behind the scenes, never allowing the public press to connect his name with any public office. He was getting ready to try for a place in the Senate, even though he would have to oppose General Fitzhugh Lee. How could a little-known country lawyer hope to beat the nephew of Marse Robert? Martin knew the answer: money, pressure, bargains. He knew, and acted accordingly.

Martin men and money worked in every corner of the state. One of his lieutenants, Walter Watson, explained in a letter just how the matter was to be handled: "What we must do is in a quiet sort of way . . . let our friends in the district know that Martin's name will be before the Legislature so that they will not obligate themselves to somebody else and so become embarrassed."[10]

At the December 8, 1893, Democratic caucus held in Richmond, Thomas Staples Martin was chosen U.S. Senator over General Fitzhugh Lee.

Most people were shocked, most Confederates enraged. A man hardly known beyond the sound of his mother's cowbells had beaten a Lee—a former general and governor—in a contest for the highest national office.

Martin not only reached the Senate; he stayed for twenty-four years. Disgruntled Democrats demanded a committee investigation of his victory over Lee. The chairman of the committtee, a Martin man, deftly ruled out of order any questions which threatened to strike at the charge of collusion with railroad interests. No irregularity was definitely proven, and Martin was officially absolved of any complicity. With the party and the patronage behind him, he would not have to face investigations again. He, more than anybody else, was responsible for the undercover political organization which came to be known as the "Byrd Machine."

Martin's bluntness and honesty were legendary. Mr. William White described a trip to Washington to ask a favor of the Senator. Having heard his request, Martin replied, "Mr. White, I would like to do this for you, because I'm a friend of your father. But I can't. The reason is that I've promised it to someone else."

Later on Woodrow Wilson called Martin to the White House to discuss the question of the President's attending the Paris Peace Conference. Martin listened attentively and then said, "Do not go, Mr. President."

"I am going," President Wilson replied.

"Mr. President, why in the hell did you want my advice?" Martin answered, as he arose and took his leave.

Virginia's Democratic machine was close to, if not dominated by, corporation and railroad interests. Businessmen controlled the Democratic party, squelched the Republicans, and turned back the Populists. By various means they kept the farmers in line, while vetoing a number of their basic demands.[11] One of America's most effective state machines operated so quietly that casual observers couldn't tell it was there.

Martin's major instruments were jobs, patronage, and an uncanny ability to influence men. His blandly unassertive personality was the agent of a masterful will. Some know Martin as an able man, others as an excellent organizer; only a handful realized what a penchant he had for politics and power. He covered his tracks so cleverly that even today there is no good study of him.

Extremely partisan, the machine's top men let it be known that spoils and party support would fall to those who saw eye to eye with Martin and his friends. No young and ambitious politician was allowed to take over from Martin, as he had done from Barbour. Until his death in 1919, the country boy from Albermarle was the political czar of the state.

Social recovery was as difficult as the political one. Too poor, too clannish, too debt-ridden, Virginia did not attract many of the immigrants who were pouring into the Northern ports. In addition, because of better opportunities and conditions elsewhere, Virginia's chief export for a generation was brains. The migration was in four directions—from the state to northern and eastern cities, from non-mining districts to mining districts, from the county to the cities, and from the mountains to the valleys. The 1880 census reported that the number of people born in Virginia but living elsewhere in the United States was higher by 407,608 than the number born elsewhere and living in Virginia. In her study of *Virginia's People,* Sara Gilliam estimates the cumulative net loss from migration during the 1880's at 600,000, which means that 28 per cent of all native Virginians were living in other parts of the United States. The net annual population increase from 1880 to 1900 was only half of the national rate of increase.

Naturally this lag reflected in all phases of state life. In 1870, for example, the state was still producing less tobacco, wheat, and corn than she had in 1860. Farm prices were sinking, and would continue to do so until they reached their nadir in 1896. The only area of rapid growth was in the number of sharecroppers, tenant farmers, and rural failures. By the time Franklin D. Roosevelt came into office, half of Virginia's agricultural workers were tenants or wage earners. The land was washed out and the farm children were as gaunt as the scrawny cornstalks in the drought-plagued fields.

The farm problem, in Virginia and the whole nation, was inherently difficult. While industrialists could regulate and control production, farmers could never predict the demand, regulate the supply, or contend against the natural forces over which they had no control. They lived in a world of overproduction or scarcity; of floods, blights, droughts, and depressions.

A decline in rural prosperity did not, however, greatly alter farm psychology. True enough, many farmers went off to new cities and factories; but they usually went out of necessity rather than desire. Though they may not be very articulate about it, most Virginians think that farming is the job for which God intended most of His children. The fabric of their life, religion, and thinking is agrarian. This, more than any other factor, explains the conservatism which is the hallmark of the Old Dominion. If any of the farm boys are ambitious and talented enough to make their fortunes in the city, they will inevitably use their new economic resources to buy a handsome place in the country.

Throughout Reconstruction the state of Jefferson, Taylor, and Ruffin took much less enthusiastically to the "New South" doctrines than her sister Confederate states to the South. There was considerable "progress" in a few places. Danville and Richmond were key points. As a New-South textile center, Danville grew from 3,500 to 13,000 between 1870 and 1885. By 1890 Richmond was America's third-ranking center for tobacco products. Chewing tobacco was falling from favor, and the newly introduced cigarette was sweeping the market. The plant which had saved the colony in the early seventeenth century rehabilitated its economy two and a half centuries later.

There were dilemmas which all the smokers, politicians, and intellectuals put together couldn't solve; but Virginia was further along by 1900 than other Southern states which had been less devastated by the war. If many places had been destroyed, many more had been rebuilt or else built anew. Conditions were more encouraging in the cities than in the country, more favorable in the realm of physical than social repairs. The Negro had definitely lost his fight to win real equality. A broad reform movement, so noticeable in other parts of the country, hardly permeated Virginia. That the railroads controlled the Democrats, the Democrats the machine, and the machine the people, was plain to see and hard to change. The infamous Walton Law made it possible for voting officials to control unwary and ignorant voters, black and white. Long after the "emergency" had passed, emergency measures and methods continued. Worst of all, there was no strong opposition party to complain, since the Republicans were doomed to be linked universally with "Yankees and niggers."

The only hope was a constitutional convention which would encourage the Democrats to set their own house in order. Many people militated for this. Finally, in the summer of 1901, it materialized. The Democrats concentrated attention on eliminating the power of Negro voters. "The great task before us," said John Garland Pollard, a politician who would be rewarded with the governorship, "will be the elimination of the corrupting influences of the Negro vote. The malignant cancer must be removed from our body politic." "Let us go back to the old rule of the South, and be done forever with the frauds of an educational suffrage," the University of Virginia's Paul Barringer told the Southern Education Association in 1900. "The rigid principles of segregation should be applied in every relation of Southern life," the Richmond *Times* added. "Since God Almighty drew the color line, it cannot be obliterated."

The new constitution made the payment of three years' poll tax six months before general elections a prerequisite to voting. Within three years the number of qualified Negro voters shrank from 147,000 to a registered number of 21,000. Poor people, white and colored, couldn't vote in the state that had once revolted to obtain liberty and equality. Nor was the poll tax the only restriction put in the voter's path. There was the "understanding clause," replaced in 1904 by the "intelligence test."

To appease the vigorous new cities, the convention made them politically independent of the counties. The machine would center its attention in the rural areas. "Country boys" have been the backbone of the Democratic.party ever since. The constitution was never submitted to the citizens for ratification. It was "proclaimed" by the convention and "approved" by the legislature.

With its adoption a new century and a new era were ushered in. The tone was decidedly conservative, on occasions reactionary. Virginians are suspicious of professional reformers anrd liberals because they have (or at least think they have) suffered so much at the hand of men of this ilk. The state's two chief spokesmen in this century have been Carter Glass and Harry Byrd; and two more inveterate enemies of the New Deal and Fair Deal would be hard to find.

The Virginia Democrats have had little sympathy with the social service state. Governor Charles T. O'Ferrall noted that prisoners in the State Penitentiary were "crowded as thick as cattle in a railroad car. In all seasons they breathe the fetid and poisonous air, and in summer pant for breath when locked up for the night."[12] No Department of Health existed until 1908, when a miserly $40,000 was voted for this activity. For years there was no state sanitarium for tuberculosis, the state's fourth most deadly killer. Finally one was opened at Catawba—with a thirty-bed capacity. Governmentally, the twentieth century has been for Virginia the Age of the Pinched Penny.

After 1902 the threat of political and social revolution disappeared. Virginia was "in hand" again—too much so for her own good and that of the nation.

14 *Civil War II*

PYRRHUS USED TO SAY THAT CINEAS HAD TAKEN MORE TOWNS WITH
HIS WORDS THAN HE HAD WITH HIS ARMS.—*Plutarch*

"Hold on to your Confederate money, boys. The South will rise
again!" Granddad used to say when he wanted to provoke a laugh.
The laugh may not have been on Granddad, but on those who
thought the Confederacy was finished. Dixie has risen, and launched
Civil War II. From present indications, she will win it, too.

Civil War I, a military affair, was fought with blood and guts
and shrapnel, and left us the vision of Appomattox. Civil War II is
a literary affair. It is being waged with words and metaphors and
legends, and conjures up the vision of ante-bellum Eden and heroes
on horseback. Best-seller lists confirm the report from the battle
front: the Yankees are everywhere in retreat. Inch by inch, page by
page, film by film, the literary Confederates are sweeping the field.[1]

Paragons of Civil War I are well remembered. Transported to the
Confederate Valhalla, and memorialized in stone along Richmond's
Monument Avenue, they are frequently resurrected for use in movies
or TV. Their memories and mementoes are guarded by Vestal
Virgins of the United Daughters of the Confederacy. Their story and
strategy are constantly re-examined by Southern historians and
praised by Southern publicists. They have begun to smack of the
mythological.

Confederate soldiers were hardly buried before their comrades picked up their pens and charged into print. When no more bullets whined across the Potomac, words flew thick and heavy. By 1888, Albion W. Tourgee acknowledged that the Confederate soldier was the beau ideal of American fiction. American novels tended to be Southern in type and Confederate in sympathy. A culture which had been anathema to the North while alive was revered once it was dead. Northern patriotism overcame Northern retribution. Pride in the whole nation couldn't stand the onus of eleven states dwelling in perpetual disgrace; so they were welcomed home. For better or worse, Southern writers, with the aid of Northern editors, critics, magazines, publishing houses, and theaters, drove out the unfriendly picture of the South implanted there in the 1860's.[2]

These latter-day strategists are the stanch campaigners in Civil War II. Some of them, veterans of the First Civil War, were among the earliest recruits for the second struggle. They deserve first mention.

George William Bagby managed to sleep through the Battle of Bull Run. Once awakened, he fought and viewed a lot. He saw Virginia under fire and eventually under heel. Watching the new day come, he never forgot the old. His vindication came not by the ephemeral sword, but the enduring word.

Born on a Buckingham County plantation in 1828, Bagby volunteered for the Confederate army, but was eventually discharged for ill health. He edited the *Southern Literary Messenger* before purchasing *The Native Virginian*. As a writer, he had a mission: "to describe everything distinctive and without parallel in Virginian civilization, which culminated in the War and perished at its close." Bagby's best sketch was *The Old Virginia Gentleman*. "There was in our Virginia country life a beauty, a simplicity, a purity, an uprightness, a cordial and lavish hospitality, warmth and grace which shine in the lens of memory with a charm that passes all language at command," Bagby claimed. "It is gone with the social structure that gave it birth." Despite such romantic nostalgia, Bagby was essentially a realist in his descriptions and attitudes. He marveled that so chivalrous a group of peers as those described in Civil War novels could have produced so many scoundrels as he saw about him in his lifetime; he had a sharpness of vision that made his work fascinating to a twentieth-century writer like Ellen Glasgow. "His sketches have always been a part of my Virginia heritage," she wrote. "The vital warmth and humanity of the writing give him a permanent place in the literature of Virginia."

Yet there is no satire in Bagby's poem about General Lee, called "After Appomattox." It was as though, in the rear of Lee's tent, had been the Ark of the Covenant. Like most Virginians, Bagby simply stood in awe of the Great Leader, as he imagined Lee on his knees just after the surrender to Grant:

> The cries that upward went that night
> Unto the great White Throne,
> The tears for guidance and for light
> To God alone are known.
>
> Sacred throughout all coming time
> These sleepless hours shall be;
> For who can tell in words sublime
> The agony of Lee?*

If he couldn't tell, John Esten Cooke, was at least willing to try. Born in northern Virginia and admitted to the bar in 1851, Cooke was a gentleman-novelist. His aim was "to paint the Virginia phase of American society, to do for the Old Dominion what Cooper has done for the Indians, Simms for the Revolutionary drama in South Carolina, Irving for the Dutch Knickerbockers, and Hawthorne for the Puritan life of New England." In 1854 Cooke wrote *Leather Stocking and Silk* and *The Virginia Comedians*. Then followed *Ellie; or the Human Comedy, The Last of the Foresters,* and *Henry St. John, Gentleman*. These books showed what the Southern aristocrat was like, and how he lived. The war gave Cooke the chance to find out, in addition, how he behaved in battle.

An ardent secessionist, he turned all the Confederate generals (including the Calvinistic Jackson) into Cavalier knights. Somehow, between battles in which he participated, Cooke managed to write *The Life of Stonewall Jackson* (1863). Enemy forces never interfered with his literary chores or his meals. Continuing to eat from a plate near his horse until the Yankees were within two hundred yards, he would gulp down his coffee and gallop away. Southern readers warmed to an author who scribbled in his diary: "I tried to write in a tent, on the outpost; the enemy yonder, almost on us—but with Jackson, alas, no longer in front. Oh, to write in a quiet study, with no enemy anywhere in view."[3]

Cooke came home from Appomattox, where he buried his spurs as

---

* From *The Old Virginia Gentleman* (Dietz, 1938). Used by permission of Ellen M. Bagby.

a last act of defiance, to write Civil War novels. *Surry of Eagle's-Nest* (1866) and *Mohun* (1869) show the romantic possibilities of Civil War fiction. Cooke, whose long point was not plotting or organizing, frequently stopped his story to throw in documentary information. Thus, *Mohun* contains one of the best descriptions of Richmond just before its fall. In his latter years William Dean Howells and other writers were popularizing a type of realism which was antithetical to Cooke's work; but it did not bother him. "I was born too soon, and am now too old to learn my trade anew," he said. He kept writing, and Virginians kept reading what he wrote. Many of them still do. He was a Cavalier romancer to the end.

Younger and more talented than Bagby or Cooke was Thomas Nelson Page, in whose veins ran some of Virginia's best blood. Two of his great-grandfathers had been governors. His father served on General Lee's staff. Only twelve when the war ended, Thomas saw the old regime in his most impressionable years, and idealized it all the rest of his life. At Washington College he knew and revered General Lee. Brilliant and personable, Page turned his talents to literature, and gave the phrase "before the war" a special meaning. Borrowing from Russell, Cable, and Harris, he pioneered in local-color writing, working out a literary formula which captured the North as well as the South. This is how it went:

Take a white-haired ex-slave, yearning for "de best days Sam eber see." Have him describe the plantation Eden, stressing the justice and juleps of Old Marse, the dash and swagger of Young Marse, and the sweet perfection of Southern ladies. Throw in a few barbecues, christenings, and Christmas feasts.

Then—de wah.

Out with the trumpet and the Confederate flag! Off go Old Marse, Young Marse, and all Marses in the neighborhood, to lead an army of gentlemen and poor whites to daring victory against incredible odds. Young Marse dies on the field of honor. Now only Sam, young Marse's faithful dog, and a Lady-Who-Will-Never-Tell keep alive his gallant memory.

Page wrote novels, short stories, and poems using the format. A typical example is "Uncle Gabe's White Folks," which appeared in *Scribner's Monthly* in 1876:

> 'Fine old place?' Yes suh, 'tis so
> An' mighty fine people my white folks war—
> But you ought ter a' seen it years ago
> When de Marster an' de Missis lived up dyah;

When de nigger'd stan' all roun' de do'
Like grains o' corn on the cornhouse flo'.

Page's poems found a national audience by extolling the virtues of slavery, which the United States had spent four agonizing years destroying, and of reconciliation to the new freedom. To this end he developed the "blood will tell" formula. The refined Yankee soldier saves the refined and defenseless Southern lady from Yankee scum. After the war he comes back, weds the girl, saves the homestead, and bridges the bloody chasm. Or else (as in *Two Little Confederates*) the well-bred Southerners befriend the dying Yankee of good stock. After the war the Yank's folks repay the debt by saving the old homestead. Better than anybody else, he expressed the spirit of the Old South in a way which captivated the New.[4]

Unquestionably Page was sincere in believing that his picture was accurate and fair. "In the simple plantation homes was a life more beautiful and charming than any that the gorgeous palaces would reveal," he insisted. "Its best presentation was that which had the divine beauty of truth." His books are Virginian to the core. For him, character is determined by status. Heroic characters are gentlemen; villains are outside the charmed circle.

In Ole Virginia (1887) is pre-eminently the Virginia classic. Anyone who wants to understand the working of the Virginia mind, and the persistence of certain attitudes into the twentieth century, should read it. *The Old Gentleman of the Black Stock, Befo' de War,* and *Marse Chan* are other favorites of Page devotees. Mark Twain poked fun at the formula by having a Negro woman reply to a Yankee's praise of the Southern moon: "Ah, bless yo' heart, honey, you jes' ought to seen dat moon befo' de wah!" In *Red Rock,* Page gave his reply: "For those who knew Virginia as it was then, and can contrast it with what it has become since, no wonder it seems that even the moonlight was richer and mellower 'before the war' than it is now."

Page's golden memories appeared in the Brown Decades. Apparently Grant's cohorts, having captured Richmond, were determined to take over the Washington mint as well. The greedy, lawless, and capable coupled startling audacity with immense wastefulness. Leaders of the day, as Vernon Parrington has pointed out, fought their way encased in rhinoceros hides. They had stout nippers. Jim Fisk, for example, bragged that he worshiped in the synagogue of the libertines; and when he failed in his Erie Railroad stock swindle, he announced cheerfully that nothing had been lost save honor.

Southerners looked back to the happy plantation days with wistful eyes. They turned from the prosaic daily world to the fiction of Thomas Nelson Page. His stories rang true. "Write what you know about," he advised his nephew. "Write as you feel; write simply, clearly, sincerely, and you will write strongly." This is why, far into the twentieth century, the ghost of Page still haunted Southern writers, keening in Negro dialect over Virginia's fallen glories. Through his prose shone the patriarchal glow of days that never will return.

Not all those who made the transition after the war were concerned primarily with defending Old Marse. Among the important, if lesser known, ex-soldiers were two veterans of Civil War I, and of Yankee prison camps, John Tabb and Michael Miley. Both illuminated the period in which they lived, leaving artistic reminders of what they had seen and done.

Born in 1845 on an Amelia County plantation, John Tabb served on a Confederate steamer which made twenty successful runs through the federal blockade. Finally the ship was captured and the crew sent to the Union prison at Point Lookout, Maryland. There, Tabb met Sidney Lanier, whose friendship was one of the chief pleasures of his life. Released in 1865, Tabb studied for the Episcopal ministry; in 1872 joined the Roman Catholic Church, a faith which he held for the rest of his life.

"Why don't you come back into the Episcopal Church, John, where you belong?" a friend asked.

"I'll be damned if I do!" Tabb replied.[5]

The young convert taught at St. Charles College (near Ellicott City, Maryland) until 1881. Ordained a priest in 1884, he spent the remainder of his life at St. Charles College. Several summers he visited and preached in Virginia. Father Tabb was noted for his wit and epigrammatical flair. His own English grammar text was dedicated "To my Pupils, Active and Passive, Perfect and Imperfect, Past, Present and Future." Once, when Bishop Foley of Michigan was visiting Cardinal Gibbons of Richmond, Father Tabb was asked to invite two prelates to the St. Charles campus. To the Cardinal he wrote:

> "Dear Cardinal Gibbons:
> With all your red ribbons,

Pray lend us the light of your face;
And bring with you Holy
John Michigan Foley
(Who hopes some day to be in your place.)"*

Despite lack of recognition and an encroaching blindness, Tabb created delicate and beautiful poems, cameolike in their perfection. Primarily a poet of nature, he drew from his memories of Virginia fields, hills, streams, and clouds. Tabb combined the natural with the scriptural, though his was never a consciously intellectual poetry. "I always see in flashes," he wrote, "and rarely change the first draft of a poem." "The Immaculate Conception" is a gem:

> A dew-drop of the darkness born
> Wherein no shadow lies;
> The blossom of the barren thorn
> Whereof no petal dies;
> A rainbow beauty, passion-free,
> Wherewith was veiled Divinity.

Tabb explained the rejection slips he received from *Harper's* and *Scribner's* by admitting that he was a Southern rebel, "and a thoroughly unreconstructed one."[6] The attack of Northern critics on Virginia's Edgar Allan Poe angered him. In 1850, when Tabb was a boy of five, Poe published in *Sartain's Union Magazine* his essay on "The Poetic Principle." He defined poetry as the rhythmical creation of beauty, and denied that a long poem could exist. In claiming that the "ultimate, perhaps, if we except the dramatic, the only authentic art form is the lyric," Tabb reflected the views of Poe. He wrote six poems in praise of his master, whom he thought had found the true poetic principles. When the fiftieth anniversary of Poe's death was celebrated, one of Tabb's poems was placed in Poe's room at the University of Virginia:

> To Edgar Allan Poe
>
> Dead fifty years? Not so;
> Nay, fifty years ago
>   Death, obloquy, and spite
> To curse his ashes came.
>   But lo, the living light
> Beneath the breath of shame
>   Indignant, spurned the night.
> And withered them in flame.

* Poems of John B. Tabb are quoted by permission of Francis C. Litz. The standard edition, *Poems, by John B. Tabb*, was published in Boston, 1900, by Small, Maynard & Co.; and in London, 1903, by J. Lane.

Michael Miley's life, problems, and achievements paralleled Tabb's. Though Tabb was a "Tuckahoe" and Miley a "Cohee," they fought similar battles in both Civil Wars. Tabb left his enduring images on paper; Miley transmitted his to glass plates.

Miley was raised on a Shenandoah Valley farm and educated at the hearth. Only nineteen when he joined the Stonewall Brigade, he was captured at Chancellorsville the day Jackson was shot and taken to the northern prison at Fort Delaware. Weighing less than a hundred pounds when he was released, Miley returned to the Valley, found his home destroyed, and decided to become a photographer. After a few lessons from an itinerant artisan, he went to Lexington. The magnet that drew him was General Lee, and the opportunity of becoming the General's semiofficial photographer. The series of Lee photographs which he took between 1866 and 1870 are a major addition to the American archives.[7]

Fascinated by Virginia's past, Miley devoted days to copying daguerreotypes of early pioneers, officials, judges, and preachers. He captured on glass many phases of Southern small-town life during Reconstruction. He turned his lens on the village fool and the Negro quarters. Eventually he had 15,000 glass plates.

Miley's landscapes are full of spirituality and hope, pointing toward a new art with its own language and idiom. Hemmed in by the Blue Ridge and Allegheny Mountains, which he called "the central feature of our whole life here," he was aware of their overwhelming power, majesty, and timelessness. Miley's camera was no mere machine, but an instrument sensitive to things he could not verbalize. In his best work, Miley combined the two main streams of photography—the utilitarian and the aesthetic.

Michael Miley pioneered in color photography, receiving a patent for his color process on October 21, 1902. Ben Cable, New York businessman and former chairman of the Democratic party, was so impressed that he offered to finance Miley's work if he would come North. Miley declined. His prints could not be mass-produced and sold commercially; not wanting his name associated with inferior craftsmanship, he stayed in the Valley. His untiring experimentation and modifications are documented by hundreds of scrawled notations on the back of unsuccessful or damaged proofs. In these minute scribblings can be read the tedious evolution of his process, and the unending quest for a more vivid and flexible medium.[8]

There was no photographer present in 1918 to record Miley's funeral rites, as he had done General Lee's a half-century earlier.

The Miley Studio remained open until 1935, when his son Henry sold the whole collection of negatives to the Virginia Historical Society. Like John Tabb and all the other Southern soldiers, Michael Miley rests now in a grave marked with a small iron Confederate cross. On it are two words: *Deo Vindice.*

These men were the generals; the neo-Confederate army has many lesser officers and outside allies as well. Prominent Northern writers like Henry Adams, Herman Melville, and Henry James exhibited sympathy toward certain aspects of Southern culture. Yankee visitors were convinced that Southern life had a unique flavor and charm. Aristocrats of Europe, especially England, had favored the Confederacy in Civil War I, and continued their allegiance long afterward. The best biography of Stonewall Jackson is still that of an Englishman, G. F. R. Henderson. The statue of Jackson behind the Capitol in Richmond was erected by donations from English admirers.

Virginia sculptors and painters did much for the Lost Cause. Edward Valentine studied in France, Italy, and Germany, but came home to do statues of Jefferson Davis and Robert E. Lee. Though Moses Ezekial, a talented Virginia artist, stayed on to work in his Italian studio, he sent home a Confederate Memorial group. William Sheppard spent years studying in Paris; but his bronze masterpiece, *The Color Bearer,* glorified the Army of Northern Virginia. From Florence, William Couper sent back a statue of Captain John Smith. Their bronze and marble added form and distinction to Civil War II.

So did the pigment of John Elder and Conrad Chapman. Elder, a protege of Emmanuel Leutze at Düsseldorf, returned to Richmond to portray battle scenes and leaders. Chapman also made the long voyage home to do thirty-one monumental canvases which now hang in Richmond's Confederate Museum. The spell which the war cast over the imagination of Virginians was incredible.

Natives have known about Civil War II for a long time, but it continues to surprise and perplex European visitors. This was true of the English historian, Dr. Arnold Toynbee, who wrote:

A foreign observer who visited the Old South in the fifth decade of the twentieth century would assuredly pick out Virginia and South Carolina as the two States in which there was least sign or promise of recovery; and he would be astonished to find the effects of even so great a social catastrophe as theirs persisting so starkly over so long a period. In these States the memory of that catastrophe is as green in our generation as if the blow had fallen only yesterday; and "the war" still means the Civil War on many

Virginia lips, though two fearful wars have since supervened. In fact, twentieth-century Virginia makes the painful impression of a country living under a spell, in which time had stood still.[9]

He is both right and wrong. What he calls an "attitude" is in part a pose, tied up not only with regional psychology and history but also with economics. Being "Confederate" pays off. Tourists want to visit ante-bellum gardens, tour battlefields, buy trinkets. Historians, novelists, reporters, and artists thirst for rebel water and themes. More and more visitors want a postcard, a stamp, or a trinket which will show how "different" Virginia is—just as people like to buy Scottish souvenirs when visiting Britain. To be Confederate today isn't dangerous, as it was a century ago. No risk, no marching, no bleeding are involved. The pose is there for the taking. Thousands of Virginians, white and colored, use it as their chief source of revenue (Yankee greenbacks, redeemable at any federal bank).

Tourists and visitors spent an estimated $660 million in Virginia during 1957. In the following year $25 million was invested in facilities to house the traveling public and accomodate the "tourist boom." By then eager promoters were looking ahead to 1961-65, the Civil War Centennial years. William H. Stauffer, president of the Virginia Civil War Centennial Corporation, discussed the prospects in the April, 1958, University of Virginia *News Letter*. "From the coldly business point of view," he wrote, "the forthcoming Centennial should be welcomed by many. The Virginia Travel Council is already at work on the economic phases of the anticipated influx of visitors. . . ."

Plans will be carefully drawn. When, a hundred years after their antecedents came to Fredericksburg, Chancellorsville, and Richmond, the Yankees reinvade Virginia, they will find descendants of the Boys in Gray waiting for them. That the visitors will leave poorer, if not wiser, is certain. Possibly they will retreat to the North, just as Dr. Toynbee returned to England, with small Confederate flags tucked away in their suitcases. Thus is the victor vanquished.

15 *John Bull vs. Uncle Sam*

WE'VE GOT A LOT MORE TO LIVE FOR THAN FOLKS USED TO HAVE.
GRANDPA SAYS WE'VE GOT EVERYTHING BUT HAPPINESS. HE'S OLD,
THOUGH, AND HE DON'T SEEM TO TAKE TO THE NEW WAYS.

Ellen Glasgow, IN THIS OUR LIFE

The big question in post-Civil War Virginia has been whether to
follow John Bull or Uncle Sam. John Bull represents past glories.
Uncle Sam represents current progress. The pull of British versus
Yankee spirit has been constant and critical.

For years John Bull was the easy victor. Virginia's great centuries
were the seventeenth and eighteenth, and four fifths of those two
hundred years were spent under the British flag. Only after World
War II had Virginians been under the Stars and Stripes as long as
they had been under England's banner. Virginians know where they
come from. Theirs is a land of long-established patterns, slow growth,
and the visible survival of many ties with the past. That is why they
erected a memorial to the Earl of Cornwallis at Yorktown, inscribed:

> A Testimonial of the Affection of Virginia
> For the Mother Country.

People on the other side of the Atlantic know of this attachment,
too. Last summer I sought aid from a reference librarian in the
British Museum. "Will you help me locate a book?" I asked.

"Of course, sir. You're a visitor here?" she asked, noting my un-
British drawl.

"Yes, I'm from Virginia."

"Welcome home!" she replied.

What has been said and done in London has influenced Virginia more than what has been done in New York—perhaps, in the perspective of her whole history, more than events in Washington. Virginia's "way of life" was borrowed from English country gentlemen, justified by English political theory, and practiced by rich and poor alike. In the early eighteenth century Hugh Jones reported that colonial Virginians "live in the same manner, dress after the same modes, and behave themselves as English Gentry." Much has changed since then. Plantations have been turned into suburbia. But if you will notice the street signs, you will see the British names: Avon, Hawthorne, Raleigh, Berkeley. Pronunciation in the back country is still Elizabethan. Virginia tailors remain in bondage to Bond Street. The high point of the 1957 Jamestown Festival, for Virginians, was the visit of Queen Elizabeth II.

Knowing this, the British have a special regard for the Fifth Dominion. Thackeray says of the Virginian, in his novel of that title, "He was the best of you all!" In 1914, Winston Churchill sent a dispatch to Lord Kitchener which read in part: "I hear from many sources of the keen and widespread desire of individual Americans to take part in the war on our side. It has been stated that 50,000 to 60,000 Americans have volunteered, including a number of Virginians."[1]

The mutual admiration was documented yet again in a clothing advertisement, published in the July 11, 1956, *New York Times,* which reported on a buying trip to England:

> We were invited to a dinner. Quite informal. Don't dress. And there at last was our beau ideal. His clothes, with just a faint echo of the Edwardian, were beautifully tailored. The gold watch and chain had obviously been his grandfather's. His linen was faultless. His English accent was what is now classified here as U (upper class) as opposed to non-U. We asked our host about him. "Oh, George. Been here a couple of years, I believe. Comes from Virginia. Brilliant chap!"

Although the influence of other groups should not be underestimated (especially of the Negroes and the Germans), it can safely be said that the folk culture of Virginia is Anglo-Saxon. Never since the Civil War has Virginia had over 2 per cent foreign-born in her population. The new immigration which transformed many other states hardly affected her. What has survived is an organic folk culture, built solidly on a land that is loved and understood. This veneration is indigenous, rooted like the oak trees. The soul is wedded to the soil. No one can or would separate them.

Every Virginian, John Randolph commented, holds as his ideal of perfect felicity acquiring a plantation and spending the remainder of his days on it, "in the enjoyment of the rural pleasures, which are among the few human pleasures that leave no bitter taste in the mouth."

This is the English country squire speaking. Visitors quickly perceive it. To cross the Potomac, T. S. Eliot has observed, is as definite an experience as to cross from England to Wales, almost as definite as to cross the English Channel. "I think that the chances for a native culture are perhaps better here than in New England," he went on to say. "You are farther from New York; you have been less industrialized and less invaded by foreign races."

The land Eliot found so unlike much of America is aristocratic in manner, orthodox in religion, courteous in daily intercourse, and conservative in politics. The landscape and the dwellers thereon still retain their primitive moral connection; men still live by a semblance of order, obligation, and dogma. Overseeing affairs is the "Colonel" or the "Judge," a hearty, responsible fellow, more at home in the fields than in the books, a spiritual descendant of English country squiredom. Though he may never have led a regiment or sat on a bench, he has a generally acknowledged title which everyone uses. The plain people tip their hats to him on the street and vote for him in the elections. In time of crisis they follow him in war or politics, even when he is defending a system such as chattel slavery in which they have no stake. Dirt farmers and squires enjoy a sympathy of experience that makes for social unity and easy communication. The weather, hunting season, and road programs concern them all. Shared interests draw people together, though they may be legally segregated in hotels and schools. Consequently, practically no class consciousness exists in rural Virginia. Only the visiting professors know what the word proletariat means.

In rural Virginia class is not so much a matter of economic position as personal description. Among the poorest Virginians, John Peale Bishop has noted, there is a self-respect and sense of their worth as men, regardless of what they have done or accumulated, which set them apart from the many Americans who are lost without bankbooks and who recognize no price but that of achievement. It is in the unhurried tranquillity of the hamlet that personal quality dominates, and eccentrics are tolerated. The stress is not on becoming, but on being.

Here the old-time aristocracy has not given up, or sunk into decadence, as Southern novelists suggest. The Snopeses may come to town, sit on their haunches, and tell ribald stories about jackasses; but they will quiet down when the Colonel walks up. Unless he approves a change or a crusade, they will not endorse it either. This is why the Ku Klux Klan in one generation, the New Deal in another, and the integration crusade today have not taken root in Virginia.

Because they have such great power, country gentlemen are not now, and have never been, noted for humility. Though he defends the rural aristocracy, John Pendleton Kennedy admits in *Swallow Barn* that squires tend to become as "infallible as the Popes, to be impatient of contradiction, and to be very touchy about honor." The less sympathetic Yankee Moses Coit Tyler called them "loud-tongued and jolly fox-hunters and militia heroes."

Some scholars fail to realize that the upper class, as well as the lower, creates a folklore. In old Virginia, more folk tales and songs came from the veranda than from the slave quarters. The class which is most dedicated to English ways and beliefs is the upper class. Of all the English patterns which came to our shores, that adopted for Virginia planters has been the most enduring.[2]

No need to go to rural England to see how the English squire thinks and acts, or constructs his code around the cardinal virtues of fortitude, courtesy, prudence, and justice; just saunter down one of Virginia's roads.

Virginians, though hostile to outside ideas, are polite to outsiders. They cultivate cordial instincts, manners that are a unique combination of studied informality and acquired etiquette. They dress plainly, when they need not, so as not to depend on dress or social form to accentuate distinctions. In the Revolutionary assemblies delegates from other colonies commented on the "plainness" of Virginia dress and manners. Henry, Jefferson, and Marshall were castigated by the press for too great informality. Lax and lounging manners persist; the Episcopal Church which has carried on in the days since the Establishment is in Virginia extremely "low church."

They are a gossiping people. Relishing the minute and particular, they talk of polecats, chitterlings, scandals, and the year it snowed in September. They have the English preference for hounds, Hereford cattle, wood fires, Christmas festivities, legends of this or that local

celebrity, political arguments, and fox hunts. They like family reunions, family feuds, and bizarre manifestations of human frailty.
Over a century ago an English visitor, George W. Featherstonhaugh,
F.R.S., F.G.S., stood on the veranda of White Sulphur Springs Hotel
and listened as Virginia gentlemen argued about Bacon. How admirable, he thought, to find such concern about philosophy—until
he realized that the talk was about the hindquarters of a hog.

Folkways and folk talk go beyond scholarly documentation, en-
compassing dressing, eating, belonging. Any Saturday afternoon on
the Courthouse Square proves it. On one side are the country whites
of modest means; on the other, the Negroes. All will be leaning and
squatting and gossiping. Someone may be whittling away at a stick
with a pocketknife, but more likely the object being whittled will be
a plug of tobacco. Talking goes on in an easy unhurried fashion.

"Ain't seed you for nigh onto a month. . . . He growed up and
run off. . . . That government man said to raise 'em under electric
lights, but if it ain't no sunshine it ain't no meat. . . . I heerd them
Tolliver girls took to running around wild. . . . He drove that third
woman clear to her bury hole. The Lord he always gits his way."

"All them cows bloated up and died. Tristest thing ever was. Yep,
she knowed I was coming. I wretched out my hand and wove. . . .
Anybody brewing up any corn up on the ridge this season?

"Jake had the three day chill an' fever. . . . Another dry spell
would put the fixin's on us. . . . I didn't mind helping with the barn,
I was beholden to him. . . . She heads right for that peach brandy
every time a marryin' comes round. That stuff puts you right in
your prime!"

After standing around for an hour or so, country people amble
on to the bank corner, the Western movie house, or the five-and-
ten-cent store. Women follow their gnarled patriarchs, talking about
family ailin's or the preserves they put up for the winter. About twilight the whole family moves to the edge of town. They sit in the
tent where a traveling preacher sweats and battles the sins of the
world. Colored folks have moved on to their shoddy honky-tonk,
where they joke and feed nickels to the juke box which features
colored bands. They are oblivious of the terrible thrashing Satan is
taking a block or two away. On a good night, two or three sinners
might come out and be saved. That will make up for those who have
slipped off into the soft grain fields and got lost.

These Saturday visits and pleasures supply needs that must be met
by elaborate educational schemes, spectator sports, and recreational

programs in more "advanced" societies. Away from the big cities and highways people can still amuse themselves. There is no big sell here.

Not fully understanding this, well-meaning reformers and missionaries from the urban centers become discouraged when they try to import the New Order. They find that their newspapers, books, and crusades are ignored. The few cosmopolites who have chosen to live with these rural people have usually been absorbed into their way of life before changing it very much. The best method has been to entice the young people off to the factories or cities—that does the job. The advocates of progress can rejoice, too, in the effectiveness of the new scientific gadget, the television set. It is penetrating as books, newspapers, court decisions, and government decrees never did. In the piny woods and the hollows are the same gaunt faces and the same poor shacks. But on top of them are new shining antennas.

Back in 1708 Sir John Oldmixion noticed that "a sort of fatility attends the towns of Virginia. They have nothing so little on their thoughts as the building of towns." Outside the northern belt which services Washington, and a dozen cities, fatility is still in the air. As we send up our missiles and satellites, most Virginians continue to live close to the earth, and to trade with rural people.

The pattern of agriculture has not changed much. Tobacco is the big crop, followed by grains and vegetables. Production of fruits, timber, beef, milk, and eggs has expanded. Tourists have become an excellent item, in and out of season. The rhythm of the earth and the growing season continue to set the tempo.

Morality, meanwhile, is carefully defined and patrolled by Protestant fundamentalism. Virginia life for two centuries has been marked by an unrelenting piety and the domination of a still-thundering Jehovah. A deeply religious society is always a traditional society. One key to Virginia is faith.

No institutions rival the importance of the churches in the Old Dominion. They command more members and more man-hours than all other volunteer organizations combined.[3] Marx called religion the opiate of the poor; throughout Virginia and the South, it is the opiate of the rich as well. In Dixie, morality and religion are adjudged one and the same thing. Good character is taken as obvious proof of genuine faith. Not to attend church is frowned upon or outwardly criticized; decent people keep the Sabbath. Faith in the

Biblical heritage ranks second only to white supremacy as a means of conserving the "way of life."[4]

The success of nineteenth-century orthodox theologians like James Thornwell and Robert Dabney in swinging the Southern mind away from deism and reconciling the teachings of orthodox Protestantism with the Southern culture has been recognized by historians. Militant Presbyterians, Baptists, and Methodists won the state over to evangelical Christianity during the eighteenth and nineteenth centuries, and have held to it for generations. The Social Gospel and Ethical Culture have not destroyed old attitudes. Country people continue to believe in a fountain filled with blood. "Ministers swarm through the South like locusts, and can with astonishing facility get deep into the hearts of the folk everywhere and under all conditions, beng clown or curate as the need for religious guidance demands," Edwin Poteat, Jr., reported in 1935.[5] In religion, not politics, the South is solid.

Virginia's Protestant ethic has been strong enough to outlaw bars, mixed drinks, and parimutuel betting, giving a puritanical tone to the Cavalier State. Less damaging practices, such as smoking, cardplaying, and dancing, have also come under heavy attack. A Lexington citizen found the local school commencement exercises "shocking and disheartening" because they included folk dances and singing games. "Is this a sample of what they are teaching children in Virginia's public schools?" he wrote to the newspaper. "Old Satan himself is writing the instruction book."[6]

The United States Constitution makes explicit the separation of church and state, insisting on keeping religion out of the public schools. Not so in Virginia. Daily prayers, hymns, and Bible reading are common in state schools. Children begin early in December to decorate their classrooms and prepare pageants to celebrate the coming of the Christ Child. My daughter, who attends the fourth grade, recently brought home two report cards. One evaluated and commented on her academic work, the other on her Bible course. True enough, the local Bible teacher is paid from church, not state, funds; but this is not apparent to my daughter. The trend is toward increasing, not decreasing, religious instruction in public schools.

Technology, often assumed to be the enemy of the old-time religion, has sometimes proved to be a handmaiden of faith. Now Christians can have radio programs, TV programs, and neon-lighted

Bibles. They can fill their churchyards with manger scenes which would have been impossible before the advent of spotlights and plastics. Nor will secular prosperity and growth kill the old orthodoxy. Religion already has grabbed hold of the rising graphs, so that it may prosper accordingly. The lasting and effective changes come not in statistical tables, but in people's hearts and minds. As long as Virginians believe as they do, only the surface of their culture will be transformed.

This is the traditional, the fundamental Old Dominion. Beside (actually inside) it is the New Dominion, offspring of the wedding of impoverished Bourbons and ambitious industrialists. John Bull stayed in the country; Uncle Sam took over the cities.

To sum it up so neatly is an oversimplification, for the two forces often merged. The northern factories were not only adopted, but adapted, in Virginia. The "New South movement" was not so much a revolution from the past as a modification of the old code. The new factory took the place of the old plantation. Field hands spun, instead of picked, cotton. Advertisements of the Craddock Terry shoe company of Lynchburg pictured Confederate veterans admiring "stately" factories which were proud landmarks. As corporations and railroads expanded, they backed the Democrats, and thus allied themselves with the old Bourbons. Paternalism fits as well in an industrial society as in a rural one; it merely assumes a new guise. The ghost of the Old South stalked through the gardens of the new, and refused to rest in its premature grave.

This does not mean that Virginia culture did not change. It did. Invading armies disrupted Virginia life, but invading technology gradually transformed it. The long-range effects of Reconstruction were as telling as those of the Civil War. A look at the economic history of Virginia in the last half-century will make this clear.

16 *You-All Hurry Back*

COTTON GOES WEST, CATTLE COMES EAST,
NEGRO GOES NORTH, AND YANKEE COMES SOUTH.

In March, 1883, a loaded coal car moved triumphantly from an Allegheny coal mine to the sea. This was no routine affair. The New River had been conquered by the iron horse; the first black diamonds from the Pocahontas Flat Top mines were en route to Norfolk. That city was about to begin its career as one of America's major coal ports. The moment seemed, to those sending and those receiving, historic.

The car itself was gaily bedecked with flags and bunting. On its side was an inscription: "From Pocahontas to Norfolk for Mayor Lamb." The Mayor and his associates were in the reviewing stand as the car moved majestically across town. School children cheered, bands played, and spectators grabbed chunks of coal for trophies. There were, of course, speeches. "Norfolk," Mayor Lamb predicted, "will be a city of apartment houses, like Washington or New York!"

Virginia was adopting the time-honored strategy of New York's Tammany Hall in her fight with her Yankee foes. If she couldn't lick 'em, she would join 'em.

Actually, the strategy was not entirely new. Virginians had teamed up with northern commercial interests long before the Civil War. Yankees held many state bonds and controlled much of Virginia's wealth in the 1850's, when railroads and industry made notable progress.[1] With secession all economic ties were severed. With invasion, most of Virginia's industrial potential was destroyed. For the railroads and factories, Reconstruction meant exactly that—starting all over again.

Confusion and corruption multiplied the economic problems. Civic law and procedure were subservient to the military. Bayonets were the final arbiters. What meager gains the state was able to register in the first postwar years were largely wiped out by the Panic of 1873. These were times of declining prices, minimum profits, starvation wages, and tight money. Sacrifice was not acclaimed as it had been during the war; heroism was not announced by booming cannon. Conditions slowly improved. The empty larders were filled, and the hungry were fed. There was nothing in Virginia to match the Big Barbecue served by the Robber Barons in the victorious North and West, at least there was plenty for the well-to-do.

As manufacturing sprang up from the Atlantic to the Appalachians, confidence replaced despair. Confederate generals who had defended old Southern railroads invested in new ones. Newspapers began to write about the Enterprising Eighties and new opportunities. Virginia could become the northern outpost of the New South. Her workers would challenge the spinners of New England and the ironmongers of Pennsylvania.[2]

The Yankee bandwagon had already begun to roll, and was picking up momentum. Perhaps Virginia could hop on, if she imitated the action of her sister states to the south. Many Virginians traveled to the 1881 International Cotton Exposition in Atlanta, which received excellent coverage in the Virginia press. Senator A. B. Vance struck the Exposition keynote when he endorsed the idea of progress in appropriate Southern rhetoric. "We have renewed our youth at the fountains of industry," he said, "and found the hills of gold."

The sentiment was echoed by Virginia's chambers of commerce, state bureaus, boards of trade, and railroads. The slogans and assertions of the time would do credit to the ingenious ad men who operate today on Madison Avenue. The Virginia boosters were forceful and fervent. Remembering their heritage, they were cavalier with facts. That a great many people read and believed them is obvious by the actions taken in dozens of Virginia towns. This was the era of boom and brag. Only in retrospect would it look like the era of boom and bust.

In a few instances the anticipations of the expansionists were realized. Their chief show place was Roanoke, in southwest Virginia. Until 1880 it was Big Lick, a sleepy village of 400. Because of Roanoke's favorable location, and the eagerness of its inhabitants for new enterprises, both the Norfolk and Western and the Shenandoah Valley railroads decided to locate their machine shops there. The boom was on. A farm which sold for $800 in 1878 brought $125,000 five years later. By 1892 the population was 25,000 and rising. Roanokers found an appropriate nickname ("the Magic City") and motto ("from acorn to oak, watch Roanoke"), and kept bragging.

The factor most responsible for this was the Norfolk and Western Railroad, which ran across the state from the Tennessee border to Norfolk, and tapped the rich coal fields. Philadelphia capitalists poured a sum estimated variously as from $75 million to $150 million into the railroad and the country around it. Consequently local freight traffic increased over 400 per cent between 1881 and 1887. Coal delivered to the Norfolk docks, the New York *Evening Post* noted, ended up as far north as Maine, as far south as Havana. Other industries followed the railroad into Roanoke, which looked and acted more like a Western than a Southern town. Chamber of Commerce leaflets spoke of a city "teeming with wealth, culture, industry, energy, and vim." Perhaps the motto had not been carefully chosen; and oak tree grew too slow for Roanoke's taste.

Despite such expansion, which has continued at a slower pace in the twentieth century, Roanoke has shown symptoms of a notable inferiority complex. The city fathers have topped Mill Mountain with an eight-story neon-lighted star, "the largest artificial star in the world." Their new businesses make outlandish claims; one shop, for example, advertises as "the antique center of the South." Their actions seem to most nearby towns quite un-Virginian. When a national magazine chose Roanoke as the "All-American City" in 1952, signs proclaiming the fact were erected at the city borders. To celebrate Roanoke's seventy-fifth birthday, thousands of Roanoke males grew beards to reflect the "old days"—a trick borrowed from the Western rodeo towns. Yet Roanoke was not anxious to be Western or even All-American. She wanted to be Southern. On the back of the city boundary markers was an invitation to those leaving the Magic City: "You-All Hurry Back!"

Though the tourist will find less that is traditionally Virginian here than in any city in the state, he should make a point of visiting Roanoke. Williamsburg will show him what Virginia was, Richmond what Virginia is, and Roanoke what it is becoming.[3]

For every town that boomed, there were a dozen that busted. Look at what happened to "Coming Cornwall," "Bustling Brownsburg," "Pushing Basic City," "Glorious Goshen," and "Beautiful Shendur." The pattern was the same for each of them—flamboyant literature, a corporation to grab up the land, suckers to buy it, the resort hotel to take care of the expected visitors. The three magic words —mining, manufacturing, and improvement—were constantly invoked. After the smoke cleared, the alchemists had no gold, nor any base metal, to show; only land, as tranquil as it had been before boom days came.

The history of "Bonny Buena Vista" is typical, and well documented.[4] The moving spirit in the area was D. C. Moomaw, a preacher of the Dunkard sect. On his large farm in Rockbridge County he decided to build a town. After he had done a little reading and thinking, he changed his terminology. He was going to found the Pittsburgh of the South.

A few miles away stood the ruins of the old Buena Vista iron furnace, so named because metal from the furnace was used at the battle of Buena Vista in the Mexican War. Moomaw was convinced that the nearby ore deposits could still be worked successfully. The new city of Buena Vista would produce more ore in a day than the old charcoal furnace had in a month.

Moomaw believed this, and convinced others it was true. The fact that his site was on the north branch of the James River, at the junction of the Chesapeake and Ohio and Norfolk and Western railroads, added weight to his arguments. The Buena Vista Company was chartered by the state legislature. Subscription books were opened at a public meeting in nearby Lexington in January, 1889. Ten days later $750,000 had been subscribed. Men mortgaged their homes so as to have money to invest in lots. Farmers sold their land at country prices, then bought back small sections at city-lot prices. Professors, preachers, and lawyers scrambled to get the best lots.

Buena Vista was laid out, with streets, roads, parks, and alleys extending out of the valley on into the foothills. One-acre wooded portions were designated as "Villa Sites," and were meant for the wealthy and aristocratic. People who bought them changed the name to "Villainous Sites" later on; but while the boom lasted, they could almost see mansions on their fine land. Lots solds so rapidly that a large bulletin board was erected in a public place, so that sales could be quickly posted. When the company president, A. T. Barclay, announced that a large foundry was coming to Buena Vista from Columbus, Ohio, the bulletin board was insufficient to record the sales. In one morning a hundred thousand dollars worth of property changed hands. Over in the County Courthouse, the Clerk of Court had to hire ten assistant recorders to keep up. Finally he had deed forms printed, which could be filled in quickly. The West Buena Vista Company bought the Paxton farm and built a high bridge over the railroads and the river. Now patrons could move easily to their sites. Tales of fabulous profits circulated like land deeds. One told how an assistant ran up to a real estate agent who had just tied his handsome two-horse surrey to the hitching post outside and yelled, "Your team's running away. They're tearing down the street!"

The agent dismissed him with a flick of the hand. "Let 'em go," he said. "I'm making a horse a minute now."

Such stories bring to mind tales of Jedidiah Hotchkiss, "The Father of Booms." This colorful operator was a Yankee who occupied himself during the Civil War years making maps for Stonewall Jackson. During Reconstruction he toured England advertising the advantages of his adopted home, Virginia; in 1876 he compiled an impressive *Geographical and Political Summary of Virginia* for the Board of Immigration in Richmond. After that he published his own magazine, called *The Virginias: A Mining, Industrial, and Scientific Journal.* It told of the Commonwealth's "immense far-stretching beds of iron ore that rib with metallic wealth the sides and flanks of the mountain ranges that border our land of agricultural plenty." It was enough to make a Scotch immigrant farmer part with his last Angus cow.

Major Hotchkiss had plans. He was going to commence mining operations by leasing a hundred thousand acres in the Valley of Virginia. Here iron ore would be extracted for exactly $44.44 a ton (a figure mysteriously arrived at, but wonderfully easy to remember), at the same time paying miners the handsome wage of seventy cents a day. The ore could be shipped by barge down the Shenandoah to the railroads. (Navigational difficulties on the Shenandoah River were not discussed in the Major's literature). The earth was to be opened up, so that wealth might abound.

One of Major Hotchkiss' triumphs was persuading the American Institute of Mining Engineers to hold its annual meeting in Staunton. He wanted his visitors to hear about, but not to examine, his project. To that end he staged one of the Institute's memorable annual meetings. Southern belles supplied the charm, and colored retainers the bourbon. The evenings were anything but dull. The band from the old Stonewall Brigade was reassembled to make music. A gala ball was held in the newly built state Asylum for the the Deaf, Dumb, and Blind, and there were no cynics nearby to comment on the choice of the building. A good time was had by all, and the Boom Plan emerged intact.

If Hotchkiss was impractical, there is no indication that he was dishonest. Like most boomers (including such prominent Virginians as General Lee's son and nephew), he seems to have believed what he claimed. This was not always the case. A mysterious visitor arrived at Lexington one day announcing that he was going to build a tool plant. Much impressed, local businessmen agreed to share part of the expenses. The newcomer made as positive an affirmation of faith as a man can make in the Scotch-Irish valley; he attended the Presbyterian church and went on to join the choir. Bold to the toes, he pushed ever onward, and walked the prettiest soprano home after choir rehearsal. He did not walk after the townsmen had produced their share of the money; he ran. Neither the man nor the money were ever seen in Lexington again.

No one is sure what causes booms, or what stops them. Virginia's subsided as mysteriously and as rapidly as it had arisen. No major mineral deposits were discovered. Despite the claims of resort hotels, the winters continued to be cold and the summers hot. Signposts marking nonexistent boulevards stood in the cornfields, or fed some farmer's wood stove. By mutual consent, people didn't talk much about their investments. A few of the deserted Victorian hotels were converted into girls' schools. The rest decayed on their solitary hilltops. The Shendur streetcar, built to take commuters to the suburbs, was used for a while to haul hunters out to shoot squirrels and quail. Occasionally a man would come out to visit the spot where his dreams died. Jim Aldred, who backed "Glorious Goshen," made such a pilgrimage. He found his lot on Main Street occupied by a bear.

Just after the bust came the Panic of 1893. In a state that was 80 per cent rural, bad farm conditions became worse. Ellen Glasgow tells how it was, in *Barren Ground*. The old aristocrats had become slaves to the land, harnessed to the elemental forces, struggling against the blight of poverty and remorse of defeat. Their sons yearned to leave the dreary farm for the city, to abandon their farms to their tenants. Endless work brought no relief from drudgery, no surplus funds for improvement. Farmers lashed out at the railroads, the government, the monopolies, but refused obstinately to adopt the new ideas about farming. They ridiculed the idea of enriching their soil with alfalfa, the midwestern weed with the highfalutin name.

C. N. Berkeley pointed this out in his 1884 pamphlet called *Why is Virginia Poor?* He saw that his people had become even more tradition-bound than the English whom they had so long admired and imitated: "Fenced in by a bristling array of old traditional sophisms, practices, and unwillingnesses, our planter occupies a position from which it is impossible to force him. . . . If custom in England is a power, in Virginia it is the most awfully absolute, uncompromising tyranny, despotism, which could have taken hold."[5]

Of the various organizations which attempted to help the farmer, the Farmers' Alliance was the most effective. "Organize and cooperate" was its battle cry. Co-operatives were formed, factories established, and tobacco and peanut warehouses opened. Only the fear of the "black Republicans" kept the thousands of Alliance farmers within the state's Democratic party. That they greatly influenced that party, despite its ultraconservative leadership, can be shown by examining the 1901 Democratic platform: "We declare unalterable opposition to the criminal trusts, and every illegal combination of capital. . . . The rights of American freemen must not be sacrificed in the interests of corporations banded together for their destruction."

Jarred but not wrecked, the Democratic organization gave in to certain agrarian demands and kept going into the new century,

Conditions did not improve markedly until the First World War, which had major and immediate effects on the economy. Agricultural prices soared. Tobacco consumption, which had stood at four pounds per capita for the United States in 1900, passed the seven-pound mark in 1917. Norfolk became a major naval base, and exported 11 million tons of material in 1917 alone. In that same year the American Viscose Company opened what was then the world's largest rayon manufacturing plant in Roanoke. These tremendous stimulants to the economy carried over into the 1920's, as the chemical and textile industries expanded. During that decade Governor Harry F. Byrd's "pay-as-you-go" highway plan went into effect, giving the state one of the best road systems in America. This helped link farms to markets and encourage industry to move out into the country, where there was untapped surplus man power.

Then came the devastating Depression, which wrought changes that were psychological as well as economic. The number of state manufactures, which had topped 6,000, fell to less than 2,000 in 1933, when industrial wages were less than half of what they had been in 1919. Studies by sociologists like Howard Odum and Rupert Vance have documented the physical damage and scarcity; but we do not yet know how to tabulate the effect on the minds and spirits of those who lived through the Decade of Fear. In *I Live in Virginia*, Julian Meade tells us what it was like in a large mill town like Danville. The Christmas season was not filled with cries of greeting, but of "Yellow dogs! Scabs!" Brutal strikes divided families and destroyed lives. The song in the air was not "Peace on Earth," but "We're out to win the strike." There was discord everywhere, and signs that read:

WE ARE THE UNDESIRABLES
55 HOURS WORK FOR $13.50 WAGE
COULD YOU LIVE ON THAT?

In the half-century prior to the Great Depression, Virginia lost more than a third of her natural increase in population—the excess of births over deaths. Between 1920 and 1930, the state population rate dropped to an all-time low; only seven states in the Union experienced lower rates of increase. Men as different and dynamic as Woodrow Wilson, Booker T. Washington, Richard Byrd, and William Styron left twentieth-century Virginia to find their fame. Migration has taken the cream off the milk.

The situation did improve after the nadir of 1937, when 40 per cent of Virginia's people were living off an average income of only $183. The much-resisted New Deal brought a new day. Bureaucratic Washington spilled into northern Virginia counties. By the 1950's the Old Dominion had the greatest dependence of any state on the federal payrolls, which put 15 per cent of Virginia's income into the state. World War II saw the Norfolk port area bulge, and military installations spring up throughout the state. This sudden burst of prosperity does not change the over-all picture of Virginia's economy since 1865. It has been marked by a shortage of physical and financial resources; of suitable industry, training facilities, and opportunities. Low standards of living, exploitation of labor, physical and mental imbreeding have prevailed. Geography has made her the gateway to the New South, but circumstances have not made her its workshop. Though Virginia started industrializing before some of the Deep South states, she had not kept up with them.

This was made clear in a study of the state economy which was released in 1957. During the previous year, Virginia had been able to attract only $200 million worth of new industrial plants out of the $37 billion expended for that purpose. On a per capita basis, the figure would have been more than three times as large in the Old Dominion.[6]

Those in favor of more intensive industrial development pointed out that neighboring North Carolina spent twice as much, West Virginia and Kentucky four times as much, as Virginia to encourage such growth. Virginians simply lacked enthusiasm for industrialization.

Perhaps it would be more accurate to say that the Commonwealth wanders between two worlds, one dying, the other powerless to be born. In the former are Georgian mansions, gentle folk, and white-haired darkies. They may be viewed (for a fee) at Mount Vernon, Monticello, or Westover. The colonial charm disappears, however, in the traffic snarls of Washington, Charlottesville, and Richmond.

The world struggling to be born is hygienic, progressive, and automatic, and has footholds in many new industrial areas. It should be noted, however, that in every instance much of the money, brains, and equipment for the plants must be imported from the North. Always a committee from the local Chamber of Commerce, and a long line of potential workmen, greet the newcomers. Money-short natives welcome the machines and the wages; but they still talk about killing hogs, and eat the overcooked, overjuiced food which has plagued the South for years. They *work* in the factories without fully *believing* in them. This is no mere academic distinction. Virginians are either unwilling or unable to bring about these innovations themselves. They stand politely by, watching Yankees plan, finance, and oversee the new factories.

Virginia's factory hand has not yet become an industrial worker in the sense of an urban proletariat. His individualism and social interpretations have remained. Unions have fared badly in Virginia. The workers prefer to stick with their own kith and kin. No matter how they are abused, they never feel lost in the crowd. The people in the crowd are their cousins and neighbors.

This attitude explains Sherwood Anderson's ineffectiveness when he appeared on the scene of the Danville mill strikes in 1935 to talk to the workers. Julian Meade, reporting the incident, noticed that Anderson's hair was longer and bushier than most Virginians, making him seem "different." His midwestern accent confirmed the workers' suspicion.

"He ain't no Virginian," sneered a weaver in the auditorium. "He looks like a furriner to me." Meade said that Anderson had bought the Marion, Virginia, newspaper and was living there. "Anyways, I knowed he won't no born an' raised Virginian," the weaver replied.[7]

Very likely the weaver's son was better educated and more cosmopolitan than his father; the factories and unions may prevail. Yet even the state Chamber of Commerce sees that this would not necessarily be good. That organization has voiced its opposition to new "little Pittsburgh." The state does not offer tax reductions or rebates to new industries, as do some Southern states. The prevailing idea is to spread industry throughout the state in localities where a payroll would give strength and regularity to the economics of the area. "Sweatshops" industries and fly-by-night companies are not wanted.

Factories-in-the-country, in which workers commute by car or bus rather than congregate in mill towns, have sprung up. One of the most successful is the James Lees rug plant, in southeast Rockbridge country. The 2,600 workers come from all parts of the county, and three adjacent ones. Half the workers have been farmers, and many of the others were raised on farms. Part-time farming is encouraged. Attempts to unionize the plant have failed. The relationship of management and labor has been good in years of expansion and prosperity.

There are still Virginians, some of them influential ones, who believe that Virginia could do without any more industry. Members of old families scorn a man who would "sell out" to the Yankees. Some, like Lyon G. Tyler, deplore the coming of the New South: "In the eager desire to attract Northern capital, Southerners have put present interests ahead of historical values. Todayism is an increasing factor. The Old South furnished men for the ages. The New South cares more to rival the North in producing millionaires."[8]

The most articulate defenders of the dying order have been the Southern Agrarians, whose 1930 manifesto, *I'll Take My Stand*, received much attention. Significantly, the group centered around Nashville, not Richmond. Virginia conservatism has been more dogmatic than articulate. A group of men living and teaching outside Virginia formulated this brilliant reaffirmation of Jeffersonian principles, rejected scientific abstractions, and urged Dixie to hold out against an encroaching industrialism. Donald Davidson, John Crowe Ransom, and Allen Tate warned Americans that production had become an end, not a means; that their cities were mantraps; and that progress was an illusion. Two Virginia novelists, James Branch Cabell and Ellen Glasgow, had incorporated some of these ideas in their early fiction. "Why," Ellen Glasgow had asked, "is almost everything connected with progress so ugly?" Cabell had been content to satirize rather than condemn.

Instead of seeking answers to these and other vital questions, a sizable number have retreated into a misty, misunderstood past, taking their stand with the vanishing Virginians. Some have tried to be all things to all men, and ended up with soul-searing ulcers. Others have struck out for the Promised Land, dragging their filing cabinets, sales charts, and Miltowns behind them. A fourth segment has decided to wander about a little longer.

None of the groups has found a formula for blending the fading past with the emerging future, a way to reap the benefits of new methods without giving up old distinctions. Virginia, and the world, face a new era in history; but most Virginians are with the rear guard, looking not at the dawn, but the sunset.

17 *Tradition in Search of Meaning*

EVEN WHEN A MAN TRIES TO ESCAPE, HE IS MARKED BY HIS SOUTHERN
HERITAGE; FOR HE IS THEN, BY THE VERY CONDITIONS OF HIS MIND,
MORE CONSCIOUS OF IT THAN EVER.—*James Southall Wilson*

The problem of the fairy tale is what a balanced man will do in a
fantastic world. The problem of the modern novel is what an un-
balanced man will do in a commonplace world. To these questions
James Branch Cabell, Virginia's leading writer of this century, devoted his long and creative life.

More specifically, he conjured up the complicated and anachronistic kingdom of Poictesme. It is a land of endless loveliness and
drollery, "where almost anything is rather more than likely to
happen save one thing only: it is not permissible for anybody to
cease, for one moment, remaining a human being." His aim is
to climb through the misty upland of self-deception to life's summit,
where dwell the eighteenth-century virtues of "distinction and
clarity, and beauty and symmetry, and tenderness and truth and
urbanity." Cabell, whose philosophy emerges in books like *Beyond
Life* and *Straws and Prayer Books,* is no mere escapist. He holds that
the romanticist begins where the realist leaves off; while the former
represents like a photographer, the latter reveals like an oil painter.
A better way to designate James Branch Cabell would be the
intellectual realist posing as seer.

Despite his efforts to free himself from time and place, Cabell

184

cannot disguise the tendency of the romantic Virginian to pose as a knightly crusader, devoted to the concept of *domnei,* or woman worship. Dorothy B. Schlegel is right: "The chivalric thread of Southern romanticism has enabled Cabell to create his never-never land of Poictesme, that region so much like Virginia and yet so different from it, wherein the artist may move at will and breathe freely without fear of recrimination from his readers."[1]

"He had an air of legendary remoteness, as if he lived in a perpetual escape from actuality," Ellen Glasgow wrote later of Cabell the William and Mary undergraduate in the 1890's. "I admired his aristocratic detachment, the fine thin modeling of his features, and the enigmatic quality of his expression."[2] Born on Richmond's aristocratic East Franklin Street in 1879, James Branch was the first of three children. After private schooling, he attended the state's oldest college, to major in Latin and Greek—the traditional pattern for a cultivated person of the old stock. Afterward Cabell worked on the Richmond *Times* and the New York *Herald,* finding New York "virtually village-like." Back in Richmond, he composed the ballades, rondeaux, and sestinas that were then in fashion. As a potential Virginia author, he inherited the trappings of chivalric romance. He wanted to write popular fiction like that of Henry Harland and Anthony Hope, to deal with "beautiful fine girls and really splendid young men, and everything would come out all right in the end."

Another early interest was genealogy, as *Branchiana, Branch of Abingdon,* and *The Majors and Their Marriages* demonstrate. His earliest novel was *The Eagle's Shadow* (1904). "The typed manuscript went northward in 1904, to be rejected forthwith by the first publishers to whom it was offered." Later on, when it was accepted, his fictional career was launched.

The books of Cabell's youth depict a thinly disguised Virginia. Fairhaven is Williamsburg; Lichfield is Richmond. In them the author, an admirer of Wilde and Shaw, pokes fun at his fellow Southerners—but in a not un-Southern way. Starting out conventionally, Cabell performs surprising pirouettes, "He writes a kind of rather Shavian comedy in which the author pulls out rugs and chairs from under the Southern conventions."[3]

The hero of *The Cords of Vanity* (1909) is the worldly Robert Etheridge Townsend. He passes a summer at a Southern resort taking clinical notes of his outdoor affair with an attractive girl. Later on he writes a novel, using the material, which he reads to a sympathetic uncle, to find out if decorum will allow him to publish it. The uncle has just read the same story in a popular novel by a woman writer using a masculine name.

The Rivet in Grandfather's Neck (1911) has a heroine with a deformed pelvis. A woman in those days was not allowed to have a deformed pelvis, or any pelvis at all, in print. Colonel Musgrave is a old-line Virginia snob, comically conceived. These are pleasant, provincial people. Their lives are "ardent, sumptuous, and fragrant throughout with the fragrance of love and roses, of rhyme and of youth's lovely fallacies."

Not until *The Soul of Melicent* (1913, revised and renamed *Domnei* in 1920) do we see the dimensions of Poictesme. Situated in the south of France, it frequently reminds us nonetheless of Virginia. Poictesme was founded by Manuel in the thirteenth century; by association with Manuel's second daughter, Jurgen becomes a cofounder. Manuel is a man of action, Jurgen of contemplation. Their descendants, down to the twentieth century, incline to action or meditation in proportion as they take after one or the other. Poictesme is populated by an Arthurian circle, complicated by endless genealogical references, and embellished with details from scrambled folklores. By substituting for Virginia a vibrant and colorful unreality, Cabell relieved himself of old settings and clichés. Instead of writing of the world outside his Richmond window, he invented one inside his own mind.

The suppression of *Jurgen* (1919) made Cabell a literary hero overnight. The merry game of finding the "key" to *Jurgen* flourished, as bootlegged copies sold for up to fifty dollars. Amy Lowell, Booth Tarkington, James Huneker, H. L. Mencken, and Hugh Walpole defended the book, and a special documentary volume (*Jurgen and the Law*) appeared after the ban was lifted on October 19, 1922. The tempo of Cabell's life slackened then, and his reputation sank quietly back to the level of the pre-Jurgen period. He was content to work quietly on his series and his genealogy, and to center his life around his library in Richmond.

In explaining how the Cabell cult flourished, Edmund Wilson reminds us that the younger generation of the 1920's was escaping from the genteel censorship that long had reigned. Iconoclasts found in Cabell a cavalier treatment of taboos; they seldom read him carefully enough to see what he really had to say. "I felt I had not earned my celebrity with fairness or through any personal achievement," Cabell confessed in *As I Remember It.* "After eighteen years of unsuccess I had become temporarily famous through accident."

Instead of pandering to popular taste, Cabell wrote books that his editors must have thought perversely unpublishable. He described wicked gallantries and discomforting infidelities in detailed fashion, so that the final impression of Cabell's books is different from that of his contemporaries. He insists that life is built on sham and illusion; that the collapse of one set of illusions only frees man to seek better ones. Perhaps the novelist closest to him in outlook is Theodore Dreiser, but the final impact is different. Dreiser's pageant is like a funeral march on a downward slope; Cabell's is like a climb up Jacob's ladder, from which numerous rungs are missing.[4]

If Cabell's heroes are not masters of their fate, they are at least equal to it. His setting is cosmic rather than national. Like other modern novelists, he has descended into the depths of life; but unlike many of them, he re-emerged soon afterward, wiser and not unduly bitter, creating his own special distilled beauty and truth.

Vernon Louis Parrington was one of Cabell's most sympathetic early readers. Writing in the *Pacific Review* in 1921, Parrington labeled him "a self-reliant intellectual, rich in the spoils of all literatures, one of the great masters of English prose, the supreme comic figure thus far granted us." Well schooled in the classics, Cabell was able to create his own mythology. More remarkable and unique, he also created a metamorphosis. The people who walk through his novels may think like Greeks; but they act and talk like Virginians. He is a mental vagabond upon the surface of the earth; a Wandering Jew who has lived, as it were, through the ages. Master of the elegant and exact phrase, Cabell himself has suggested a better label: the Peripatetic Episcopalian.

There are important similarities between the Lichfield and Poictesme novels; manifestly Virginia provided the immediate raw material of his observation. Cabell is always the enemy of outmoded etiquette and perfunctory religion. Virginia both charms and exasperates him; here people speak of a "first permanent settlement, and of a Mother of Presidents, and of Stars and Bars, and of yet many other bygones, long ago at one with dead Troy and Atlantis." Christianity is the Cinderella legend set forth in more impressive terms. If the Bibical acts are true—"if one great Author did in point of fact shape the tale thus, employing men and women in the place of printed words—it very overwhelmingly proves that our world is swayed by a romancer of incalculable skill and imagination."[5]

His conception of romance is quite different from that of earlier

Virginia writers, but he too suffers from the Sir Walter disease. Though he reacts against the deification of upper-class ladies, his thought is *domnei*-dominated. Though he yearned to return to the Middle Ages, he went no further back than do most Virginians: to the eighteenth century, the age of style, measure, and good taste. This, for his people, was the Golden Age, when men assumed the gallant attitude toward life which enabled them, in Cabell's words, "to accept the pleasures of life leisurely and its inconveniences with a shrug."[6]

"The austere perfection of his art, with its allegorical remoteness and strangely hollow ring," wrote Ellen Glasgow in *A Certain Measure,* "could have sprung only from a past that has softened and receded into the eternal outline of legend. Certainly it is an art that belongs by inheritance to the South."

Like the cosmopolitan eighteenth-century essayist, Cabell has been careful not to claim too much for his books. "But for all that," he was quoted as saying in 1949, when his fiftieth book appeared, "my fifty books are merely the results of an attempt to outrun the monotony of existence." The statement fits in perfectly with the image he has created. It is amplified in *Quiet, Please,* which tells how it feels to fall out of literary fashion; and in *Let Me Lie,* which deals puckishly with Old Dominion history. Virginians, he notes, shape their history with discretion, and refuse to endorse anything unless it is edifying and pleasing. "That our forefathers were in reality a rather commonplace set—and far more that they were a gang of thieving opportunists—would be a creed from which none could derive any profit," he points out. "No history is a matter of record; it is a matter of faith."[7]

His essay on General Lee best shows what sort of Virginian Cabell is. He assures the General that he was "born of your people and of your caste and of your adherents." Lee's unbending, invincible, and somewhat stolid integrity thrills Cabell. "My blood warms to you, betrayingly," he writes, "and reason, defeated by atavism, quits the field." Lee's saying that his one purpose was to accomplish something for the benefit of mankind and honor of God is "a phrase which Valiant-for-Truth would have uttered, if only John Bunyan had been so happily inspired as to think of it." Should Lee's career reveal any mistakes or shortcomings, Cabell promises to stand with that considerable band of Virginians who would revere them also.

Chafing at the social and intellectual vacuum which Richmond seems to have become for him, Cabell filled his autobiographical *As*

I Remember It (1955) with irony that bordered on cynicism. "The dreadful thing is everything's finished," he wrote. "There's not time to start another trilogy. It looks as if the whole thing is finished. It would probably be a mistake to try to add anything to it." He was right. Suffering from various maladies, he "disintegrated with a variety that I find interesting," dying quietly in his Richmond home on May 5, 1958, of a cerebral hemorrhage.

Summarizing his long literary career, Edmund Wilson pointed out how deeply his whole philosophy was involved in the history of his state and region. "His bitterness is the bitterness of the South at having had its dream proved a fiction, and then somehow having had still to live on it," Wilson wrote. "His career commands special respect by reason of the courage and consistency with which he pursued his work."[8]

A close neighbor of Cabell, Miss Ellen Glasgow, wrote the Tragedy of Everywoman as it was enacted in the Commonwealth of Virginia. Even more than Cabell, she was a prisoner of her inheritance.

Born in a gray stone ivy-covered manor in 1874, Ellen Glasgow was given every advantage that upper-class Richmond society afforded. The primer from which she learned her alphabet was a volume of Sir Walter Scott. At sixteen she made her formal debut at the St. Cecilia Ball in Charleston; next she was formally presented to Richmond. Summers meant trips to fashionable White Springs. At eighteen she went to the opera with a Southern lady who "chaperoned her severely." Virginia was a hall hung with rare and wonderful tapestries, a cathedral illumined by blue and wine-colored stained-glass windows. She could be thankful for where and what she was— a Virginia lady.

Yet young Ellen Glasgow decided what she must oppose throughout her career: the false, the affected, the sentimental, and the pretentious in Southern life and fiction. All around her truth and illusion were intricately mixed. She would devote her life to separating the two, and infusing into sweet and insipid Virginia literature a measure of blood and irony.

Whatever one thinks of that effort, he must admire her confidence. In 1897, when she was twenty-four, she wrote Walter Hines Page: "I am working on my book and I have absolute confidence in its dramatic development. . . . I shall not divide my power or risk any future reputation. I will become a great novelist or none at all."

She decided to attempt a multivolume social history of Virginia, written in the more freely interpretative form of fiction. The series is divided into three parts: six novels of the Commonwealth, three novels of the country, and four novels of the city. While American fiction entertained itself with historical pageantry, she set about writing a history of manners that would embrace all aspects of the life around her. She began the work in 1899, and finished shortly before her death in 1945. "In looking back over the years, Miss Glasgow wrote in 1938, "I have often wondered whether any other obstinate author could ever have received so little understanding encouragement. Of encouragement that was misunderstanding, I had, I think, a little more than my share."[9]

The Battleground, first novel of the series, attempted to portray the last stand in Virginia of the aristocratic tradition. It covered the period from 1850 to 1865, and in method and theme laid out the pattern the later books would follow. Not the fortunes of war, nor the moral order of the universe, but economic necessity doomed the South to defeat. In the industrial age that inevitably followed, the aristocratic tradition survived only as an outmoded memorial. Forsaken by time, it was condemned to stand alone and unnourished.

Before writing, Miss Glagow visited every scene of her narrative, and studied the background meticulously. She did not want to write about a town until she "knew every buttercup in spring on the courthouse green." In her room were extensive newspaper files for the years she was covering, and she always strove to draw houses, landscapes, and communities directly from life. We have no trouble identifying her Queensborough as Richmond, Kingsborough as Williamsburg, and Dinwiddie as Petersburg. She transmits what she saw, felt, heard, and smelled. As Elizabeth Monroe points out: "Miss Glasgow's whole art has been oriented by the culture to which she was born—she has criticized it but has made her art out of its systems of tradition."[10]

The Voice of the People, which covers the Reconstruction epoch, is set in Williamsburg, *Virginia* in Petersburg, and *The Deliverance* in south-side Virginia. *Barren Ground* depicts the Piedmont, *Vein of Iron* the southern portion of the Shenandoah Valley. Seven novels take place in and around Richmond—*The Romance of a Plain Man, Life and Gabriella, The Builders, One Man in His Time, The Romantic Comedians, The Sheltered Life,* and *In This Our Life.* The background of *They Stooped to Folly* is a composite of several Virginia cities, including Norfolk and Danville. *The Miller of Old Church* deals with the back country.

Miss Glasgow knew Virginia intimately. Though reared in Richmond, she spent long periods either in her father's place in Louisa County or at the Glasgow homestead in Rockbridge County. Trips through Tidewater and the Valley were frequent. She cultivated a feeling for the land which became a part of her as a person and artist. "If I were to walk out into the country and pick a scene for a book," she wrote in the preface to *The Sheltered Life,* "it would remain as flat and lifeless as cardboard. But the places I loved or hated between the ages of three and thirteen compose an inexhaustible landscape of memory."

Across this vivid landscape pass people, as thick and fast as dead leaves, whirling and dancing, disappearing from view. Many linger on in memory: half-pathetic aristocrats, like Judge Honeywell, General Archbald, and Mrs. Lightfoot; old Cyrus Treadwell and his Negro mistress; Virginia Pendleton, the product of a tradition and education founded upon the theory that the less a girl knew about life, the better prepared she was to contend with it; Grandmother Fincastle, recreating her life in hopeless reverie. There are powerfully drawn Negroes, unlike the Southern stereotypes, human, tender, trapped: Big Abel in *The Battleground,* Aunt Mehitable Green in *Barren Ground,* Memoria in *The Sheltered Life,* Parry Clay in *In This Our Life.* Master of the art of parenthetic malice, her prose reminds us of Jane Austen or (because of her ironic view of man and nature) Thomas Hardy.

Not only Virginia's people but also the social order come under constant scrutiny. The major theme is the rise of the middle class as the dominant force in the state. The *Romance of a Plain Man* deals with the poor whites from the rural districts. *The Voice of the People* follows the class struggle in politics. Outward and inward processes are examined. Her motive in these social studies is to analyze "the enduring fibre of human nature under the law of continuity and the sudden impetus of dramatic occurrences." She wants to show the South as it really is. But this, in her opinion, does not mean filling her books "with multitudes of half-wits, and whole idiots, and nymphomaniacs, and paranoiacs, and rakehells in general, that populate the modern literary South."

Obsessed though she was with the local scene, Ellen Glasgow was no mere "local color" writer. In that her acknowledged masters of fiction were Balzac, Flaubert, de Maupassant, and Thackeray, she was closer to them than to Americans whose subject matter and range was, on the surface, wider than hers. "I am not writing of

Southern nature, but of human nature," she wrote to Allen Tate in 1932. "As you perceive, I was not concerned with the code of Virginia, but with the conventions of the world we call civilized." She evokes the local atmosphere and spirit to serve her purposes as an artist striving for universal meanings. For this reason her work is of far more than regional interest.

Still, the travails of her characters are Virginia's struggles; the philosophy inherent in her books belongs more to her state than her nation. The two recurrent themes are the effort to survive in and renew an exhausted land, and the struggle to preserve the integrity and individuality of rural life in an urban surrounding. The land she writes about is worn out and eroded; the families on it have struggled for generations to overcome poverty and isolation, and to create a good life.

A stoic philosophy emerges from her studies; the spirit of fortitude triumphs over the sense of futility. Her world is one in which dreams seldom come true, and in which good intentions are not enough to bring happiness. Yet it is not a dark world which evil dominates. Discussing her views on life, Ellen Glasgow wrote: "I believe that there are many evils, but that the only sin is inhumanity; and I believe, too, that benign laughter is the best tonic for life. If life is sad, it is also a laughing matter, and it has its moments of rapture."[11]

Failure is the consistent lot of many of her characters, especially her women, whose lives are founded on lies and illusions. One after another, her heroines come to say, "There ought to be something more real and permanent than physical love to live by." The half-legendary gentlewomen of the Victorian era inevitably encounter stark tragedy. The trade-mark of their tragedy is waiting—waiting for the first words of love, waiting for the return of their lovers, the birth of their children, the last word of the dying.

Ellen Glasgow had to wait for literary recognition and fame. Her career, which stretched from the closing years of the nineteenth century to World War II, divides itself into four phases. Her early novels, culminating with *The Deliverance* in 1904, were generally well received. Critical acclaim came from the North and South. In the next decade, there was a decided decline in her reputation. She was trying, rather unsuccessfully, to explore new philosophical backgrounds and writing techniques. In addition, her personal life was marked by such tragedies as her brother's suicide and her favorite sister's death. When her stories were set not in Virginia but New York, they did not succeed.[12]

Nor were efforts to deal with contemporary affairs, as she did during World War I, entirely successful. Her romantic interest in a Richmond lawyer also affected her writing unfavorably. Not until *Barren Ground* (1925) did she seem to find herself. Her ensuing novels represent full maturity: *The Romantic Comedians* (1926), *They Stooped to Folly* (1929), *The Sheltered Life* (1932), *Vein of Iron* (1935), and *In This Our Life* (1941). In 1942, she won a Pulitzer prize. Death came in 1945, when she was seventy-two years old.

By then, she ranked beside Willa Cather and Edith Wharton as a leading feminine author of her day, and the best chronicler of the Virginia mind. Since her death, however, her reputation has sharply declined. Only four articles on Ellen Glasgow appeared between 1945 and 1953, one of those not exclusively about her. Enthusiastic critics such as James Branch Cabell, Henry Seidel Canby, and Alfred Kazin lost their zeal for her work. In 1954, only two of her novels remained in print.

In that same year her literary executors decided to release her autobiography, *The Woman Within*. It served as a disillusioning coda to her life's work. She stressed "the slow vengeance life reserves for those who refuse to surrender their innermost sanctuaries." Ellen Glasgow claimed she had lived "a lonely and agonizing life among the mountains of grief and despair." She did not share the invulnerability and fortitude of her own fictional heroines. A morbid sensitiveness stalked her, in a panic terror, for the greater part of her life. Instead of being unconquerable, her proud isolation eventually became intolerable. Wounded and caged, she was called upon "to endure the unendurable." Self-pity set in. Her nerves became harp strings, "played upon day and night by stumbling fingers." Committed to realism, she was anything but realistic. Posing as a modernist and rebel, she was repelled by literary and social innovation, a victim of self-deception.

Equally disconcerting was her tendency to strike out bitterly at her friends. For no apparent reason, she revived an unproven story about a homosexual charge against James Branch Cabell while he was a student at William and Mary. Today many Richmonders simply refuse to talk about her life or her work.

Not by her fear-haunted autobiography, but by her stronghearted novels, will she be judged and remembered. Very likely her reputation will rise to a higher niche; for her social histories catch the flavor and feeling of Virginia better than most formal histories. Ellen Glasgow grew up in a society haunted by aristocratic illusions. The rising lower and middle classes attracted her interest, and their lives her sympathy. She personally belonged to the old regime, and she frequently gave away her own predilections about the New Order: "Like other Southern cities, large and small, Dinwiddie has sold its charm to industrialism, and has grown modern and commonplace. Industry, as usual, has proved to be a poor creditor."[13]

In her books, but not in her life, she insisted that fortitude and integrity would outlast asphalt and gadgets. There was a vein of iron in her fictional characters, but not in her.

What, then, sustained her? Donald Davidson asked the question when he reviewed a 1957 compilation of Ellen Glasgow's letters. "Perhaps it was, after all, the Scottish Presbyterian heritage against which she early revolted," he concluded, "and the Southern or Virginia tradition that she officially denounced as 'evasive idealism.'"[14]

At first glance the work of Mr. Cabell and Miss Glasgow seems worlds apart. Not so. They fought the same battles, often with the same weapons. Both used irony, as General Grant used artillery, to attack self-contained Richmond; yet both defended it vigorously when others attacked it. Both interpreted Virginia's past with candor and courage, yet liked it well enough to spend their lives among those whom they criticized. Despite their growing animosity in the late part of their lives (Cabell claims, for example, that he actually rewrote much of *In This Our Life*, for which Ellen Glasgow won her Pulitzer prize), they realized their basic similarity. "Ellen Glasgow and I are the contemporaneous products of as near the same environment as was ever accorded to any pair of novelists. From it she has built her Queensborough, and I my Lichfield." Though not on road maps, these are two important Virginia cities—a better word might be monuments—founded on tradition in search of meaning.

The search was continued after World War II by William Styron, the brightest new star on Virginia's literary horizon. Styron was born and grew up in Newport News, where the odor of magnolias was impinged upon by hot rivets, live steam, and crude oil. He has admitted that so far as his inheritance is concerned, "I am somewhat schizoid about it all. Certainly the attitudes that I was brought up in were largely 'Southern,' but never really 'Virginian' in the old Monument Avenue-Westover-Marse Bob Lee scheme of things."[15] In an interview printed in the *Paris Review,* Styron conceded there was a Southern literary tradition—"that old heritage of Biblical rhetoric and storytelling." He insisted that his own widely acclaimed first novel, *Lie Down in Darkness,* could have been set in any part of the country; that his heroine would have ended up jumping out of the window no matter where she came from.

John Aldridge, who wrote discerningly of the book, was not so sure. There are strong Southern elements in the book—fundamentalism, racial guilt, contrast of classes—and the Loftis family is very Virginian. Not until Peyton Loftis marries and goes North does she become overtly psychotic and finally kill herself. Only that portion of the novel dealing with the North is presented in the form of interior monologue.[16] Perhaps, like Cabell, William Styron shows in fact what he denies in theory.

About his moving to Connecticut to live, Mr. Styron has said: "I have not so much revolted against my inheritance as simply slid gently out of a way of life that, lacking the real and ancient traditions, could scarcely be called an inheritance at all. For instance, I feel little desire or need to write about Virginia *per se* any more. Yet oddly enough—or perhaps not so oddly—I still feel fairly strongly attached to the South. The hero of the book I'm working on is an expatriate in Europe from the low-country of North Carolina."

Virginia's inability to produce a flourishing literature at the time when the South is enjoying a notable literary renascence is definitely one of the signs of the times. In literature, as in politics, education, and art, the state traditions seem too binding, and the efforts to transform the past into a usable literature too meager. The old glories are dead; the old symbols and superstitions no longer communicate. Until a transformation is effected, the history of writing in Virginia will be the tale of isolated individuals fighting heroic but futile battles.

18 *F.F.V.'s*

WELL, WHERE DO YOU START,
WHEN YOU START COUNTING F.F.V.'S?
*Stephen Vincent Benét**

"People in all nations are naturally divided into two sorts, the gentlemen and the simplemen," John Adams observed. "The gentlemen are generally those who are rich, and descended from families in public life." Southerners who seldom seconded a Massachusetts Adams enthusiastically agreed. "I am an aristocrat," said John Randolph of Roanoke. "I love liberty. I hate equality." "We of the South," Robert Toombs contended, "are a race of gentlemen."

Virginians have, at various times, claimed this and more. The First Families of Virginia (F.F.V.'s) are, said William Caruthers, "that generous, fox-hunting, wine-drinking, duelling and reckless race of men, which gives so distinct a character to Virginians wherever they may be found." They are to society what the mint is to the julep: they dwell triumphantly on top.

Their history extends back beyond the settlement of Jamestown. Adventurers who came from England brought with them a whole set of social usages. Nothing could have been further from their minds than the establishment of social equality. Class structure was embedded in custom and written into law.

In 1673 James Bullock, a York County tailor, raced his mare against a horse belonging to Mr. Matthew Slader, but never collected his winnings. The county court judged the race illegal, "it being contrary to Law for a Labourer to make a race, being a sport only for Gentlemen." Indeed, the court went further and fined Bullock one hundred pounds of tobacco and cask for his insolence. Suspicious of Virginia's abundant gentlemanly claims, diligent scholars have exhumed the records to show how few patricians actually migrated. What their findings do not show is how much influence these few had, and how many others sought and achieved aristocratic status in the New World. Their titles, dress, education, manners, and church seating reflected it. By William Byrd II's day, the class line even had caste overtones. Of a well-born girl who eloped with a plantation overseer, Byrd wrote: "Had she run away with a gentleman or a pretty Fellow, there might have been some excuse for her, tho' he were of inferior Fortune; but to stoop to a dirty plebian, without any kind of merit, is the lowest Prostitution."

Equally revealing, so far as the subject of gentlemen's conduct is concerned, is the series of letters which John Randolph of Roanoke wrote his foster son, Theodore Bland Dudley, between 1806 and 1822. Intended to instruct the young man in aristocratic behavior, they set forth a well-constructed code.[1] "Let me recommend to you another perusal of Lord Chatham's letters to his nephew," Randolph wrote. "Attend to his precepts respecting *deportment* to inferiors, equals, and superiors. . . . Remember that labour is necessary to excellence."

Daniel Hundley, like Dudley a graduate of the University of Virginia, analyzed aspects of the gentleman's training in his *Social Relations in Our Southern States* (1860). "Scarcely has he gotten fairly rid of his bibs and tuckers," wrote Hundley, "before we find him mounted a horseback; and this not a hobby-horse either (which the poor little wall-flower of the cities is so proud to straddle,) but a genuine live pony. By the time he is five he rides well; and in a little while thereafter has a fowling piece put into his hands, and a little black boy of double his age up *en croupe* behind him. So accoutred, he sallies forth into the fields and pastures in search of adventures."

This social pattern was imported from English country squiredom, and strongly influenced by European romanticism. Life in the Old Dominion and the South was built on a three-legged stool: plantation, slavery, and romanticism. The first and second have gone, but the third remains. Neither poverty nor defeat have destroyed the gentleman's code, although life has been complicated by social changes in the New South. *Noblesse oblige* cannot be displayed or rewarded so easily as in earlier days. Yet some values do not change. Thomas Jefferson's statement about honor is considered as germane today as it was in 1800: "Never suppose that in any possible situation, or under any circumstances, it is best for you to do a dishonorable thing, however slight it may appear to be."

Other statements of Jefferson, such as those on democratic education, did not set so well with the upper echelon. The University of Virginia should, said Jefferson, "reach every description of our citizen from the richest to the poorest." Yet he was hardly in his Monticello grave before the faculty was criticizing practices "which are not considered proper habits for a gentleman; and the University is intended exclusively for that class." The students took for their sobriquet "Cavaliers," and acted accordingly. They were, Alexander Bruce's official university history says, "more inclined to kick up their youthful heels wantonly in the University pasture than to compete for academic or intellectual distinction." Nonetheless, the university flourished. By 1855 the enrollment reached 558, which was only 61 less than Yale's and 110 less than Harvard's. University faculty members were not modest in their claims about the role of gentlemen in history, or Southerners' place in their ranks. "The belt of earth corresponding to the South makes Moses one of the first Southern gentlemen," claimed the late Professor Walter B. Hill. "It takes in Greece, and gives us Homer, Plato, Aristotle, and Dante. The southern gulf stream makes possible the civilization of England; so that Englishmen are only Southerners at long distance!"[2]

The upper-class world was and still is family-centered and perpetuated. Masculinity, class consciousness, conformity of dress, ancestor reverence, and scorn of competition are also stressed. To be properly molded, Virginians are usually sent to such preparatory schools as Woodberry Forest, Virginia Episcopal School, or the Episcopal High School, founded in 1839 on a hill outside Alexandria.

Though the University of Virginia is the gentleman's most obvious selection among the colleges, Washington and Lee, William and Mary, the Virginia Military Institute, and Hampden-Sydney are sound choices. Certain Northern schools, such as Yale and Princeton, are also acceptable. Most Virginia schools and colleges have honor systems. If a student cheats, lies, or steals, his fellow students expel him from their ranks. It is as simple as that. While he was president of Washington College, General Lee was asked by a new student for a copy of the rules. "We have but one rule here," Lee said, "and it is that every student must be a gentleman."

Another president, Henry Louis Smith, gave about the same advice to students entering half a century later. "He wanted us to understand," wrote Thomas Sugrue, "that there was a more important fact than our enrollment as college students. We were gentlemen of Washington and Lee. To that ideal we must surrender ourselves completely; henceforth our honor was to be the apex of our values."[3]

Northerners helped to foster this aristocratic image by dividing Southerners into three classes—aristocrats, poor whites, and Negroes. As the Southern quarrel with the Yankees grew in intensity, white Southerners themselves defined and refined the image in the mirror in thousands of articles, orations, poems, and novels. The dominant myth for the Southern apologists was Southern aristocracy. Actually the Virginia Byrds were offspring of a London goldsmith, and the Carters could find no ancestor at all; such facts got lost in history's shuffle.

Since women were the keepers of the home fires and guardians of the purity of the white race, they were substituted for the Platonic absolutes. They were the good, the true, and the beautiful; or, to be more Euclidean, the center, circumference, and periphery of all affections. The end result, in this land of romantic chivalry, was downright gyneolatry.

Virginia poetry is dedicated to and obsessed with fair maidens. This was as true in colonial times as later on. "The Belles of Williamsburg" is an early example:

> Wilt thou, advent'rous pen, describe
> The gay, delightful silken tribe
> That maddens all our city?
> Ye girls, to you devoted ever
> The object still of our endeavor
> Is somehow to amuse you;
> And if instead of higher praise
> You only laugh at these rude lays
> We'll willingly excuse you.[4]

Not only poems, but orations, essays, and sermons often began and ended with tributes to the lily-white paragons who dwelt on high.

"At the last, I verily believe," says W. J. Cash in *The Mind of the South,* "the ranks of the Confederacy went rolling into battle in the misty conviction that it was wholly for her that they fought."

In upper-class Virginia society it's never leap year. Short or tall, slim or plump, all ladies are expected to play the role of the white goddess, aloof and disdainful, approachable only after a long and gallant campaign. Not all ladies have enjoyed the stylized role. The October 22, 1736, issue of Williamsburg's *Virginia Gazette* contained "The Lady's Complaint":

> They plain can their Thoughts disclose
> Whilst ours must burn within;
> We have got Tongues, and Eyes, in Vain
> And Truth from us is Sin.

Few colonial ladies were bold enough to assert such sentiments. Most of them were like the wife of William Byrd III. When told in a letter from her absent husband to take their sick baby to his mother's house, she replied: "I am very sorry you have limited poor, sweet Otway, so that he has but a short time to stay with me. But Sir, your Orders must be obeyed whatever reluctance I find thereby."[5]

The third William Byrd came naturally by such patriarchal views. His father always expressed his disapproval of strong-minded women. To a henpecked overseer Byrd let it be known "that he was to Correct his own Errors, since the power certainly belonged to him, in Verture of his Conjugal Authority." When the overseer shook his head dubiously, Byrd inferred, with disgust, that "the Grey Mare was the better Horse."

Of all the eighteenth-century belles, none excelled Byrd's own daughter, Evelyn. Her perfection matched that of Westover. She stood off an army of gallants, had her hand kissed by Lord Chesterfield and Lord Oxford, dined with Pope at his Twickenham villa, and was noticed by Beau Nash, the autocrat of Bath. The family still has the carved Chinese ivory fan she carried when she was presented at Court. Perhaps (as the romancers would have us believe) she did fall in love with the dashing Earl of Petersborough and, separated from him by her father's objections, died of a broken heart.

Thanks to Godfrey Kneller's portrait, we have a good notion why she captured so many hearts. There she stands, listlessly, dressed in a silver-blue gown, caressing the exotic flowers on her leghorn hat.

Such beauty as this was far too ethereal to be subjected to the buffetings of a tobacco-filled world.

Her premature death in 1737 started a series of poetic laments that has continued into the twentieth century. One of the many unsuccessful suitors did this acrostic for the December 2, 1737, *Virginia Gazette:*

> E ver constant to her friend
> V igilant in truth's defense
> E ntertaining to her end
> L ife, brimful of eloquence.
> Y outh in person; age in sense
> N ature gave her store immense.
>
> B ut she's fled and is no more
> Y onder soars in fields of light!
> R obbed of all our little store,
> D eath oh death! We're ruined quite.

The legend of her beauty and tragedy lives on. Those who sit around the Yule fire at Westover, some say, can still hear the soft step of Evelyn's high-heeled slippers on the stairs down which she was carried to her grave.[6]

There was a more prosaic side to the world of the plantation lady. Not all the time could be devoted to the fluttering of fans. There was a large and complicated house, kitchen, and staff to be managed, and an endless number of meals to supervise. At Nomini Hall, for example, the annual consumption of food included among many other things 27,000 pounds of pork, 20 beeves, 550 bushels of wheat (excluding the corn eaten by servants and slaves), 4 hogsheads of rum, and 150 gallons of brandy. More than once did Philip Fithian, the Yankee tutor who lived at Nomini Hall with the Carters just before the Revolution, find Mrs. Carter out in the yard after dark, "seeing to the Roosting of her Poultry."

No matter what her responsibilities, the lady always dressed with precise elegance, and so far as possible in the latest London fashion. Young Fithian was much impressed by Mrs. Carter's whalebone: "Her stays are suited to come up to the upper part of her shoulders, almost to her chin; and are swaithed round her as low as they can possible be, allowing Her the liberty to walk at all. To be sure, this is a vastly modest Dress!"

Vastly modest, and often vastly confining, an ever-increasing number of twentieth-century Virginians have decided. Mrs. Lila Meade Valentine headed the fight for women's suffrage. Mary Johnston wrote *Hagar* to assist the feminist efforts. Ellen Glasgow depicted women's plight in a number of her novels. James Branch Cabell had his heroine ask, in *The Rivet in Grandfather's Neck:* "Ah, who will write the tragedy of us women who were 'famous Southern beauties' once? We were queens of men while our youth lasted, and diarists still prattle charmingly concerning us. But nothing was expected of us save to be beautiful and to be made much of, and that is our tragedy."

In *The Fathers,* Allen Tate's novel, we meet a lady whose life is based on a pattern as formal as that of her dishes. In the simplest habit, such as washing the china, she seeks a fixed regularity. Every piece she immerses in the suds of one basin, and rinses in the water of another, after which each piece is dried with a separate napkin. "If this little ritual of utility—not very old to be sure, but to her immemorial—had been questioned, she would have felt that the purity of womanhood was in danger, that religion and morality were jeopardized, and that infidels had wickedly asserted that the State of Virginia (by which she meant her friends and kin) was not the direct legatee of the civilization of Greece and Rome."[7]

Skeptics have cropped up within the gentleman's domain, too. Thomas Jefferson, himself one of the chief glories of the aristocracy, acted in such a way that many Virginians had no choice but to conclude that he was a traitor to his class. The irascible John Randolph observed that "Self-conceit and indifference . . . both flourish in Virginia as if it were their native soil. A petulant arrogance, or supine, listless indifference, marks the character of too many of our young men. Placed in the society of *real* gentlemen, and men of letters, they are awkward and uneasy; in all situations, they are contemptible."

The ranks of the gentlemen have changed as wealthy Yankees have moved into the Old Dominion. A pleasant life, low taxes, and quick transportation to urban centers have brought the Chryslers, Whitmans, Harrimans, Iselins, and many others to northern Virginia. Known to some natives as the Horsy Set, they have reintroduced tournament lances, pink coats, and emblazoned dinner jackets. Over carefully preened fields the insatiable hounds pursue the inedible fox.[8]

The green, gently rolling Virginia countryside, full of foxy crevices, is ideal for such carryings-on. There is plenty of historical precedent, too. For generations the horse has been in the saddle here. The fourth Baron Fairfax, whose father furnished Charles II with his mount when he returned to the British throne, spent many of his happiest days galloping over Virginia's Northern Neck. Having decided in 1740 to make the Old Dominion his permanent home, Fairfax dedicated himself to the life of a country squire. Neighbors claimed that he kept a fox under his bed at night. Whether or not that was true, he was the only resident peer in Virginia during the Revolution, having received by special act of the Assembly all the privileges of a citizen. His body is buried in the chancel of Frederick Parish Church, Winchester; his legend is still riding out to hounds.

Although many colonial gentlemen hunted foxes on horseback with their dogs, there seems to have been no chase of the pink-coat variety before the Revolution. There were, however, jockey clubs in Williamsburg, Dumfries, Fredericksburg, and Portsmouth.

The Williamsburg club was founded by the Reverend Dr. James Blair, "Father of the Virginia Turf." This illustrious cleric, the first president of the College of William and Mary and owner of a private race track, has joined Fairfax as a patron saint of Virginia horsemen. During his lifetime horses like Byerly Turk, Darley Arabian, and Godolphin Arabian were being brought to the British Isles and bred to the royal mares. From them sprang the horses that are the foundation stock of thoroughbreds brought later to Virginia.

Even before the thoroughbreds arrived, the horse cult was thriving. In 1724 the Reverend Hugh Jones, chaplain of the General Assembly, wrote: "The Virginians are such lovers of riding that almost every ordinary person keeps a horse; and I have known some to spend the morning in ranging several miles in the woods to find and catch their horses only to ride two or three miles to church, to the courthouse, or to the horse race."

Six years later James Patton brought the first thoroughbred—Bulle Rock—to Virginia's shores. Other noble steeds, like Yorick, Nonpareil, Selim, and Merry Tom, helped to sire an equine aristocracy.[9] By 1800 there were a hundred thoroughbreds in the Old Dominion. Names like Shark, Diomed, Saltram, and Gabriel were household words for horse fanciers like John Tayloe, Benjamin Harrison, William Byrd III, Samuel Galloway, and Arch Randolph. It was good blood all around.

Virginia horses probably had some infusion of Spanish blood, since there were Spanish horses in the back country. An early English traveler described them as "not very tall but hardy, strong, and fleet."[10] Presumably these horses came from the Spanish district Guale, which composed the southeastern section of the present United States. By 1650 there were seventy-nine missions, eight towns, and two royal ranches there. Raids on the Spanish stock were a favorite sport of Virginians and North Carolinians. With the crossing of Spanish and Anglo-American blood, the quarter horse came into his own.

In 1752 Dr. Thomas Walker of Albemarle County began hunting with especially bred foxhounds, descendants of which still hunt in twentieth-century packs. The oldest surviving hunt in middle Virginia is Piedmont Foxhounds, which dates from 1840. At this time Virginia was the horse-breeding center of America. Not until Reconstruction years did the ark of covenant move west to Kentucky, where it resides today in fields of blue grass.

At the end of the "golden era" of equine F.F.V.'s appeared the horse which became Virginia's Bucephalus. Oddly enough, he was not a thoroughbred. His name was Traveller; as Robert E. Lee's steed he won a special place in state history and legend. Born near the Blue Sulphur Springs in 1857, of Grey Eagle Stock, Traveller was owned by Thomas L. Broun when the Civil War broke out. While serving in western Virginia, General Lee took a fancy to the colt, and eventually purchased him. Throughout the campaigns the charger was under constant fire, but he was never scratched. Johnny Rebs told tales about both the man and the horse around their campfires, and much of Traveller's tail was tweaked out by soldiers and souvenir hunters. Lee rode Traveller to Richmond after the surrender, and to Lexington when he became president of Washington College. "Traveller is my only companion, I may say my only pleasure," Lee wrote at the close of his life. "He and I whenever practicable, wander in the mountains and enjoy sweet confidences." The horse outlived his master, and died on a feather mattress contributed by admirers. His bones are mounted and displayed in the Lee Memorial Chapel at Lexington today, the nearest thing to a relic one will find in Protestant America.

After breeding supremacy passed, interest in hounds and horn continued. The Loudoun Hunt, Orange County Hunt, Warrenton, Casanove, and Middleburg hunts were all established before World War I. An event which contributed greatly to the rehabilitation of fox hunting was the famous 1905 Foxhounds Match, in which the superiority of James Gordon Bennett's American hounds over the

English was demonstrated. The ceremony of "blessing the hounds" was reintroduced by rural Episcopal ministers, and has continued to the present.

Though it did not rank particularly high with the horsy set until the twentieth century, the town of Middleburg has come to think of itself as "the Leicestershire of America." Publications like the *Loudoun-Fauquier Magazine,* the *Chronicle,* and the *Northern Virginian* feature the races, hunts, and auctions that occur throughout the year. Grooming and schooling of jumpers, hunters, and hacks goes on constantly, as do breeding, selling, and exercising. Schools and riding stables sponsor special horse shows. There is truth in the quip of a visitor from Fauquier County who said, "Where I come from, social standing isn't determined by who you are or how rich you are, but how much you smell like a horse."

Ridiculed by many, the squirearchy has nevertheless helped the state. These people have built up the land, raised realty values, attracted tourists, provided jobs, supported libraries, and sponsored charity projects. If they have wined and reveled more than some might think proper, they can at least claim ample precedent from the colonial squires who went before them. If they have disturbed the equanimity of northern Virginia, they have transformed parts of it into a subsidized rural paradise.

Not all twentieth-century gentlemen are able to finance themselves on out-of-state earnings, nor spend fortunes on sleek horses and cows. The three most acceptable callings, if one must work, are law, church, and army. The inner sanctum of the state remains the lawyer's office. George Wythe, Thomas Jefferson, John Marshall, Patrick Henry, and James Madison gave the profession a tone and appeal it has never lost. Though training facilities in most fields of study are limited, there are law schools in Williamsburg, Lexington, Charlottesville, and Richmond. In most Virginia towns, "Lawyers' Row" is the social and political center.

The prestige of the ministry has also held its own in Virginia, despite the inroads of secularism and modernism. Most Virginia churches mix evangelical zeal with patriarchal dignity. Occasionally this zeal has got out of hand, as with the "Dry Messiah," Methodist Bishop James Cannon, Jr. In the main, the ecclesiastics have been faithful to their high calling, and have deserved the respect and status accorded them.

There's something about a soldier that captures Virginia's imagination; Richmond has always been a haven for heroes. In the eighteenth century an English visitor reported: "Almost every person of the better class is at least a colonel, and every tavern-keeper is at least a major." Those who could hold no title by desert got one by courtesy. The Richmond Light Infantry Blues, formed in 1789, claim to be the nation's oldest continuously active military organization. Virginia supplied many fighting men for the frontier and Indian wars. One of her sons, Sam Houston, led the Texans to victory. As the Confederate capital, Richmond accumulated still greater military memories. Monument Avenue commemorates heroic Civil War leaders. Today the state is full of battlegrounds, military cemeteries, monuments, and military schools.

Another indication of militarism is the historical data featured on the state highway markers. Though she has lagged in many areas, Virginia pioneered in erecting handsome metal inscriptions. Of the first 700 erected, 410 dealt with war, soldiers, and battles; over 300 were concerned with the Civil War.

This helps to explain why the Virginia Military Institute holds such a special place in the state's affection. Every cadet is taught, by words emblazoned on the wall, that his task is to be "attached to his native state, proud of her fame, and ready in every time of deepest peril to vindicate her honor or defend her rights." He is reminded that the teen-aged Corps marched into battle against the Union forces at New Market. On the anniversary (May 15), the names on the 1864 roll books are called. When the name of a casualty is called, a cadet steps forward, salutes, and says, "Died on the field of honor."[11]

Just what such rituals mean, or will continue to mean, in the Age of the Common Man, is hard to know. The gentleman has always been, at best, a mixed blessing for the society in which he has flourished. For example, he has not been very kindly disposed toward his New England neighbors to the north, who were more interested in establishing new havens for themselves than in dreaming of those they left behind. Virginians prefer to think of themselves as a continuation of the fine old breed; as a band of exiled Cavaliers, "ever ready to resist the strong, to help the weak, to comfort the afflicted, and to lift up the fallen," as the editor of the *Southern Literary Messenger* put it in 1835. By insisting on this interpretation, Virginians have not had to live in the past—they have made the past live with them.

Even unsympathetic historians have been impressed by the achievement. The consensus is that the cream of American colonial society was "indisputably the Virginian, celebrated not only for elegance in dress, speech, dining, and sport, but also for that graceful lotus-eating in a land where the abundance of nature made hard work seem almost an act of ingratitude."[12] The lotus has given way to the locust, but the myth remains.

Lomax Hunter III was one of those who labored that this might be so. During the 1930's and 1940's he wrote a popular newspaper column called "The Cavalier." A self-styled "farmer who does a daily column before breakfast to whet my appetite," Hunter praised the squirearchy of bygone days. Scorning the city and damning the New Deal, he argued that increasing the poll tax and lengthening the hunting season would improve affairs considerably. He intertwined the mythology of Virginia and Greece, as other Virginians had done before him: "Here hide the hamadryads, and down the dim tree aisles we hear the hooves of Pan. The forest creatures call me at all seasons, but never so insistently as when young Spring comes smiling through the wood."

Such nostalgia smacks more of the Old World than the New, and it is interesting to note how many Europeans have been more at home in Virginia than in most other states. Herman Keyserling reported (in the *Atlantic Monthly* for November, 1929) on "The South—America's Hope." The Virginia aristocrat, he believed, was "truly responsible for Virginia's greatness in the past." The Southern gentlemen and their ladies were the only types of "complete souls that the United States has as yet produced."

Writing a generation later, Frenchman Jean Gottman found Virginia "an oasis of calm and quiet. The Virginia way of life has a real mission: if it came to play a greater part within the American civilization it might mellow it somewhat."[13]

Mellow—a good word for the world of the F.F.V.'s. There are other things one likes about them: their cohesiveness, their dignity, their flair for life, their sense of pageantry. Silver trumpets which are inaudible to lesser breeds urge them constantly on. And who, in this unpredictable twentieth century, would deny that there might just *possibly* be one more crusade?

19 *Poor White*

YOU CAN'T RAISE COTTON ON SANDY LAN'
I'D RATHER BE A NIGGER THAN A PO' WHITE MAN.

Listless Lem Buckra faced up to another day. July 4, 1930. Lem stood on the porch of his mountain shack and looked out over the Alleghenies. Curtains of yellow dust hung over the hollow. The scorched-out grass clung to the parched earth. Flowers were withered; the mountain laurel had dried up. Already the sun bit into the mountain like a hungry fice dog gnawing a bone.

Lem nipped the corner off a plug of tobacco, put it back in his pocket, and scowled. "Well," he said deliberately, "another go'dam scorcher." He did not know July 4 was a national holiday.

He approached this and every morning without pleasure or plan. Something was wrong with his life, but he couldn't do anything about it. So he sat down.

Phebe, his wife, came out on the rickety porch. At thirty she was old and broken. Fifteen years ago she had been a bride, singing ballads like "Pretty Polly" and "Little Mose Groves." She didn't sing any more.

Phebe Buckra was a servant. She served her husband standing up in the day and lying down at night; toted water from Frying Pan Creek; dragged kindling from the woods; tended the brood; put out the corn crop and husked it. Corn was all that kept the Buckras

208

from starvation. Nothing that was soft or feminine remained. Phebe didn't complain. She had expected nothing better.

Behind her was her daughter Sarah, fifteen, stoop-shouldered, pregnant. Her calico dress was taut about her stomach and her eyes were lusterless. Marryin' time had come. She would give herself to a shiftless lustful male until she could bear him no more children and carry no more loads.

"Phebe, go fetch the water," Lem ordered.

"Going down now. Watch out for the young 'uns."

Lem spat tobacco juice over the porch rail and clenched his fist. There was no love, no passion, between them. All that had passed away.

"Keep 'em out of my way, Phebe," Lem said. "Specially the one with the swole-up jowls. I can't stand to be pawed on a go'dam hot day like this one."

The next-least one had the thrash. Her mouth was so sore it was bleeding. Phebe hoped to meet up with the conjur' woman, who carried herb medicine. Or she might have spring water poured by the conjur' woman from her shoe into a bottle. Thrash is right hard to cure in hot weather.

"Take your whore with you," Lem ordered.

"She don't feel like walkin', Lem. You leave her alone."

"If I did, I'd be the first. She's laid with every man this side of Mouth of Wolf."

Lem had been angry when he discovered Sarah was pregnant; angrier still when she didn't know who by. He would try to bluff the Tolliver boy into claimin'. It wouldn't be easy.

The fatalism of the mountains finally overcomes self-improvement and morality. Every fifteen years or so the process is repeated, and the same old verses are sung with new meaning:

> Once your heart was mine, my dear,
> And your arms lay acrost my breast,
> You made me believe by the oaths that you swore
> That the sun rose in the west,
> That the sun rose in the west.
>
> I never will believe what another man says,
> Though his hair be black or brown,
> Unless he's on some high hill top,
> And swears he will come down,
> And swears he will come down.

Phebe started out for the water. She had two pleasures in life. One was sucking on the wad of snuff under gums. The other was the occasional visit of the Preacher. He wasn't a real preacher, but he had the calling. He talked about the other world, the one of ever-lasting joy. He told her about the clothes she would have, and the hog meat, and the streets of gold.

Lem heard the creaky front door open. Will, the fourteen-year-old, came running out. He had snatched the last stick of corn pone off the table, and the other boys were chasing him. Their faces were so lined and sharp they seemed to have been born old. Barefoot, they ran with a strange ungainly gait, yelling as they went. One-gallus Big Bens, too short in the legs and too full in the waist, were their only clothing.

Will escaped into the brush. His two brothers walked back slowly, because there was nothing else for them to do.

Their faces brightened a bit when their hound dog came out of a thicket. Since there was no food for him at the shack, the dog had been hunting for a rabbit. His ribs almost poked through his tight brown skin as he looked for a spot to rest where no one would take the trouble to kick him.

"Will stole all the corn pone, Pa."

"I'll slap him down, boys," Lem promised. He had tolerable good times with his boys, training them to hunt, to gather chinquapins, and to hate the Chessers over by Council. The hate went back a long way, and the feud between the Buckras and Chessers was fierce and fiery. Neither side would give or take any quarter. This was the one subject in all the world about which no Buckra would com-promise.

Back a spell the Chesser boys had caught Lem's uncle unarmed, clubbed and kicked him to the ground, and shot him twenty times in out-of-the-way points so he could spend a long afternoon dying.

Afternoons like that have to be avenged.

Lem could tolerate the boys, but not Grandma. She made him retch. Always telling him to leave home and take a job in the mines, or tend to the bratlin's, or work in the fields like a nigger. Lem hated niggers too. Hadn't seen many, but Grandpap had told him about 'em. The Federals who came to Buchanan County to draw maps in 1925 had brought a nigger cook. Folks had been so riled up that the Federals flew a United States flag over him to be sure there wasn't any trouble. Down at Grundy Lem had seen an old man dress up like a nigger at Christmas and call himself Santa Claus.

Lem couldn't stand niggers. They made him retch.

He couldn't do much about niggers, but he could make it hard for Grandma. She wasn't nothing but a doorjamb around the place anyway. So why should he try to feed her? No matter if she ate or not, she kept on living.

"Gawdamighty, it's too hot to die," Lem muttered, as little driblets of perspiration formed on his forehead and followed the dirty furrows towards his eyes.

How the Buckras had ever been pushed back up the side of Big A Mountain, almost to Buzzards' Roost, Lem wasn't sure. Probably Grandpap's fault. He'd had a better place, over in Booger Hollow. Then he had to get mixed up with the law. There wasn't anything to do but move back onto Big A.

Buchanan County is at the western edge of Virginia, bordering on Kentucky and West Virginia. Named after James Buchanan, this wild and unworkable county embraces thousands of acres, the largest level tract of which is eight acres across. In 1930, there were eight persons in the county who paid federal income tax, and one private telephone.

The population is almost all of Anglo-Saxon descent, practically 100 per cent native born. Three branches of the Big Sandy River drain the county. In the summer of 1930, they were sluggish brown trickles. Dust drifted in yellow clouds. Breathing was difficult. The heat was ferocious and continuous. Most of the springs dried up. The big one at Bear Wallow, which supplied the mission school, was so low that the people were allowed only a pint a day. They could choose whether to drink it or wash their faces. Not many faces were washed.

The lumber camps and coal mines were mostly shut down, so there wasn't much money in Buchanan County that summer. "With the drought killin' the crops, what we gonna do?" the women asked.

The men didn't answer. They didn't know.

They gathered stunted blackberries with their gnarled, cracked hands, and brought them to the Mission School to sell. Their families were hungry, but no one would think of eating berries if he could get a little cash for them. The Mission Lady bought them, not because she wanted the dried, withered pellets, but because the people had to have the money and didn't want to be beholden.

Finally the corn died. And when corn dies in Buchanan County, that's bad.

Each day the heat seemed worse, and the dust clouds thicker.

The jack-leg preacher came and talked about the sixth chapter of Hosea. He said that until the sinners repented there wasn't going to be any improvement. The sinners must not have repented. There wasn't any change.

The summer of 1930 was a fright. When your backbone and your navel shake dice to see which is going to have the last black-eyed pea, you know it's a fright. A piece of fat back would like to scare Lem Buckra's children to death.

Lem looked out toward Will, who was sitting under the shade of an oak tree, throwing the dried-up clods of dirt that cluttered up the yard at his brother. Will had always been his pa's favorite.

"Hey Will, is it nigh to Sat'day?" Lem asked.

"Two more days, Pa," Will said.

Saturday was Lem's day to go to Grundy. It was a long hike, especially in the heat, but he always went. By the time he reached the Courthouse Square about noon the benches would be full. Lem would squat down on his haunches and discuss the weather, crops, and shootings with his buddies.

If he was lucky, Lem might hear a good political speech. One election year he heard "The Man" speak in the Square. This was a high moment for Lem. The speech had guided his thought ever since that day. If there wasn't a talk, Lem would amble over to the dives around East Grundy. Maybe there'd be a good fight or a knifing. Near the corner of Jefferson Street, Si Brown dispensed his mule-kick wild tiger. Lem might start back home late that night, unless the cops started using night sticks. Then he'd probably spend the night in jail.

"Sure is a long time between Sat'days," Lem said.

Lottie Lou hollered something from inside the house. Lem couldn't understand her. "Keep quiet. You sound like a hog in heat," he yelled back. Lottie Lou had difficulty speaking. Her palate had been deformed since birth. She grunted and motioned to communicate. Thoughts wasted away in her mind. She had the "big lazy" and the bloated stomach that always comes with malnutrition. After a while she would walk down to the creek, loll on the bank, and scoop a handful of wet clay out of the water. She would squeeze it, put it in her mouth, and nibble away at the mud-cake. Lottie is twelve. Lem knows that she'll be needing a husband. Because of her mouth, it's doubtful that Lottie Lou will qualify for the rural whoredom of the other girls. Maybe she'll be lucky and die.

The Buckras have very little future, but quite a past. They have lived out an American tragedy.

The first one who set foot on America left his London hovel in 1732, having heard there was gold in the streets and water that bubbled like wine in Virginia. For a while Ephraim was a teamster in Williamsburg; but he didn't mix well with the people there. He had the urge to move west and own land.

Buying a wife out of her bondage as an indentured servant, Ephraim moved out into the Disputed Bounds between Virginia and Carolina. The Buckras, lazy and dirty, were soon living the life of "white Indians" in Lubberland. Only rarely did visitors come to their shack. One day a whole party stopped by and asked for water. The leader said he was Colonel William Byrd; his men were surveying a dividing line. Ephraim didn't understand. The Colonel put some notes in a little book before he left.

Lem Buckra, squatting on Big A Mountain in the summer of 1930, didn't know there was a Revolutionary soldier among his ancestors. Neither did the Daughters of the American Revolution. Probably this was just as well.

Nevertheless there was one. The second son of Ephraim joined the "crow squad" which fought under the Swamp Fox, Francis Marion. The boy didn't like to march, but he was a tolerable good shot. When the Revolution was over, he went further west, into the Piedmont, and built a cabin in Albemarle County. Being the game-follerin' kind, he didn't plant any corn.

His son was in the War of 1812. Jim Buckra, Ephraim's grandson, fought under General Gaines at Fort Erie. Jim couldn't tolerate the officers; so he deserted.

Back home, he wore out three wives and bred fourteen children. One of these boys, Bill, didn't like the cabin stuck on the side of the Blue Ridge; so he ran away and eventually became overseer at Colonel Carter Fitzhugh's plantation. That was the highest pinnacle any Buckra ever reached. Yet Bill Buckra found out it was not an enviable job. He was respected neither by the Negroes nor the plantation whites. Bill made up for social snubs he received from the whites by venting his spleen on "uppity" niggers. Some of them had the nerve to sing smart-aleck songs. But if Bill heard them, they never sang them again:

> Cawn bread en de black molasses
> Is better dan honey en hash,

> For de fahm-han' coon
> En de light quadroon,
> Along wid de po' white trash.

Then the Yankees came. Bill Buckra and his kind had little to gain from defending the "nigger lords." But the hatemongers reminded Bill about the cheating Yankee peddlers who wanted to make niggers and white men equals. The recruiter told him how much fun it would be to hunt for Yankees instead of squirrels. So Bill enlisted, a private in the Stonewall Brigade.

His primitive life had conditioned him well for the long marches, the unstable conditions, and the sharpshooting. For a while everything went well. By '62 Bill was tired of the long marches, convinced that this was "a rich man's war and a poor man's fight." He deserted, just as his father had done, and went back to the Blue Ridge. The next few years he spent avoiding the conscription squad and terrorizing the neighborhood with his bushwhacking raids.

Bill figured the Rebels couldn't win once he drooped out, and he was right. The surrender news didn't bother him. The Buckras lost nothing because they had nothing to lose. The land had been decimated. Northern troops came to town to see that niggers were treated like white men. Down in Charlottesville one day Bill heard a nigger singing out:

> My folks war'n none o' yo' po' white trash,
> No sah, dey was ob high degree—
> This heah darkie am quality!

What could Bill do, with a Yankee soldier across the street fingering the trigger of a rifle? Nothing but pack up the kids and the pots and move on out to white man's country.

During the packing his wife gave out. Bill had to move quick to find a new woman for the family. He picked up one who had been living near the federal army posts. She came into the Buckra family, bearing her illegitimate son in her arms. The Buckras started out for the Alleghenies.

He never made it, being killed in a street brawl in Fincastle. But the Buckras kept moving. J. C., the oldest boy, took over. J. C. was Lem Buckra's grandfather.

When they reached Buchanan County, J. C. tried for some good bottom land, but without success. All he wanted was good hunting, solitude, and independence; but they were becoming harder and harder to find. A relentless cycle of hard scrabbling and deterioration set in. The first settlers had taken the rich bottomlands at the mouths of the rivers. Their sons, looking for more game and land, followed the smaller streams to their heads, built cabins, and populated the wilderness right smart. This process repeated itself until people like J. C. had to go to the very heads of the hollows, and up the sides of mountains, where only backbreaking toil would produce any food. All the game was gone. Razorback hogs provided the only chance for meat. If they went any further, they would cross the ridge and meet other families coming up the other side.

Thus it was that the mountains closed in on the Buckras; the world of rocks and trees and hookworm shut out everything else.

J. C. wasn't much of a farmer. He raised more cain than corn. His hatred of the Yankees burst out to a point surpassing his father's when he discovered they were teaching niggers to read and write. J. C. was illiterate himself. So were his children. He couldn't stand the thought of the black nigs having more education than his own children.

He was glad to pitch in when the white men demanded violence. Atrocities, lynchings, and the burning of the Bureau Schoolhouse whetted his sadistic appetite. Lem still remembered the bloody stories his Grandpap loved to tell in the evenings.

Lem didn't know much about his father. He had been a hard-drinking and fighting man. One night he filled up on wild tiger and went roaring into Grundy. There was a fight. The law moved in. All Lem remembered about his father's funeral was that a lot of men came with guns, and nobody cried.

Phebe was dragging back now with the water. Lem motioned her over and grabbed the bucket so he could take a drink. It was so brown you couldn't see the bottom.

"This here is hog water," he said. "How you expect a white man to drink it?"

"Can't help it, Lem. S'all there is."

Lem swallowed a mouthful of the brackish water, handed the bucket back to Phebe, spat, and said, "Git on back in the house." He looked out over the seared mountain empire of southwestern Virginia. The sweat was running down his cheeks and into his ears.

"Yep," Lem said stoically, "another go'dam day."

The Buckras of Virginia, and the rest of the South, have been known by many different names—poor white, cracker, redneck, dirt eater, woolhat, sand-hiller, tacky. Whatever the name, the circumstances are about as Byrd recorded them in his 1728 account of

Lubberland. These are lazy, shiftless wretches, bedeviled by poverty, miseries, and the "country distemper."

They are the poor, the disinherited. Their poverty is partly material, partly psychological. They lack not only all but the barest necessities of life, but also any urge to better themselves. They have stopped trying.

The mind of the poor white is feral, fatalistic, bordering on bitterness—unable to improve, and unwilling to relent.

Since Byrd's day, many Virginia writers have devoted thought and effort to describing the poor whites in the Old Dominion.[1] In the Valley of the Shenandoah, George Tucker wrote of the cruel and lawless actions of poor whites around "Battletown," and of a tenant plodding off to Kentucky, with eight children under fourteen. William Caruthers dealt with the group in *The Kentuckian in New York,* writing of the rural poverty:

> Some half-dozen pale and swollen-face children are sitting on a bench against the side of the hut, endeavoring to warm away the ague in the sunbeams. The wife lies sick in bed. . . . The husband has in his pocket a summons for debt, contracted for sugar and tea, and other needful comforts for his sick wife and children.
>
> Had he any cause for hope? God knows he had none in the world.[2]

That the poor white was a limited asset to the Confederacy is emphasized in Thomas Nelson Page's *The Two Little Confederates.* Page describes Holetown, a poor-white settlement in the piny woods. Thinking war might be more like play than work, a number of the men join up; but Tim Mills tells his Colonel how he feels about staying: "I'm gwine back . . . an' I'm gwine to fight, ef Yankees gits in my way; but ef I gets tired, I's coming home; and 'taint no use to tell you I ain't, 'cause I *is*." And he did.

Ellen Glasgow, bent on bringing realism south of the Potomac, dealt extensively with the poor white. She published *Voice of the People* in a year (1900) when not a single Southern college or university had a department of sociology, and when most Southern writers didn't deal with "lost people." Miss Glasgow imagined one of her poor whites, Nick Burr, as being capable of bucking the aristocratic pattern of control. More often, she saw for them only futility.

Poor whites hover in the background of Virginia life and fiction like sinister shadows, which will not go away. They are made the butt of crude and sardonic humor, reflecting the authors' inability to shut the door on a room which everyone wishes were not in the house. The blood of these people, as well as the Negroes, is on the white aristocratic hands.

Virginia has done very little for the poor whites. True enough, she has not allowed them to be exploited politically to such extent as they have been in Alabama, Mississippi, and Georgia. The state's failure lies not so much in things done as things undone. So far as public welfare figures are concerned, the state of Virginia ranks near the bottom in every category. Not until a system for gathering nationwide statistics was set up under the Federal Emergency Relief Administration in 1933 were full figures available. By 1940, Virginia was still spending less than $2 million for its total public assistance, averaging only $1.29 per capita. In Buchanan County, the per capita figure was an incredibly low 56 cents. A decade later, in the midst of post-World War II prosperity, 22.5 per cent of Virginia's farmers were making less than $500 annually, and more than half the state's rural farm families reported incomes less than $1,500. In 1956, Virginia, with a miserly $1.75 expended per inhabitant for any kind of assistance payment, was not only last among the forty-eight states —she even lagged behind Hawaii and Puerto Rico.[3]

The vast rural underworld of poor whites is much ridiculed but little understood. Fanny Kemble called them "the most degraded race of human beings claiming an Anglo-Saxon origin that can be found on the face of the earth—filthy, brutal, proud, penniless savages." In our own day, Dr. Arnold Toynbee has said the Appalachian mountain people are "no better than barbarians. They have relapsed into illiteracy and witchcraft. They are the American counterparts of the latter-day white barbarians of the Old World— Rifis, Albanians, Durds, Pathans, and Hairy Ainus."[4]

One wishes the learned doctor condemned less and forgave more. Though the Buckras are every bit as retarded as he says, they are more sinned against than sinning. They have been told to make bricks without straw; have tried, failed, and given up. Like the Negroes against whom they have often competed, the poor whites have needed support and understanding. But where is the N.A.A.W.P. which will do for them what the N.A.A.C.P. has undertaken for the depressed Negroes?

The poor white stands alone. He has little feeling of class unity. Denied adequate income, education, and respect, he has been victimized by the hate-mongers, the negrophobes, and the city cartoonists. He seeks outlets for his fears and hungers as best he can. Told to farm on land that will not produce crops, he naturally fails. Told to seek out jobs where no jobs are to be had, he goes idle. Driven finally to the factories of Detroit and Pittsburgh, he is almost as isolated as on the side of Big A Mountain.

That this level of society has produced such men as Davy Crockett, Abraham Lincoln, Andrew Johnson, and Sergeant York is seldom acknowledged. The portrayals of Erskine Caldwell or William Faulkner are those we choose to emphasize. Yet Jeeter Lester, the chief character in Caldwell's *Tobacco Road,* had an innate and almost religious feeling for the land. The first to catch the smell of plowed fields in the spring time, he would not sink to being a "durn woodchopper." Faulkner's poor whites, no less than his Negroes, endure.

What will become of the Lem Buckras, the marginal men with inadequate income, food, clothing, shelter, and social contacts? Some will be absorbed in the nation's expanding industrialization. These are the ones who

> Want to live in Bristol, where all the lawin' goes;
> To look about them settlements, and wear them foreign clothes!

Others will be helped by improved agricultural techniques, or expanding social and religious agencies. Yet it would be mere wishful thinking to say that the problem of the poor whites will soon be solved. As late as World War II, sociologists estimated that there were over 100,000 white rural Virginia families, and 65,000 Negro families, living on the marginal plane. A quarter of a million Virginia families and unrelated individuals reported total money incomes of less than $1,000 in prosperous 1949. The Buckras remain very much in evidence throughout Virginia.[5]

Chambers of commerce point proudly to the state's new industries, and the miraculous rise in income. But neither factories, paved roads, nor higher wages can alter the fabric of society overnight. It took generations for the Buckras to come to act and think as they do; it will take them a long time to learn to act and think differently.

One of the paradoxes of history is that the people who might benefit most from change are those who oppose it most resolutely.

Nor should we assume that change is always necessarily beneficial. There are, in Lem Buckra's life, certain factors and feelings which should not be discarded. Some of the endurance of the hills rubs off on the mountain people. Not so far removed from the Buckras, in space and time, was the editor of the Big Laurel, Virginia, paper which he called the *Cumberland Review*. "I came into the world, and the world was hills," he wrote in a 1932 editorial. "I was nourished on the fruit of the hills. The hills have measured my life; the hills have made me what I am. I have learned the language of the hills, and I must write. So I will write of the hills."

For over three centuries, and in every part of the land, Virginia's poor whites, like the poor in the Bible, have been with us. Many American stories tell us what it means to win in our society; the tales of the poor whites tell us what it means to lose.

One of the men who understood this was a sensitive and little-heralded twentieth-century poet, John Peale Bishop (1892-1944). Descended on his mother's side from Tidewater stock which settled in Virginia in the seventeenth century, he was born in Charles Town, West Virginia. In his essay on "The South and Tradition," he observes that not only the various white groups but also the Negroes have "an ancient and complicated culture of their own." This is what makes Bishop's lines about "Southern Pines" so poignant, and so true:

> Cut pine, burnt pine,
> The fourth man's eyes burned in starvation,
> Bone-back cattle, razor-back hogs
> Achieve the seedling, end the pinewoods.

20 *Marse Chan vs. the N.A.A.C.P.*

'OUGHTS AN 'OUGHT AND FIGGER'S A FIGGER;
ALL FOR DE WHITE MAN AND NONE FOR DE NIGGER.

A proud young Negro lad who served in the Governor's Mansion returned home late one night after a splendid dinner party. "What do those quality whites talk about at big affairs?" his mother asked him.

"Oh, mainly about us colored folks!" the youngster replied.

So they do. Eventually any conversation, on any social level, moves around to Negroes. Some approach the racial issue via the myth of Marse Chan, others via the reality of the National Association for the Advancement of Colored People. Sooner or later, everyone arrives.

Though legally segregated, Negroes are well integrated into Virginia history. Since 1619 they have been working and laughing and breeding, mixing their blood and aspirations with their white master's, lifting heavy loads, accepting inequality, tempering anguish with patience. Sometimes they have protested. Then violence and tragedy have followed. Yet if you enter a Virginia town and listen for the laughter, it will usually come from the colored quarters. The Negro inevitably stands as a judgment on the men and civilization which enslaved him.

Because their labor made the tobacco economy flourish, Africans played a critical role in colonial history. Slavery, developing as an extension of indentured service, existed in practice before it was recognized by law. The slave trade was greatly increased with the establishment of the London Company of Royal Adventurers in 1662. Patrons included the Queen Dowager and the Duke of York. Eventually white indentured servants could not compete successfully with cheap slave labor.

By 1720, New England shipyards were building vessels especially designed for the slave trade. In the holds were racks, two feet by six, fitted with leg irons and bars. A typical slaver from Bristol, Rhode Island, had "ten feet in the hold, with three feet ten inches betwixed decks." Into these spaces captives were packed like fish. When the hatches were battened down, they suffocated in droves. A captain's diary describes his deck as "so covered with blood and mucous that it resembled a slaughter-house." Of 60,783 Negroes shipped by one company between 1680 and 1688, about 15,000, or a fourth, died en route.

The lucky survivors were brought to such trading centers as Hampton, Jamestown, or Yorktown. After a training period in which they were taught to obey white authority and to speak basic "pidgin English," they were sold and put to work on the plantations. By 1700 there were about 6,000 Negroes in Virginia, with others coming in at the rate of 2,000 a year.

Virginia's Slave Code defined slaves as imported non-Christians. Both fugitive slaves and servants were apprehended, imprisoned, and advertised for like any lost or stolen property. Testimony of Negroes was admissible only in the case of capital offense charged to a slave; the judge warned the colored witness beforehand that if he falsified he would be pilloried, lashed, and have his ears cut off. Negro criminals were tried by special courts without a jury. In short, they were chattel.

Historical, social, economic, and religious arguments were advanced to justify all this: the descendants of Ham had been fated to do menial work. Jews, Greeks, and Romans had practiced slavery; the Ten Commandments mentioned "servants" three times. Saint Paul had urged the fugitive Onesimus to return to his master. Unable to create a civilization of their own, the Negroes were fortunate to leave their heathen homeland. Their innate inferiority was as easy to demonstrate as the law of gravity. "It is the order of nature and of God," said Professor Thomas R. Dew, of the College of William and Mary, "that the being of superior power should control and dispose of those who are inferior." Virginia lawyer George Fitzhugh presented similar arguments in books like *Sociology for the South* and *Cannibals All!* "The free states of antiquity abounded with slaves," he wrote. "The feudal system changed the form of slavery, but brought with it neither liberty nor equality." Instead of being a necessary evil, slavery came to be regarded as a positive good and a prerequisite to aristocracy.

Many Virginians disagreed; but it was easier to condemn than to abolish a labor system on which the state's economy was based. Negroes, meanwhile, craved freedom and proved they were willing to die to obtain it. There were seventy-two revolts or threatened slave insurrections in Virginia. The 1800 plot by a Richmond slave, Gabriel, was extremely well planned. State mythology claims there was little crime or unrest among slaves. Facts disprove this. There are 1,418 vouchers on slave convictions in the Virginia State Library, and many others were never received by this collection. Of those on file, 1,117 specify the offenses—346 for murder, 194 victims being white. All but two of the 111 convictions for attempted murder involved white people.[1]

Not every slave was miserable. Those at Monticello, for example, slept in comfortable brick quarters which had wooden floors, tight-shutting doors, and glass windows. No overseer was employed, and no one had the authority to interfere with Mr. Jefferson's workers. Corn shuckings, coon hunts, barbecues, and seasonal holidays were common on many plantations. When slaves managed to visit or live in cities, they sometimes outdressed the whites, as this description of Sunday promenaders in the Richmond of 1833 indicates: "The colored females wear white muslin and light silk gowns, with bonnets, ribbons, and feathers; many are seen with parasols, while nearly all of them carry a white pocket-handkerchief before them in the most fashionable style. Their young men wear white trousers, black socks, broad-brimmed hats, and carry walking sticks."[2]

No matter how Negroes dressed, they were and still are treated as a distinct caste—and this surely is the most important reality of Virginia society. Whether or not a caste system is justified is a moot question; that it exists is undeniable.

"The slaves are never married," a shocked Philip Fithian noted when he came to Virginia in 1774. "Their lords think them improper subjects for so valuable an Institution." All that was required was for the couple to parade down the line of cheering spectators, join hands, and "jump the broomstick" as the onlookers chanted:

Dat you' wife
Dat you' husban'
I'm you' marse
She you' missus
You married!

With such a system, illegitimacy and miscegenation flourished. James Madison's sister complained that the planter's wife was but the mistress of a seraglio. The 1860 census figures gave a color of truth to her complaint. At that time 518,000 persons (one-seventeenth of the Negro population) were of mixed blood.

The only objection to the caste system came from the Church, and that challenge was only partial. There was no point in urging Negroes to read their Bible; for after the Nat Turner Rebellion, it was illegal to send slaves to school. Enough that they should memorize such verses as "Servant, obey thy masters," "Render unto Caesar the things that are Caesar's," and "Well done, thou good and faithful servant." Somehow they learned other verses, too. "Dey can law us out of church, but they can't law away Christ."

Promising slaves were occasionally encouraged to develop their special talents. A 1760 advertisement in Williamsburg's *Virginia Gazette* offered for sale "a young healthy Negro fellow who has been used to wait on a gentleman and plays extremely well on the French horn." A later notice described a runaway servant who "Plays the violin and took his fiddle with him." When Lafayette visited Monticello in 1825, the distinguished Frenchman enjoyed an evening violin concert performed by Robert Scott, a Negro.

Few Negroes were given Scott's opportunities, and few had genuine enthusiasm for the South's "peculiar institution." A Virginia ex-slave is quoted in the Slave Narrative Collection of the Federal Writers' Project as saying, "A man told me a nigger woman said she'd rather be slave than free. Anybody which says that is telling a lie. I was both slave and free, and I knows."[3]

Another important source is the vast collection of folk tales, music, and folk songs which come out of slavery. In order to survive, physically and spiritually, the Negro needed release from the resentments and frustrations created by human bondage. His songs, tales, and dances were the emotional catharsis by which he endured.

Songs like "The Blue Tail Fly," "The Gray Goose," and "Po' Laz'us" reveal the Negro mentality and outlook. In the last of these songs, Lazarus breaks a commissary window. For this he is hunted down and shot. What brave men, his white pursuers:

> Wid a great big number,
> They shot po' Laz'us,
> Shot him wid a great big number,
> Number 45, Lawd, number 45.

Though dying, Lazarus is not allowed to have a drink of water. His sister rushed back with his mother to the scene:

> Laz'us' mother she come a-screaming and a-crying,
> Laz'us' mother she come a-screaming and a-crying
> "Dat's my only son, Lawd, dat's my only son."

Yet the Negroes could look forward to better days:

> Oh laugh an' sing an' don't git tired.
> We's all gwine home, some Monday.
> To de homey ponds an' fritter trees,
> An' every day'll be Sunday!

Such verses point to the deep-rooted optimism to which the slaves clung. This outlook has been their salvation. Such optimism was disarming. It enabled them to survive under hardships, and to come psychologically close to the people who were exploiting them. Because the Negro seemed happy and properly subservient, he was able to identify himself closely with the master group. Moving into the heart of Southern culture, he left the indelible mark of his temperament on it, all the while wearing the mask:

> We wear the mask that grins and lies,
> It hides our cheeks and shades our eyes,—
> This debt we pay to human guile;
> With torn and bleeding hearts we smile,
> And mouth with myriad subtleties.[4]

Though the North waged war to free the slaves, many Negroes were loyal to Confederate masters. They built rebel trenches and breastworks, continued to do the manual labor, and stayed on when the Union armies triumphed. After the Emancipation Proclamation was issued, the Federals actively enlisted Virginia Negroes for the army, but less than 6,000 bore arms against the state. Many others enlisted with the Confederates when finally they were allowed to do so.

Negro freedom came at a time and in a way that made the whole business detestable to the Southern whites. The new freedom destroyed the old South's economy and social structure. Moreover, it was a Republican solution in Democratic states. "There ain't but two parties named in the Bible, de Publicans and Sinners," an old

Negro is quoted as saying. "I'se gwine vote wid de Publicans!" The day would come, the whites vowed, when he would not vote at all.

The quotation might be legendary; but there was nothing legendary about the colored judges, electors, and legislators who assumed power prematurely during Reconstruction. A brief honeymoon of emancipation had come. The first mixed petit jury assembled in the United States was impaneled at Richmond in May, 1867, to try ex-President Jefferson Davis—a humiliation Virginians would not forget.

At the 1867 Underwood Convention, 25 of the 103 delegates were Negroes. Two years later 27 colored delegates sat in the General Assembly. With the withdrawal of the federal troops in 1876, the Negro's political hopes and power collapsed. Only then did he realize the true meaning of vindication and white supremacy. He would be effectively disenfranchised, pushed to the bottom of the economic ladder, and segregated in all areas.

By denying federal power, a series of civil rights decisions in effect empowered the states to handle the new problem. Various laws were passed to formalize sovereign white opinion. During Reconstruction in Virginia, mixed marriages were punishable by $100 fine and a year in jail; after 1879 all such marriages were declared void. The 1879 law held that a Negro was a person with one-fourth or more Negro blood. In 1910 the fraction was changed to one-sixteenth, and in 1930 "to every person in whom there is ascertainable any Negro blood." Such a law was made by politicians, not anthropologists.

The antagonism, tension, and bitterness of the Populist revolt resulted in the rapid extension of Jim Crow laws. Up to 1890, the only law of this type adopted by the majority of Southern states applied to train passengers, and Virginia was the last to adopt this one, in 1900. Most Jim Crow laws originated in the twentieth century. They appeal to the lowest common denominator of white psychology, but once established take on the guise of a "final settlement" or "permanent solution." Discriminatory legislation mushroomed, as buses, steamboats, and streetcars were affected. Instead of resisting such action, the typical Southern progressive reformer rode to power on the white-supremacy movement. Hoke Smith in Georgia, Charles Aycock and Josephus Daniels in North Carolina, and Carter Glass and Andrew Montague in Virginia are cases in point. A crusade for stricter segregation ordinances, led by musician John Powell, resulted in laws separating the races in all public halls, theaters, and places of public assemblage. A region-wide capitulation to racism

developed, as alternative solutions were forgotten or rejected.[5]
Sooner or later the *reductio ad absurdum* would be reached. Some
Southern courts required separate Bibles for swearing Negro wit-
nesses.

Such mental attitudes naturally had many social manifestations.
Last hired and first fired, colored people had to stay on the mudsill
of society. Negro novelist Charles Chestnut observed in 1903 that
Negro rights were at a lower ebb than at any time since their emancipation, and race prejudice more intense and uncompromising. "The
county jail and Negro schools are our sore spots," Sherwood Anderson reported in his Marion, Virginia, newspaper. "Either is likely
at any time to spread disease through the entire community." The
O'Shea Commission, appointed by Governor Harry Byrd to survey
state education, noted that Negro school children were being taught
by teachers utterly untrained, and suggested that "it would be better
for Negroes not to be in school at all rather than to be taught by a
person who is herself almost illiterate." Two-thirds of the colored
pupils were being instructed in one-room shacks. The average cost
of Negro school buildings and sites was $1,329. When World War II
began a decade later, 1,616 of the 1,695 colored rural schools were
still small wooden buildings. Over a thousand had only one teacher.

In 1900, eight out of ten Virginia Negroes were rural, but economic pressure has since driven many of them into towns and cities.
By 1930 only 67 per cent and today only half, remain in the country.
Those who migrated to the cities are crowded into black ghettos
called "Niggertown," "Coon Row," or "Black Bottom"—appella-
tions of the white man. Newport News' "Bloodfield" and Richmond's "Sophie's Alley" were perhaps the worst, but colored quarters
everywhere were bad. Of course, a man could always move North
to Harlem, Washington, or Detroit. But, judging from reports of
those who went, they were also brutal, in a different way.

Such conditions help to explain the high crime rate among
Negroes. Misery and privation breed crime and maladjustment. The
Negro is under relentless pressure to search in the underworld
jungles for the relief, recognition, and reward that the upper world
withholds. For years theft and bootlegging were the leading crimes.
Since the passage of the Twenty-first Amendment, the "numbers"
game has taken the place of bootlegging. Backed by the white men
and played by the colored, it is big business in urban slum areas.

Another result of existing conditions is a high rate of illegitimacy.
In 1955, for example, there were 75 white and 754 Negro illegitimate

children born in Richmond. This represented 29 per cent of the total Negro births, and only 3 per cent of the white. Most white people condemn Negro morality without acknowledging the tradition forced on Negroes by whites of informal, nonreligious marriages.

Especially discouraging is the fact that many racial arguments have not changed or yielded over the centuries. Despite the findings of science and the progress of the Negro, segregationists continue to act as if they are dealing with the first slaves to reach Jamestown. By refusing to allow Negroes of ability to receive status and justice, they have made the current racial crisis inevitable.

If "scientific tests" are occasionally administered, the conclusions drawn are not always justified. For example, the California Mental Maturity Test was given to all Virginia's eighth-grade pupils in 1957. It showed that Negroes are not as well prepared or educated as white students of the same age. Due to economic and social factors, they are indeed inferior; but the test proved nothing as to inherent qualities.

Negroes organize secret clubs and lodges to meet their social needs. Carter Woodson, Negro historian and editor, says Virginia contains more secret societies than any other state. The influential True Reformers, organized fifty years ago, have a large banking and insurance committee. This and other groups tend to reflect pride in ancestry and status. Professional and managerial Negroes have their own "high society," with closed neighborhoods and clubs. There is a group known as the F.F.N.V's (First Families of Negro Virginia). Prominent clubs include the Dukes and Duchesses, the Congenial Matrons, the Mighty Twelve, the Big Fifty, and We Moderns. Most colored people still depend on the streets, the dingy restaurants, and the colored honky-tonks for whatever social diversion and outlet they can find. Here they joke, jive, and escape temporarily from the white man's world.

In spite of such restrictions, several Virginia Negroes have risen to state and national prominence. Dorothy Maynor, Ella Fitzgerald, and Bill Robinson are outstanding names in the musical world. Booker T. Washington, son of a Negro cook on a Franklin County plantation, became a symbol of enlightened Negro leadership. He studied at Hampton Institute in the 1870's. He was appointed head of the newly founded Tuskegee Institute, which opened in a dilapidated shanty with forty students. When he died in 1915, the Institute had a hundred buildings and several thousand students.

Up From Slavery, his biography, outsold any book written by an American Negro. He began his work with what he called "the gospel of the tooth brush," teaching cleanliness and emphasizing vocational skill. His conciliatory attitude toward segregation won him much white support. At the 1895 Atlanta Exposition he praised the loyalty of workers who had no thoughts of strikes and labor wars. Agitation of questions of social equality was "the extremest folly." The opportunity to earn a dollar in the factory was worth infinitely more than the opportunity to spend a dollar in an opera house. "In all things that are purely social we can be as separate as the fingers, yet one as the hand in all things essential to mutual progress," he asserted. At a 1912 conference of white Southern University presidents, he went further: "We are trying to instil into the Negro mind that if education does not make the Negro humble, simple, and of service to the community, then it will not be encouraged."

Just three years earlier an interracial organization named the National Association for the Advancement of Colored People had been formed, with a totally different philosophy. Lynching and discrimination were its targets, and aggressive action was its chief weapon. Receiving considerable support from the white world, the N.A.A.C.P. grew so rapidly that by World War II it could claim 500 chapters and half a million members. In 1919 the Commission on Interracial Cooperation was organized "to quench, if possible, the fires of racial antagonism." The National Urban League and National Negro Congress came later, and expanded to the point where they had national political significance. Even more militant were the Southern Conference for Human Welfare (1938) and the Southern Regional Council (1944). "If the antagonistic forces are destined to dominate and bar all forward movement," James Weldon Johnson told his people, "we must make our isolation into a religion and cultivate a hard, keen, relentless hatred for everything white."

Added to all this internal pressure was the external example of racism in Nazi Germany. How could America fight Hitler's policies and yet segregate millions of her own citizens at home? This question has continued to embarrass Americans until the present day.

One of the answers to it came on May 17, 1954. The Supreme Court of the United States ruled unanimously that segregation of whites and Negroes in public schools was unconstitutional, and must end. The long-standing separate-but-equal doctrine set up in 1896 was invalidated. Separate educational facilities, the Court held, were inherently unequal. The Negro plaintiffs in the five cases involved had been "deprived of the equal protection of the laws guaranteed by the Fourteenth Amendment."

Within a few hours, the Voice of America had broadcast the news to foreign countries in thirty-five separate languages. Domestic papers and radio stations carried it to the seventeen states which segregated approximately two-thirds of the nation's Negroes. Couriers took it across the street to the Senate Office Building, where Senator Harry Byrd, head of Virginia's political machine, warned that the decision would bring "implications and dangers of the greatest consequence."

When the decision was announced, Virginia had twenty-three counties in which the Negro school population was greater than the white, and seven in which it was more than 65 per cent. Most of these were in south-side Virginia. The next day the Richmond *Times-Dispatch* commented: "Segregation in the South is not about to be eliminated. Final achievement of that objective is years, perhaps many years, in the future." Later on the Supreme Court ruled that integration must be undertaken with "deliberate speed," but set no dates for its culmination.

"The nation's highest tribunal obviously became convinced that the opposition to integration is such as to require time for adjustments to be made," observed the *Times-Dispatch*. "It saw that in areas where Negroes outnumber whites, any effort to force mixed schools now could only bring trouble. . . . The Court's decisions have created the most difficult and complex situation that has faced us in three-quarters of a century."[6]

The problem confronting the white man had been difficult and complex to the colored man for generations; in many ways, the "Negro problem" was actually a "white problem." For it is the white man, not the colored, who has barricaded himself in the path of social change. "As long as the black man is the victim of caste, the politician, capitalist, and labor leader will refuse to share any real power with him," Francis Simkins wrote. "He will be forced to remain a mere beggar for favors in a country not consciously unkind in its attitude."[7]

The N.A.A.C.P., with the moral and legal authority of the Supreme Court behind it, did not wish its constituents to remain mere beggars. In the summer of 1955, the organization filed desegregation petitions in seventeen states, signed by local Negroes with 170 school boards.

The result was mass fear and insecurity throughout the white South. Race relations deteriorated. Resistance stiffened. The Citizens Councils movement, originating in Mississippi, spread through the old Confederacy. The initiative passed over to the reactionaries.

Virginia, famed for her moderation and conservatism, lent her prestige of leadership in historic crises of the South to the side of reaction.[8] Senator Harry Byrd called for "massive resistance." From Richmond came the "interposition plan," by which the state attempts to interpose her sovereign power between the Constitution and the alleged usurpation of power by the Supreme Court. The idea was adopted by Alabama, Georgia, South Carolina, Mississippi, and Louisiana. Alabama resurrected the phrase "null, void, and of no effect." The key to this position is that court orders must be directed to *someone*. If, by interposition, these orders are ultimately issued to the Governor or legislature, how can they be enforced?

In the fall of 1958 public schools in several Virginia communities, including Norfolk and Charlottesville, were shut down by state leaders who had no better solution to offer citizens in the state that had once produced a Thomas Jefferson.

The solution favored by many Negroes was to migrate; in a decade, the number of Negroes living outside the South has jumped 100 per cent. In 1830, half Virginia's population was colored. From 1880 to 1950, the Negro population increased only 17 per cent as compared to 193 per cent for the whites. Only 22 per cent of the state's population was colored in 1950, and a third of the Virginia born Negroes were living outside the Old Dominion.

Those favoring new policies have not received much sympathy in their state at large. They have watched as the once-cordial relationships between white and colored deteriorated along with the willingness to judge individuals on their own merit or lack of it. Despite the insistence on gentlemanly manners, certain delegates at the 1958 General Assembly treated Delegate Kathryn Stone so rudely when she opposed segregation measures that she burst into tears. The Richmond papers commented on the episode, and the Washington *Post* devoted its leading editorial to it on March 2, 1958.

"She wept," the editorial writer suggested, "for what Virginia was, in the presence of men whose silence while a lady was insulted attest to what Virginia is. . . . No wonder the lady wept. The wonder is that the whole House did not weep. The wonder is that the whole state does not weep."

21 *Mountain Music*

THE MUSIC IN MY HEART I BORE
LONG AFTER IT WAS HEARD NO MORE.—*William Wordsworth*

The English visitor was more than enthusiastic. He was ecstatic. "It is a paradise!" wrote Cecil Sharp when he visited western Virginia in 1918. "I don't think I have ever seen such lovely trees, ferns, and wild flowers, or such a wonderful lot of people. The tunes of Virginia are extraordinarily beautiful, of greater musical value than those I have taken down anywhere in America."[1]

The world-renowned ballad collector and president of the British Folk-Lore Society found the part of the state most eastern Virginians apologized for very close to a state of bliss. "In an ideal state of society each child learns to sing the songs of his forefathers in the same natural and unselfconscious way in which he learns his mother tongue. It was exactly this ideal state that I found existing in the mountain communities."

Despite the un-British snakes, heat, and thunderstorms, Cecil Sharp spent forty-six weeks tramping around, listening, and copying. He did more than collect a treasure trove of folk music. He proved that what was marginal land for the sociologist was a happy hunting ground for the folklorist.

The pioneers who pushed west were poor in property but rich in folk memory. They brought many European ballads with them,

231

adapted the songs to their new environment, and made up new ones. Here was the basis of much American music and American folk expression.

Though none of them spoke with the authority of Sharp, many Virginians before his visit had been impressed with the ballads in the mountains, and had endeavored to collect them. In 1913 the Virginia Folk-Lore Society was founded to "discover, collect, and thus preserve the folk-lore of Virginia and of the states recruited by immigration from Virginia." C. Alphonso Smith, Professor of English at the University of Virginia, guided the project; schoolteachers throughout the state did the legwork. Their devotion to their task was admirable. Mr. John Stone of Mt. Fair made this note on one of his findings: "I walked fourteen miles, raised four blisters, and walked lame for a month. The next day, in spite of my blisters, I walked seven more miles to get a ballad."

The men who heard and studied the music wondered if that was generally described as the Highlanders' arrested development might not be arrested degeneration.

Moving from this speculation to a genuine liking for the ballads is not easy. Newcomers to the field are frequently disappointed. The tunes, themes, and performers are seldom "pretty." To one raised in the climatic blessedness of Hollywood background music and juke boxes, mountain ballads seem crude, severe, and unmusical. They use the "gapped scale," which leaves out certain of the seven available tones, and the ancient modal scales of preharmonic music. The unexpectedness of the intervals and emphasis on unusual degrees of the scale make for surprising originality. The whole emotional expression finds its sole utterance in melodic line and structure.

As for subject matter, the ballads stress gory murders, poisonings, adultery, desertion, and incest. Folk singers don't separate tunes from the story of the songs; the tune is a medium rather than an end in itself. Variations in the tone and rhythm are used to accentuate the story. Performers, often toothless old women or white-haired patriarchs, depend as much upon their method of singing as upon content for effect. To perceive just what they are doing, and to appreciate the freshness and unparalleled charm seldom heard in "popular" music, requires an effort on the part of those who usually get their culture canned.

Curling up with a book of early ballads or a phonograph album by a night-club singer is no solution. Now the potion has been diluted. There is no way of feeling the full impact from printed or watered-down versions, or from hearing the song properly sung once. "A good tune," Evelyn Wells explains in *The Ballad Tree*, "is known only through many repetitions."[2]

Variations, the real art of the folk singer, allow for wide creative range. Scores of Virginia variants of "Barbara Allen" have been found. This pathetic tale recounts how a young girl scorns her lover, Sweet William (who might emerge as Willie, Sweet Jimmy, Young Johnny, or Jimmy Grove in Virginia). "Barbara Allen" has been as much enjoyed in isolated cabins as in fashionable London, where in 1666 Samuel Pepys praised the rendition by the celebrated actress, Mrs. Knipp. He would hardly have believed that years later a mountaineer thousands of miles away would sing:

> Way down South where I come from
> Is where I got my learning.
> I fell in love with a pretty little girl
> And her name is Barbey Ellen.

Argument over the origin, authorship, and transmission of folk songs is endless. How do such songs start? Is a specific author, or are the "folk," as a community, responsible? Scholars like Herder, Grimm, and Langer have endorsed the communal theory; such opponents as Scherer, Brandl, and Pound have been equally sure of the individualist position. Currently the attackers of "the notion of the immaculate conception of poetry" dominate. Whatever the prevailing theory, the actuality is before us—hundreds of gripping and compelling songs which have existed for generations by oral transmission. Not on the printed page, but in the hearts of the people, have they survived.

In order to live, ballads must grow. What was "The Twa Sisters" in Britain became "Sister Kate," "The Miller and the Mayor's Daughter," or "I'll Be True to My Love" in Virginia. In it a jealous girl pushes her younger sister into the millstream because she has stolen her suitor. A miller recovers the body and exposes the crime. In Old World versions, he performs magic on various parts of the corpse, which become musical instruments which play and denounce the murderess. Virginians left out what seemed to be far-fetched magic and turned the story into a children's game. They transformed magic into merriment.

Another major shift was affected on a well-known English ballad, "The Gypsy Laddie." A fair lady gives herself to a roving gypsy. Her Lord returns, finds her gone, races after and rescues her, and hangs fifteen gypsies. In adaptations discovered in Virginia, the retribution and hanging are omitted. Instead, the lady casts her lot with the roaming vagabonds—a decision that would have appealed to the hard-pressed pioneers moving into frontier territory:

> "How can you forsake your house and land,
> How can you forsake your money O?
> How can you forsake your sweet little babe
> To go with the gypsy laddie O?"

> "O, I can forsake my house and lands,
> O, I can forsake my money O,
> O, I can forsake my sweet little babe
> To go with the gypsy laddie O."

> She was used to a feather bed
> And servants all around her,
> And now she has come to a bed of hay
> With gypsies all around her.

Similarly, "The Three Ravens" became in Virginia "The Three Crows." In the Appalachians the gripping song moves forward with powerful cadence:

> There were three crows sat on a tree
> As black as any crows could be

> One of these crows said to his mate,
> "What shall we do for food to eat?"

> "There lies a horse in yonder lane
> That has been only three days slain

> We'll sit upon his bare backbone
> And pick his eyes out one by one."

Always willing and able to make the punishment fit the crime, Civil War survivors wrote parodies of "The Three Crows":

> In eighteen hundred and sixty-two
> The Rebels put the Yankees through.

> In eighteen hundred and sixty-three
> You ought to seen them Yankees flee.

> In eighteen hundred and sixty-four
> Them Yankees cried, "We want no more!"

In eighteen hundred and sixty-five
We all thanked God we was alive.[3]

Mountain people distinguish between "hymns" and "love songs." One of the best informed "hymn" scholars was George Pullen Jackson (1874-1953), professor at Vanderbilt University. The hymns, Jackson discovered, were old folk tunes which everybody could sing, with words that spoke from the heart of the devout in the language of the common. During his lifetime, Jackson discovered the organic relationships of over one hundred and fifty hymn melodies to an even greater number of traditional secular folk tunes. He also demonstrated that white spirituals were the progenitors of many of the best-loved Negro spirituals.[4]

Common themes of Appalachian religious ballads, often told in the first person, are the poor wayfaring stranger, the departing preacher, the backslider, and the convert. The songs frequently begin with a religious experience and end with a warning to those who embrace "this vain world of sin." They flourished during the eighteenth and nineteenth centuries. Emotionalism and renunciation swept the hills like a forest fire. Music had to match the occasion, when evangelical preachers decided:

To pitch my tent on this rough ground
And give old Satan another round!

At first none of the folk hymns existed in print. Eventually, as the revivals became better organized, booklets appeared with such titles as *Hymns and Spiritual Songs/For the Pious of all Denominations/As Sung in Camp Meetings.* Sensing the enormous value of rousing hymns, preachers encouraged publications of more elaborate books; *The Christian Harmony,* one of the most popular, appeared in 1805. From the Valley of Virginia—especially the little town of Singer's Glen, near Harrisonburg—thousands of copies of hymn books appeared, entitled *The Kentucky Harmony* (1814), *Choral Music* (1816), *The Virginia Harmony* (1831), *Genuine Church Music* (1832), and *The Union Harmony* (1848). Throughout the Old Dominion, "Hard-shell songs" and "Methodist jigs" flourished like the loblolly pine.

These books made use of "shape notes," so called because the pitch of the note is determined by the shape, independent of the lines and spaces of the music staff. Devised to simplify the reading of music, the books employed the Four Shape and the Seven Shape systems. In the former, the first and fourth degrees of the scale, called *fa,* are represented by a right triangle;; the second and fifth, *so,* by a circle. For the third and sixth, *la* is used and symbolized by a square head, leaving a diamond for the seventh, *mi.* The Seven Shape system has a different form of notation. Both spring from the sol-fa method of sight reading used in Elizabethan England, and referred to by Shakespeare in *King Lear.*

The singers of folk hymns, long considered substandard by the professional hymnists, actually have a goodly heritage. Their defenders profited, moreover, from the attack by the supporters of ordinary staff notes; for the country people struggled to keep the "good old tunes" alive. That is just what they did. Eventually city-trained musical authorities acclaimed the folk hymns' honesty and directness as central religious singing and worship. Musicians like John Powell and Charles Vardell, Jr., Virginia's foremost twentieth-century composers, have woven folk tunes into their best-known compositions.

Though it is impossible to catch the haunting beauty of these hymns without hearing them, a reading of the words to the "Garden Hymn" suggests the quality:

> The Lord into His garden comes,
> The spices yield a rich perfume.
> The lilies grow and thrive.
> Refreshing showers of grace divine
> From Jesus flow to every vine
> And make the dead revive.
>
> Oh, that this dry and barren ground
> In springs of water may abound,
> A fruitful soil become.
> The desert blossoms as the rose,
> When Jesus conquers all His foes
> And makes His people one.
>
> Come, brethren, ye that love the Lord,
> Who taste the sweetness of His word,
> In Jesus' way go on;
> Our troubles and our trials here
> Will only make us richer there,
> When we arrive at home.
>
> The glorious time is rolling on,
> The gracious work is now begun,

> My soul a witness is;
> I taste and see the pardon free
> For all mankind as well as me,
> Who come to Christ to live.[5]*

Sometimes well-known parts of the King James Bible were adapted. In a lovely mountain version of the Twenty-third Psalm, the Valley of the shadow of death became the lonesome valley:

> You got to cross that lonesome valley,
> You got to cross it by yerself.
> There hain't no one
> Gwine cross it for you;
> You got to cross it by yerself.

Often filled with the quiet sadness and resignation of mountain life, the songs were not altogether devoid of humor and satire. The backwoods Presbyterians, unhappy when Alexander Campbell and his friends formed the Campbellite Church, told about it in a new verse for "The Ram of Derby:"

> The horns upon his head, sir,
> Were higher than I could reach.
> They built a pulpit up there
> For the Campbellites to preach.

When Virginia-born Henry Clay, first a candidate for the Presidency in 1824, was still trying for the office twenty years later, the people understood him well enough to make up stanzas like:

> Henry Clay he climbed a tree
> And stuck his bill in for to see.
> The lizards caught him by the snout
> And he hollered for the coons to pull him out!

Virginia's local characters, as well as her national ones, figured in songs and legends. A good example is Joe Clark, veteran of the War of 1812. He was the Blue Ridge's Paul Bunyan. Going to the war from Henrico County, Joe and Nelson Clark were later given grants of land as a reward for military service. Their tracts, as the Rockbridge County deed book shows, were in the rugged Irish Creek area of the Blue Ridge Mountains. The Clark boys were elated with their acquisition—until they saw the land.

It was mostly straight up.

* From *Twelve Folk Hymns*, edited by Anna Morris Buchanan (J. Fischer & Bro., 1934). Used by her permission.

But the Clarks didn't discourage easy. Having pulled up their roots and moved to new territory, they intended to stay. They mixed well with the Indian settlers, who had been driven to this remote place because they had smallpox, and with Revolutionary War deserters, who had gone upcreek to avoid soldiering. Once a man was settled on Irish Creek, nobody was apt to come up after him.

The Clark boys married Indian girls and settled down to a little mountain matrimony. Whatever else Joe Clark lacked, he was a good breeder. He had twenty-odd children. Nelson did all right too. Before long the Clarks outnumbered everyone else from Wigwam Mountain to Norvells Flats. They still do. Most of them can sing a song about their tribal patriarch who came into the Unpromising Land, a song proclaiming him a genuine nineteenth-century king-sized cockalorum demigod:

> Old Joe Clark had a mule
> His name was Morgan Brown
> Every tooth in that mule's head
> Was sixteen inches around.

> Old Joe Clark had a cow
> She was muley born
> It took a jaybird a week'n half
> To fly from horn to horn.

> I went down to old Joe's house
> He was sick in bed
> Rammed my finger down his throat
> And pulled out a wagon bed.

The Great Awakening swept the mountain country, and Joe himself became a preacher—of sorts:

> Old Joe Clark set out to preach
> He preached all over the plain.
> The highest text he ever took
> Was high, low, Jack, and game.

> Old Joe Clark had a yaller cat
> She'd neither sing nor pray,
> She stuck her head in the buttermilk jar
> And washed her sins away.

With Joe, the law of love did not prevail. The fittest survived, and reaped the bounty:

> Old Joe Clark killed a man,
> Killed him with a knife.
> I'm damned glad he killed that man,
> Now I'll have his wife!

Verses of "Old Joe Clark" spread like wire grass in an April rain. By 1944, B. A. Botkin (in *A Treasury of American Folklore*) had collected verses as far west as Cleveland County, Oklahoma. Back on Irish Creek, Sam Downey made up some of the best ones. Active in the early twentieth century, Sam was a teamster for the South River Lumber Company, which owned thousands of acres of timber and operated a sawmill near Cornwall, Virginia. Sam drove the stoutest eight-horse team in the Blue Ridge, and sang the best songs. Plodding over the ruts, rocks, and mudholes, he liked to invent new verses of "Old Joe Clark":

> Sixteen horses in my team
> The leasers had no line
> I whip them around a rocky road
> To see that girl of mine.
>
> Driving my old mule team
> Leading Old Gray behind
> Before I'll see my true love walk,
> I'll pull Old Nellie blind.

The girls Sam sang about could hardly be called ladies:

> I wouldn't marry a yeller gal,
> I'll tell you the reason why:
> She'd eat a barrel of sauerkraut
> And drink the river dry.
>
> I wouldn't marry a school teacher
> I'll tell you the reason why:
> She blows her nose in yellow corn bread
> And calls it pumpkin pie.

People up the Creek still remember Sam, attributing so many verses and songs to him that no one will ever be able to unravel fact and fancy. One mountain man who claims to have worked with Sam remembers his sad demise: "Yep, I knowed old Sam. When he got too old to work he came to live with his married daughter near our home. One day Sam took a bucket of swill into the hog pen. He walked up on the ramp and poured the swill into the hog trough. As he straightened hisself up, he fell right over backwards, and when someone got to him, Sam was plum dead."[6] Thus do the mighty fall.

But Old Joe Clark, and Sam Downey's verses about him, lived on. As a child Charles Vardell, Jr., heard a servant sing the song. Years later he used it as the basis for a symphonic piece called "Joe Clark Steps Out." When the National Symphony came to Rockbridge County in 1956, this composition was performed. The concert's sponsors invited Joe Clark's grandson, by then an eighty-six-year-old mountain patriarch, to the concert.

Finding Joe Clark's offspring was not easy. When his home burned down some years earlier, he took what money he had left and bought a tractor. The idea was not to farm, but to become a knight of the road, and move from place to place. A car isn't much good on the back trails around Irish Creek.

Joe was finally found and invited to the performance. He came, sat in the front row, and heard the big band play the piece written in honor of his grandpappy. Having thanked his host and posed for photographers, he asked for a ride back to Irish Creek.

Future ballad collectors may hear about the visit in new verses to the "Old Joe Clark" tune.

Some of the men who worked and died in the mountains are more remembered in the singing than in the burying. That's the way it was with the celebrated Negro, John Henry. Good lawd, what a steel-drivin' man.

He drove steel with a ten-pound sheepnose hammer. The four-foot switch handle was greased with tallow. John Henry stood back six feet and struck with the full length of his hammer, driving from either shoulder. He made a nineteen-foot stroke, fast as lightning. When he hit, the cold steel rang out like a bell. The men swore he could drive ten hours without turning a stroke.

In the generation after the Civil War, the Chesapeake and Ohio Railroad pushed tracks through the Alleghenies, in order to connect the West Virginia coal fields and the ocean. From Big Sandy to White Sulphur the drill hammer clanged from morning to night. Gradually the sound of steam drills could be heard too. In 1873 the crews were ready to tackle the Big Bend Mountain near the Greenbriar Mountain. It was the largest tunnel on the line, a mile and a quarter long. This was tough enough for John Henry.

There was so much trouble on the Big Bend from silicosis, cave-ins, suffocation, and falling rocks that the area was closed to the press.

The Chesapeake and Ohio Company claims that the files for this undertaking have been destroyed by fire. Where history stops, folklore takes over. The wonderful folk song of John Henry is true, just as the stories of King Arthur or Robin Hood are true; and if they are not, they ought to be.

One day the white boss man brought in a newfangled steel drill, to find out just how efficient it was. He decided to have a contest between the drill and his gang leader, John Henry. In dramatic, unforgettable words, John Henry accepted the challenge:

> John Henry told his captain
> "A man ain't nuthin' but a man,
> And before I'd let that steam-drill beat me down,
> I'd die with my hammer in my hand, good Lawd,
> Die with my hammer in my hand."

The Negro had his foreman bring two new twenty-pound hammers. The steam drill was placed on the right hand, the man on the left. The contest began.

> Oh the captain said to John Henry
> "I believe this mountain's sinking in."
> John Henry said to his captain, oh my,
> "Ain't nuthin' but my hammer suckin' wind,
> Lawd Lawd, ain't nuthin' but my hammer suckin' wind."

There, in the bowels of the earth, John Henry fought for his own integrity, and that of men everywhere. He swung straight and hard and true. He drove fourteen feet while the drill went only nine.

> John Henry was hammering on the mountain
> And his hammer was striking fire,
> He drove so hard till he broke his poor heart,
> And he lied down his hammer and he died.

> Well, some say he was from England,
> And some say he was from Spain.
> But I say he's nuthin' but a po' Virginia boy
> Just a leader of the steel-drivin' gang, oh Lawd,
> Just the leader of the steel-drivin' gang.

His story catches the drama of the newly freed Negro in a white world, of the worker struggling against the machine, of the human refusing to bow to superior technology. The death of John Henry, as F. O. Mattheissen has noted, coincided with the exploitation of the frontier, just as had Paul Bunyan's with the gutting of the forest-land. The factitiousness of recent attempts to retell these stories shows that folk art doesn't adapt easily to an industrialized society. In an urban society, folklore must tap new sources, and develop new techniques to survive.[7]

Folklorists have been recording new versions of "John Henry" ever since 1909. Louis Chappell collected a whole volume of them.[8] Eventually the hucksters moved in, and produced a cheapened version for the juke boxes. John Henry is tough; he withstood even this. Last month, while trudging along a dirt road, I saw a Negro resting beside a tree. On his mouth harp he was playing his own version of "John Henry."

I stopped, listened, and gave his song the tribute of a little silence.

"That was nice. Who taught you the tune?"

"Didn't nobody taught me," he said. "Just sort of picked it up, I guess."

"A real good tune."

"Yep, that John Henry tune is right. I feels it with my mouth."

22 *Restoration Blues*

DELAY, DECAY. LIVING, LIVING,
NEVER MOVING. EVER MOVING
IRON THOUGHTS CAME WITH ME
AND GO WITH ME.—*T. S. Eliot,* "VIRGINIA"*

In 1926 Virginia was twice-captured. Rockefeller took over Williamsburg, and Byrd occupied Richmond.

This dual triumph of benevolent despotism was no mere coincidence. Neither event would have occurred had not Virginians' enthusiasm for the past excelled their belief in the future. The plan, in both town planning and town running, was to return to the Good Old Days. Rockefeller and Byrd capitalized on the desire of most of the state inhabitants to turn back the clock. Both were efficient, honorable gentlemen with good names. Thirty years later, when the 1957 Jamestown Festival opened, both were still very much in power.

To examine conditions and attitudes in the Old Capital (Williamsburg) and the New Capital (Richmond) in recent generations is to see that the dual invasions came in the fullness of time.

In 1856 a Tidewater schoolteacher, Josiah Ryland, wrote a quatrain expressing the nostalgia which had long pervaded Tidewater:

> But now the time of bronze returns
> And honest check with flushes burns.

* From *Collected Poems 1909–1935* by T. S. Eliot. Copyright 1936 by Harcourt, Brace & Co. Used with their permission.

243

Cant, affectation, gloss, begone!
Old times, old times, return, return.[1]

Stripped of its social and political leadership, impoverished by the disappearance of its topsoil and tobacco monopoly, the area which had been the cradle of the Republic a century earlier was becoming a mausoleum of deserted manors and memories. As early as 1814 John Randolph had complained that "the old families are gone" as he looked out over the ruined houses and eroded fields. The Civil War brought more destruction and ruin; even Yorktown's Moore House, in which the articles of surrender had been drawn up in 1781, was partially destroyed to provide kindling for soldiers in the winter of 1862.

Intellectually, Tidewater was reduced by the Civil War to the reality of a pleasant fancy. William and Mary, once the educational center of Virginia, closed its doors. After state aid had enabled it to reopen in 1889, the college languished so badly that the state took over in 1906. Isolated and poverty-stricken, the counties of the great coastal plain were at the century's end barely eking out an existence that was a travesty on the old plantation mythology.

Jamestown Island was in private hands in 1900, and the river was slowly engulfing the marshy land. Williamsburg was dilapidated, with only the foundations left to mark the Capitol Building. A public school was on the land which the Governor's Palace had occupied. Victorian trimmings hid most of the eighteenth-century buildings. Telephone wires were strung like cobwebs up and down Duke of Gloucester Street.

These problems of isolation and neglect culminated in the islands which lay between the peninsula and the Eastern Shore. Life on them was not only isolated, but isolating and inbred. In 1932 on Tangier Island, for example, three-fourths of the people had only nine last names. Twenty-three per cent of the inhabitants were named Crockett.[2]

In the first quarter of the century Tidewater remained a vast decaying museum to which other Americans might make a pilgrimage: "A pilgrimage it verily is! Holy ground it is, with a certain brooding presence of great spirits. . . . Surely the tall figure of George Washington will emerge in a moment from the doorway."[3] Then a cultural miracle occurred: the good old days returned. Once more wigs and bustles appeared on Williamsburg streets, harpsichord music floated from the candle-lit Governor's Palace, and Britain's

Great union flag flew over a meticulously restored Capitol. Williamsburg went forward by going backwards.

Money from one of the nation's great oil fortunes, generously contributed by John D. Rockefeller, Jr., paid for it. But an Episcopal minister, William A. R. Goodwin, brought the vision and the fortune together.

Son of a Confederate officer, Goodwin attended Virginia Theological Seminary, and was called to Williamsburg's Bruton Parish in 1902. His 200-year-old building was badly disfigured. Immediately he drew up plans to get money and restore it. King Edward VII, Theodore Roosevelt, and J. Pierpont Morgan contributed. In 1907 a restored Bruton Parish Church was rededicated.

Accepting a church in Rochester, New York, Dr. Goodwin left his native state during World War I. In 1923 he returned to Williamsburg as Professor of Biblical Literature and endowment director of William and Mary. He was horrified at what war conditions had done to the charming old town. Cheap amusement halls and restaurants had been erected, some of corrugated iron. Ancient trees had been sacrificed to make way for filling stations. Dr. Goodwin made ready for an all-out battle to restore, not a few buildings, but the whole town.

Substituting for William and Mary's President Chandler, who was too ill to address a Phi Beta Kappa convention in New York City, the Williamsburg rector told what had been happening in the Old Capital, and pleaded for help. One of those who heard him, John D. Rockefeller, Jr., asked for further details. He caught Dr. Goodwin's vision, and in the winter of 1926 announced that he would finance preliminary surveys of the town.

The architectural firm of Perry, Shaw, and Hepburn was employed, without being told the name of the sponsor. Property in the heart of Williamsburg was purchased in Dr. Goodwin's name. Mr. Rockefeller's support was announced at a public meeting on June 12, 1928.

No restoration in modern history has been more meticulous. Topography, water, trees, and soil have been studied. Archaeologists have dug up tons of artifacts. Architects have made hundreds of sketches and comparisons. Researchers have sifted historic truths in archives, courts, libraries, personal papers, and newspapers. Jefferson's drawings of the Governor's Palace turned up in California's Huntington Library. There was an invaluable copperplate of early Williamsburg in Oxford's Bodleian Library.

Thirty years and sixty million dollars later, 495 buildings had been restored or reconstructed, 720 modern buildings had been removed, and 90 acres of gardens had been planted. Eight million visitors had seen the sleeping city that was awake again.

No mere statistics can convey the impact of Colonial Williamsburg, which brought American archaeology into its own and gave America a tangible symbol of Tidewater's greatness. No estimate can be made of its effects on state morale and pride, or on the American aesthetic.

Official state sanction came on February 24, 1934, when the reconstructed Capitol was opened by a joint session of the House of Delegates and Senate. Governor George Peery praised Mr. Rockefeller. Mr. Rockefeller praised "those great patriots whose voices once sounded in these halls." The Assembly authorized subsequent sessions there. The capital had been brought to life, not by the dictates of economics, politics, or military necessity, but by the power and compulsion of vital historical tradition.

On August 14, 1938, William Goodwin conducted his last service in Bruton Parish Church. When he died the next year he was buried in the aisle of that church, beneath a simple stone bearing this inscription: "Here Rests the Rev. Dr. William Archer Rutherford Goodwin, A Native of Virginia, Late Rector of This Parish."

Williamsburg has been refurbished intellectually as well as physically. The Institute of Early American History and Culture, sponsored jointly by Colonial Williamsburg and the College of William and Mary, has sponsored study and research bearing on America up to 1815. The Institute has published books, bibliographies, and the *William and Mary Quarterly*. The Colonial Records Project, supported by other agencies as well as Colonial Williamsburg, has helped to obtain transcriptions of Virginia's colonial records in England. Today there is more brain power in Williamsburg than there has been since Governor Dunmore's day. Mr. Rockefeller has collected talent as well as timber, for which Virginia must be grateful.

Still there is a disconcerting note about Operation Williamsburg. Perhaps it is, or will soon be, *too* restored. The ever-fresh paint and unlimited expenditures have turned the mellow old town into a glossy movie set. The work illustrates the American curse of over-doing a good thing. There is more pose in the summer pageant players and the costumed employees than there was in the hard-working, earthy men whom they imitate. A restoration which surpasses the original is as false as one which does not equal it. How much Mr. Rockefeller's town men like Thomas Jefferson and Patrick Henry would recognize is a good question.

The matter has not stopped with buildings. Colonial people have been conjured up, too. The grace and charm of Georgian structures is internally convincing, without adding the trappings of a fancy-dress ball. Blacksmiths who drive to work in automobiles are apt to appear artificially quaint; their anachronistic pose in picture-book setting borders on the ludicrous.

The thoughtless transplantation of humans from one cultural environment to another cannot result in authenticity. One of the Williamsburg hostesses, Helen Campbell, has written a diary which deals with this.[4]

In her first farthingale she felt like a bird in a gilded cage. Among the tourists who came to her building were "ribald gentlemen who commented very graphically on the picturesqueness of the female form silhouetted in farthingales through a bright sun-lighted doorway." She frankly admits that the delectability of young ladies in quaint, gay costume "at times encourages certain of the sea-going gentlemen to dwell on biology rather than history." The official restoration area seems incongruous with ye olde colonial chain store in the business district, or the eighteenth-century Howard Johnson Restaurant which according to appearances had twenty-eight flavors of ice cream even in days of yore.

A lively concern with the Georgian arts and crafts is in itself commendable, requiring special study, knowledge, and skill. The people employed at Williamsburg have done a splendid job creating a living museum of America's past. Unfortunately, Williamsburg has been taken not as a museum but a model. Unhistorical restorations, antiques, and alterations have been sponsored by well-meaning, uninformed people and companies. The South, having suffered long with the boll weevil, now must contend with the Williamsburg architectural blight.

Misapplying a knowledge of the past can lead to disastrous results, damaging, if not killing, the first buds of a contemporary and functional architecture. It has already prompted merchants to build colonial drug stores, theaters, and barbecue pits in towns that weren't founded during the colonial period. Georgian houses with no relevance to modern living, material, and demands have gone up. Instead of being the "Sahara of the Bozart," as H. L. Mencken claimed, Virginia is the museum of the Bozart. Conceivably the restoration fad, once it spreads from architecture to politics, education, and literature, could be the worst cultural disaster to befall Virginia since the Civil War.

Who knows how many antique shops have opened up in Virginia in the last twenty years? The graduate student who would make a case study of what they sell, what they claim, and how they define an antique would contribute to our understanding of the state. He should surely visit my favorite antique shop, a modest place in the colored section of Orange, Virginia. This sign is in the window:

ANTIQUES—NEW AND USED

Many dealers and restorers are careless about distinguishing the old and new; in fact, they employ people to make the latter look like the former. At the brick kilns in Glasgow, one can hear a workman talk about "making bricks look old-timy for Williamsburg." Virginia carpenters and metalworkers find it lucrative to "make" antiques; merchants, to peddle them.

All this confuses and dismays the authorities. "What are we to do?" Wallace Nutting has asked. "The offenders can't be sent to jail, and ostracism is out of date. That is why we let the bad work go on."[5] There is a Gresham's law in preservation activities, as in economics. "We are afraid that the bad, tawdry, ill-considered 'restorations,' lacking historic and architectural validity, will tend to drive out interest and appreciation in the safeguarding of the sound ones," cautions Richard H. Howland, president of the National Trust for Historic Preservation.

Wealthy, well-meaning persons have compounded the crime by indulging in synthetic restoration. They choose a bit here, a bit there, from various houses and periods. The result is often monstrous. There are houses around Richmond and Charlottesville which have borrowed from half a dozen sources, doing credit to none and parodying all. A University of Virginia fraternity built its small version of Monticello—an object lesson in misplaced enthusiasm. They had, as one Charlottesville lady insisted, more dollars than sense.

Organizations have been just as guilty, with less excuse. One of the leading state groups decided to rebuild George Washington's birthplace. Unable to discover what it looked like, they copied a colonial model in the adjoining county. They have not claimed this is just what the house looked like; but many people who come to see the birthplace of the father of their country take it to be the actual house, just as many believe the Williamsburg buildings are "the halls in which great men walked." Speaking of the Washington birthplace, James Branch Cabell said: " 'Tis beyond reason to pick flaws in a relic so impressive and remunerative, upon the shallow ground that it was not builded until two centuries after Washington's birth. Through our latter-day intervention of our antiquities we have displayed our freedom at its noble utmost."[6]

An elderly Negro, employed by Colonial Williamsburg, put it more succinctly. Bedecked in satin and lace, photographed by many tourists, he looked out pensively over the manicured gardens. "It's all right," he said. "They pays good and we don' do much. But I liked the town a whole lot mo' when it was a little dirtier!"

The man who became Governor of Virginia in 1926, and who has controlled state politics ever since, did not organize a machine; he inherited and perfected one.

We have already noted how John S. Barbour and Thomas S. Martin created the state Democratic organization. They called for a holy crusade to end Negro-Republican domination, employed tactics that were hardly holy, and welded their forces into a monolithic party. When Tom Martin entered the U.S. Senate in 1895, his followers were so firmly entrenched that there was little chance they could be dislodged except by discontented or antimachine Democrats. To lessen this possibility, the organization pushed through the Constitution of 1902. The main consequence was the drastic reduction of voters. Hampered by the poll tax and other provisions, only about 11 per cent of the adult population voted in the primary elections to choose the Democratic nominee for Governor in the ensuing years. Thus, the Governor owed his victory to about 6 per cent of the state's adult population. Virginia achieved the worst voting record in the Union. By contrast, Mississippi was a hotbed of democracy.[7]

In 1915 Senator Martin became the majority floor leader of the U.S. Senate. In his home state, that same year, a young man with a famous Virginia name entered the state Senate. Born in Martinsburg, West Virginia, in 1887, Harry Flood Byrd returned to the state of his ancestors as a lad of fifteen, going to work on the Winchester *Star*. Like the earlier Byrds, he bought land as soon as he could. Throughout his career apples, roads, and politics have been his three main interests.

In the same year in which Harry Byrd moved to Winchester,

Woodrow Wilson became president of Princeton. Both would distinguish themselves in political affairs, and one would become a world leader. Wilson had ideas; Byrd had ideas and endurance.

Born in Staunton's Presbyterian Manse, Wilson was raised in an atmosphere of intense piety, and nourished on the drastic moral tonic which is known as the Shorter Catechism. He studied at Princeton and then at the University of Virginia. While president of the Jefferson Literary Society he tinkered with its constitution. Unable to establish a successful law practice, he studied history at the Johns Hopkins University, receiving his doctorate in 1886. Four years later he returned to Princeton, to serve, successively, as professor and president.

The first professional teacher to move almost directly from the classroom to the White House, Wilson served America magnificently in war and peace. He gave invaluable aid to the Allies and envisioned a League of Nations which would be a disentangling alliance; but America wouldn't join. His political enemies killed it in the United States Senate.

In the fall of 1919 Wilson sought from the American people the approval which the Senate withheld. The thirty speeches of his western tour are a high point of political oratory. Realizing that his health was poor, he was willing to risk his life to attain the end he sought. He forfeited his life, without attaining his goal.

A liberal individualist and lover of freedom, Wilson was descended from the tough Scotch-Irish who left an indelible mark on Virginia. He used his mind sternly and reverently throughout his life, to defend and bolster up a people who never understood him. Though he was proud to be a Virginian, his state neither was nor is Wilsonian. One of the most impressive lines in the shortest of his well-wrought books occurs in *Robert E. Lee, An Interpretation:* "I wish there were some great orator who could go about and make men drunk with this spirit of self-sacrifice." Wilson was himself a fine orator and theorist; but he could not make men drunk. He could not come close to people, either in word or deed. There are no nicknames for "Woodrow."

Nonetheless, he believed in democracy, and had strong feelings about men's necessary connection with the region in which they are born. "You can love a country if you begin by loving a community; but you cannot love a country if you do not have the true rootages of intimate affection which are the real sources of all that is strongest in human life," he wrote. He died in Washington. There was both a river and a gulf between the man and the state that had sired him.

In 1956, the hundredth anniversary of Wilson's birth, Virginia staged a Centennial Celebration. Most Virginians paid little attention to it; the main speakers for the biggest gatherings were imported. He, if anyone, deserves in our century the title of the Forgotten Virginian.

After the death of state boss Tom Martin, political control passed into the hands of Wilson's Secretary of the Treasury, Carter Glass. This "unreconstructed rebel," as he liked to call himself, had stood on the James River bridge and seen the barge bearing Stonewall Jackson's coffin moving beneath him en route to Lexington, where the fierce warrior would be buried. Later on Glass controlled Lynchburg's newspapers and distinguished himself at the 1902 Constitutional Convention. Cosponsor of the Federal Reserve System, Glass's consuming interest was finance. He resigned from Wilson's Cabinet to be a United States Senator. Colorful and dynamic, speaking sarcastically out of the side of his mouth, he was a decoration to the Byrd machine; but he never rivaled, statewise, the colorless, cautious, undramatic Byrd, who won for himself the nickname "Buddha of Berryville."

A bitter opponent of the New Deal, Glass' influence waned rapidly after 1932. Long before this embittered and caustic old man passed away, Harry Byrd was the real boss of Virginia.

Financially speaking, Harry Byrd was a very successful Governor. During his four years in office (1926–30) he converted a deficit of $1,258,000 into a surplus of $2,596,000. His "pay as you go" highway program drew much support in a state which had gone through the financial nightmare of Reconstruction. Byrd has always claimed to follow Jefferson, who, according to Byrd, "perceived with the vision of an inspired prophet certain eternal principles and translated them into simple language." As Governor and U.S. Senator, Byrd has made economy his central tenet. "The Democratic party should declare for lowering our government costs—national, state, and local—to the ability of the citizens to pay," he insists. "This can only be accomplished by less government in business and more business in government."

All this sounds Jeffersonian enough. Yet, when translated into twentieth-century policy, such principles have given Virginia one of the most restricted and Hamiltonian governments in the nation.[8] The state is controlled by a well-disciplined, well-meaning oligarchy of perhaps 10,000 people, many of them prosperous former inhabitants of other states. The "organization," as members prefer to call it, is elusive but no illusion, as the three and a half million people under its sway have reason to know.

Virginia is a political museum piece, more like England before the Reform Bill of 1832 than most of the United States. Country squires and city businessmen run it. Laws passed by the well-controlled legislature favor them, and restrict the activities of organized labor and reform groups of various types. Former Governor John Battle, a staunch Byrd man, has said the "so-called" machine is merely a loosely knit group who think alike and act together to give good government to the Commonwealth. If "good government" means scrupulously honest government, he is right. If "good government" is one free of buffoons and demagogues, he is right. This is a gentleman's machine. The code that governs many other aspects of Virginia's life is particularly relevant here. But if "good government" be defined as one which serves men through general suffrage and manages money as well, then there is little good government in Virginia. The present regime seems to subscribe to a combination of the tough-minded ideas of Alexander Hamilton and Adam Smith.

State expenditures for schools, mental hospitals, and public assistance offer proof. Virginia's schools are among the nation's poorest. Her 1957 average public school salary was almost a thousand dollars under the national average; 45 per cent of those giving up teaching did so to enter other types of employment. Not one of the state's four mental hospitals had in that year been fully approved by the American Psychiatric Association. The expenditure was even less encouraging. Statistics showed that in the field of public assistance, Virginia could not place forty-eighth since Hawaii and Puerto Rico were included in the survey. Virginia ranked fiftieth.[9] No wonder the late Jonathan Daniels, naughty North Carolinian, called Virginia both the cradle and the graveyard of American democracy.

The ability of the Byrd machine to control the state with little overt show of power and little visible corruption impresses political scientists. Much thought and effort are behind this condition. While Governor, Byrd sponsored a "short ballot" which allowed citizens to vote for only three state officials. All the rest would be appointed by the Governor, or his appointees. This centered tremendous power in the Governor. The man he chooses to head the

State Compensation Board fixes salaries and expense allowances for all local state offices. His hand is in the politicians' pocketbooks. A study of the state hierarchy suggests that the real power behind county affairs is the Governor in Richmond, and the real power behind him is the senator in Washington.

In a study published in 1947, Dr. Albert Porter found that the county governments of Virginia had changed little over the decades. Modern auditing and accounting methods had brought some change, but the local political spirit and temper were stable. The two world wars that had altered much of the world drastically had hardly changed the governmental structure of the Old Dominion.[10]

True enough, there have been disagreements "within the family." In 1937 a gubernatorial candidate not backed by the machine (James Price) became Governor. Machine men took a flying leap for Price's bandwagon, then confronted him with a General Assembly which was two to one against him in both branches. Price could push little legislation through. His successor, a machine man, got back on the old track.

In 1949 an anti-organization Democrat, Francis Miller, almost won again. Four years later a Republican, Theodore Dalton, polled 45 per cent of the popular vote. At this critical point in the state's political history, the Supreme Court handed down its 1954 integration decision. This decision gave the machine a "mission," the same one which brought it into being in the late nineteenth century: to save Virginia for the white race.

Senator Harry Byrd called for "massive resistance" to integrated schools. Democrats up and down the line took up the cry. The incredible luck of the machine was continuing; here was an issue that might preserve its power for years.

Making the Democratic party the Segregation party may be good politics, but it forbodes bad history. Future generations of Virginians may study the record of their leaders of the mid-twentieth century not only with regret but with shame.

In 1958 a stunned Virginia read that Senator Byrd had decided, after forty-two years of public service, not to seek re-election. He pointed out that Mrs. Byrd was an invalid, adding, "It is our desire to spend our lives together at home in Virginia." The State Assembly pushed through memorial tributes, and state politicians rushed to Washington to urge "the boss" to stay on. Coyly he agreed to do so. At the same time he urged the state to continue its massive resistance against federal encroachments and racial integration. Apparently the old work horse preferred to die pulling the same old plow.

Mr. Rockefeller could not have taken Williamsburg, nor Mr. Byrd Richmond, without active support from numerous inhabitants. Their motives may have been pure, just as certain consequences of historic and political restoration have been laudable. Yet in the light of thirty years' experience, the scholar must try to evaluate the over-all result.

The main consequence has been the glorification of the past at the expense of the present. While many other parts of America have been obsessed with the future, Virginia's mind has dwelt, too long and too lovingly, on the misty past. They are in effect deteriorationists, believing in the inevitable superiority of former times. They say with George Bagby's *Old Virginia Gentleman:* "I can but think that, since the Colonial and Revolutionary days, each generation has shown a slight falling away from those grand models of men who really existed in Virginia, but whom we have come to look upon almost as myths." The Old Dominion's history, artifacts, and legends have been loved not too wisely, but too well. Too many Virginians have forgotten Jefferson's words: "The earth belongs to the living." They spend their time looking forward to the past.

This is why, when asked to sing a song, the historian of Virginia must sing the Restoration Blues.

23 *The Virginia Lady*

FOR IN VIRGINIA, I CAN BUT REPEAT, WE SHAPE
OUR HISTORY WITH DISCRETION.
James Branch Cabell

She is Virginian in every drop of blood and every pulse beat. Her heart is more open than her mind. Yet even when rigidly set, her agile mind reflects a careful, inconsistent accumulation of prejudices. She is a dogmatist, rather than a doubter; a Rebel, rather than a conformist; a lady, rather than a female. The faults as well as the virtues of the Old Dominion are embodied in whatever she says or does. Call her the Virginia Lady.

If the state's genealogical records were suddenly and irrevocably destroyed, no major crisis would ensue; for she could reproduce most of them from memory.

Visiting her is an extra attraction available to people who live in our town. She probes, pontificates, and slanders with such naturalness, such waspishness, that both her buzzing and her stinging are delightful. One comes to her, as earlier visitors came to the Delphic oracle, not to debate but to listen. What she lacks in logic she makes up in intuition; no education which ignores her insights should be classified as liberal.

Last week I knocked on the Virginia Lady's door and received the customary cordial greeting. Her eyes danced about like those of an agile boxer wondering where he will find his first opening.

Before settling down to business, she presented the obligatory question.

"Can I fix you a highball?"

Experience had taught me the only acceptable answer. "Bourbon and branch, with just a little ice. Not enough to bruise it, though."

"Good! Water's the only companion for good bourbon. Up North they drown it in ginger ale!" She made a wry face, as if she had been made to taste the disgusting Yankee concoction. "I'll be right back."

She returned, handed me my glass, and sat in her white wicker chair. "Well. I'm still recuperating from yesterday." Her opening wedge was in.

"What happened?"

"I spent the day shopping in Big Lick." This is what she insists on calling the city generally known as Roanoke.

"Dreadful place. The people there are so common. Rushing around acting like they're in Chicago. Next year I'll just do without shoes if no local store cares to stock my size."

I laughed nervously. If her mind dwelt long on foreign and hostile places, she might speak of West Virginia. That would infuriate her for days.

She was not through with Roanoke. "Driving over reminded me of the time I gave a reception and was confronted with a guest from Big Lick. She was very plain. Had a name no Virginian ever heard of. The others were *our* people. Of course, we tried to make her feel at home. When my guests came by the lunch table, I said to them, 'Would you care for vichyssoise?' Finally the pride of Big Lick walked over. 'My dear,' I said, 'this is cold potato soup. Would you like some?' But let's get to a pleasanter topic. What are *you* doing this summer?"

"I'm trying to write a history of Virginia."

"Silly fellow. You can't put Virginia history in a book."

"What *can* you put it in?" I asked timidly.

"Oh, I don't know. Maybe in a bottle," she said, pointing toward the fifth of bourbon set at a safe but not unreasonable distance from her chair. "Why do you have to put it in anything? Who doesn't know about our history?"

"Not quite everybody, I suppose. Virginia history books aren't generally best sellers."

"Why should they be? The last one I read claimed that John Smith was a liar and George Washington a drunkard. A Yankee wrote it,

I'm sure. Reading most Northern histories is like being shot at sunrise—twice!"

"Some Southern histories, too," I added. "I've just been taking notes from them."

"There aren't many really Southern books being written these days," the Virginia Lady complained. "Our boys think they have to run off and spend years in New England graduate schools before they know anything about history. When they come back, they can't write an interesting sentence."

Thoughts of my Ivy League training kept back a reply.

"Your book will probably be all right, though."

"Thanks," I said, without much enthusiasm.

"It ought to be. We've had a most interesting history. And you can find wonderful material in the three Johns."

"The three Johns?"

"Certainly. First, Second, and Third John. John Smith, John Esten Cooke, John Fiske. The three Johns."

"Sounds very Biblical," I said. "The three Johns. They were colorful writers, but not much on research. The kind of history they put together has gone out of style."

"I'm afraid you're right," the Virginia Lady sighed. "Just like most other things that made the old days so wonderful. Maybe we live too long. What sort of book are you going to write?"

"A general survey, I suppose you could say. From the Jamestown settlement to the twentieth century. I'm trying to prove—"

"Prove? What are you, an historian or a mathematician?"

"Not exactly prove—point out is better. Point out that we have a way of life."

"Any fool can see that."

"But not everybody's lucky enough to live here. Outsiders don't know how much we have in common."

"*Some* of us have in common, you should say. What do I have in common with those people dashing around the streets of Big Lick?"

I knew better than to try and answer that one. I just smiled pleasantly and waited for her to continue. "Just as I suspected. You're bound and determined to prove a thesis. You young whippersnappers are always looking for a magic formula that explains everything from William Byrd to Harry Byrd. There isn't any such formula."

"No formula; but we have developed a sort of code in Virginia, haven't we?"

"If you mean we have better manners than people in Maryland and West Virginia, of course."

"Not exactly manners, but a whole outlook. A point of view. A—well, it's hard to put into words."

"Naturally. Everything worth saying is. Where do you claim the code came from?"

"It goes way back to the days of knighthood, I suppose. Men like Walter Raleigh and John Smith were really knights-errant. The early immigrants planted ideas as well as tobacco in the seventeenth century. Politics, economics, society, literature—it all went together."

"You're right—along with the dueling code. Wasn't it Thomas Jefferson who backed the legislation outlawing them?"

"I think so. But the duels continued. The mountain feuds are just as real today as they ever were."

"You don't have to go into the hills to find people who defend their honor," the Virginia Lady said. "Grandfather was a second to Algerman Battleheim when he fought George Thomas at Fincastle back in the 1880's. Poor Algerman. Thomas blew off his face."

"Maybe we're just as well off without *that* part of the code. You see what I'm trying to do?"

"Yes. But you won't be able to do it. All you'll describe is the pose. The code is tucked away in the heart, where scholars never enter."

"There ought to be some way to work underneath the surface and the clichés."

"It's easier for the writer or artist than for the historian. Read the three Johns—or Thomas Nelson Page. That's as close as the historian can come." We seemed to be going in circles. I looked discouraged. "But I'm glad you're going to try to do something more than collect statistics. Grandfather used to say there are three kinds of lies—lies, damn lies, and statistics. How can statistics explain why men as different as Lee and Jackson could be loved by so many Virginians at the same time? Or how much we improved our democracy in 1902 by restricting the vote? I suppose you're going to admit that we don't herd all the white trash to the polls, the way the Yankees do?"

"Yes, I'm pointing out that since less than only 11 per cent of the adult population votes in primaries, and 6 per cent for governor—"

"There you go. Statistics! What did I just tell you? That's why you're not going to tell the real truth about Virginia. You'll add up all your figures, and announce that we aren't as democratic as Massachusetts. Next you'll lambast the Byrd machine. There isn't a state in the Union as basically satisfied with the way it's being run as Virginia. Don't all the country people like Mr. Byrd?"

"Yes, but the cities don't. Up around Arlington—"

"That's not Virginia. Virginia starts at Fredericksburg. We ought to lop off these northern counties and give them to the Yankee bureaucrats who live there. People in the real cities, like Richmond and Danville and Petersburg—the ones that amounted to something in General Lee's day—are very content with Mr. Byrd. And so am I."

So much for politics. I sipped away at my highball and waited for her to charge another rampart.

"You do *like* Virginia, don't you?"

"I certainly do."

"And didn't you defend it when you were studying up North?"

"Against all comers."

"I thought so. It's always that way. You don't really know what you think of a place until you're somewhere else. That's why Virginians are always trying to come home. We fuss about conditions when we're here. But nowhere else ever seems good enough after you've been here a while."

She raised her glass to her lips, let her eyes dwell reassuringly on the still-potent bottle, and allowed her mind to move back two centuries.

"Your generation laughs at us for clinging to the eighteenth century; but why shouldn't we? It was the last one that made sense, and had conventions that matched reality. There was a style in those days, a language that everyone could understand. No matter where they went, civilized people carried that style with them. Not that they imitated one another. There was room for all sorts of variety within the mold. Those were the days." Her eyes were glowing now.

"Take architecture, for example. Can you imagine a style more sensible and graceful than the Georgian? Think of men moving out into the American wilderness and building manor houses like Westover and Shirley. And, not so long afterward, writing documents like the Virginia Constitution and the Declaration of Independence. Why shouldn't descendants of those men be proud?"

"Of course you should. My point is that times change. We have to work out new ways to build and write, so we can do the kind of job they would want us to."

"Change. Bah. The ugly Industrial Revolution had to come and ruin everything. What's so good about replacing human values with machine values? Would you like to live in Pittsburgh? Or Detroit?"

"I sure wouldn't. But I'm glad I have an automobile to drive around in. Without Detroit, there wouldn't be any."

"Don't give me that argument. I'm too old and too set in my ways to believe in progress, my dear. I'm not impressed with grimy mantraps like New York or Chicago or Pittsburgh, full of smoke-stacks and hoodlums. No wonder people go berserk. If a planter had treated his labor the way New Yorkers treat Puerto Ricans, neighbors would have driven him out of Virginia. And they say *we* were inhuman! Imagine that. If you knew more about horses, you wouldn't be so fond of automobiles in the first place.

"But I'm not so silly as to argue against change. Of course history moves on. Else we wouldn't have come to the New World in the first place. The trouble is that people try to force change down other people's throat, and that doesn't work. The New England abolitionists never learned that. Neither has the Supreme Court." Sooner or later I knew we'd get on integration—and here we were. "They don't look like stupid people. Can't they see that the more they force us to integrate on the surface, the more we'll segregate underneath?"

"I'm sorry, I don't quite know what you mean."

"The South will tolerate the Negroes as a race, but push them aside as individuals. This is the real tragedy. Instead of knowing each other and judging each other as individuals, the way they have for three hundred years, both the whites and Negroes will think in terms of race. Let me ask you this, young man. Do any colored people take communion at your church? Do you ever have a Negro preach?"

"No."

"When I was a young girl, we all came to the same altar rail. And the Negro preacher came over regularly to preach. And I don't mind telling you, he was the best preacher in town. Maybe the only Christian."

I almost dropped my glass. She kept talking.

"I don't notice any interchange of pulpits today, and not much mutual understanding, either. How many Negro families in this town do you really know? I mean, know about their background, and their problems, and all the little things you have to understand before you can sit down for an afternoon and talk?"

"Not many." She had a good point. I read and wrote about Southern Negroes. I saw them every day. But after the usual guarded
pleasantries, I moved back hastily into the white world. I didn't
really deal with them often as individuals.

"I know dozens. We understand each other. God made us different
colors, and gave us different places in life. But as individuals, we're
integrated. We have a whole lot more in common with each other
than with those julep-sipping Yankees who bought up the county
and dress up like circus clowns and try to ride horses every Saturday
afternoon. After all, we belong here, you know. We *are* Virginia."

"Gosh," I said, "you ought to be writing the book about Virginia.
I could tack on a bibliographical note at the end."

She laughed, and shook her head. "I already know all the history
I want to know, and have enough people to talk to in town to keep
me busy. As a matter of fact, I'm talking so much that I'm not being
much of a hostess. Let me freshen up your drink."

She took our two glasses and headed back for the ice tray. When
she reached the door she stopped, turned around imperiously, and
gave me her final thought on the plight of present-day Virginia.

"What Virginia needs," she said, "is less Ph.D's and more F.F.V.'s."
Then she fixed two strong drinks.[1]

24 *Jamestown Revisited*

DREAMS TREASURED UP FROM EARLY DAYS,
THE HOLY AND THE TENDER.—*William Wordsworth*

The last time I was here, Jamestown didn't amount to much. After seeing the ruins of the old church and the excavated foundations, visitors had to depend on markers, imagination, and a National Park Service guide to tell the island's story. A few remnants of the 1907 Tricentennial Celebration and two statues remained. This was no enduring city.

There was a note of quiet sadness. History had made a short, dramatic stand here, then moved on forever. Only the guide and the insects broke through the blanket of calm.

In 1957 there is more of everything—more noise, more people, more planning. A multimillion-dollar Jamestown Festival draws thousands of visitors a day. Twice as many people work for the Festival as sailed to Jamestown in 1607. The prevailing note has changed from sadness to insistence. Jamestown has been revived, revamped, and put gloriously on display.

Not only here, but for miles around, the tempo has quickened. Tidewater has learned to advertise with billboards, restaurants, motels, restored plantations, and churches. Owners of Georgian manor houses like Berkeley and Shirley not only welcome visitors; they entice them with slogans and suggestions. So, alas, do the

262

churches. "Ancient," "original," and "olde" are Tidewater clichés. Of all the signs, this one disturbs me most:

Sleep Tonight in an Early
Virginia Plantation
Vacancy

Glancing down the macadam road to the Manor-turned-motel, one expects to see Jacobin chimneys or Georgian balustrades. But no—only the gingerbread decoration and spindle railings of the late Victorian. There should be a limit, in a free country, to the freedom of historic interpretation. Freedom is not a synonym for license.

Driving from Richmond to Jamestown brings to mind Gertrude Stein's quip: "Virginia is uninhabited." Despite numerous tourist traps, the peninsula is really as lonely as ever. The land is still sandy, flat, and worn out. Scraggly pine trees flourish. The heat beats down mercilessly from April to October. Mosquitoes patrol in squadrons. My sympathy is with the first settlers. They were men who had boldness in their blood. Along the dirt roads and clearings are Negroes, darker than those in Washington or Richmond. Patriarchs sit by shacks marked with the heavy hand of poverty. Not many of their sons sit beside them. They pass me in two-tone convertibles, proud trophies of shipyard jobs and installment plans. Glistening chromobiles rest in the clearings, rainbow-bright and incongruous in front of unpainted shacks.

Prosperity, but not equality, has engulfed eastern Virginia. "White" and "colored" signs hang in restaurants, filling stations, motels. Men build memorials more easily than they alter mores.

The Festival Park memorials, I soon discover, have been well built. This is no seventeenth-century Coney Island. On thirty acres of Glass House Point, a mile from Jamestown, an Old World Pavilion commemorates the spread of English-speaking civilization; and a New World Pavilion, Virginia's part in it. A. H. Midgley designed the pavilions. Albert Bell rebuilt austere and triangular James Fort. Replicas of the *Susan Constant, Godspeed,* and *Discovery* are tied up at a nearby wharf. There is a note of authenticity on every side.

Most of the buildings and displays are permanent installations. When the Jamestown Festival Commission completes its functions, the state will establish a state historical area here. For this Lewis A. McMurran is largely responsible. He sponsored the bill which proposed the Festival and headed the commission which planned it.

Festival Park and Jamestown Island are joined by a new causeway, into which went 500,000 yards of fill. On the island's southwest tip, the most historic spot, is a handsome new Visitors' Center. Here, lectures, film strips, dioramas, and other modern techniques are used in the effort to make the past live again. Judging from the comment of a young visitor just leaving—"It's almost as good as a TV spectacular"—the Center does the job well. But before moving into the air-conditioned comfort, I walk over toward the swampy marshes. I prefer to see history out of doors. In the brazen July sun, I wipe the sweat from my eyes, glare out at the dank uninhabited island, and have a thrilling thought about this unpromising place:

In these swamps was planted the seed of the physical, spiritual, and moral power of the United States of America. This malarial suburb of the Old World became, under God, the gateway to the New.

Men died to make this so. I don't mind sweating while I remember.

"Explorers" fits the first Englishmen better than "settlers." They knew not where they came. This urge to move beyond maps sent John Smith to Pennsylvania, William Byrd to Eden, Alexander Spotswood to the Blue Ridge, Lewis and Clark to the Pacific, Richard Byrd to the Antarctic. These and others Virginians moved on, carrying their inheritance with them. They established the plantations and country squirearchy on which much of the Old South was modeled. Their state assumed unmistakable leadership in the crises of the Revolution, the new Republic, and the Confederacy. They helped to lay out and people the agrarian West, spreading Jeffersonian principles which men like Jackson and Lincoln vigorously endorsed. They kept going.

Hence Virginians, who lack many things, have an abundance of great memories. They frequently look back on their past, and wherever they look they see heroes. Heroes exist because their people want and need them. Heroes satisfy emotional and psychological needs, and reflect social and racial ideals. They are the mirrors in which people see their own image, magnified.

The Old Dominion's achievement is almost written in the overlapping lives of a half-dozen men. This gives consistency and unity to the state's story. The way to understand Virginia is to know those six men.

They are not the Deep South's heroes. Andrew Jackson, John C. Calhoun, Jefferson Davis, Ben Tillman, and Huey Long have little Virginia following. The Civil War binds Virginia to Dixie; but

Virginians see it as the heroic effort of the Army of Northern Virginia to defend the homeland from Yankee invaders. The Solid South is largely a figment of historians' imagination.

The men Virginia loves most—Smith, Henry, Washington, Lee, Stuart, Jackson—are code men, who add to the Decalogue a complex eleventh commandment concerning honor. They have the habit of command, and depend not so much upon the power of truth as upon the beauty of conduct. They are irrationally fond of everything Virginian. The forum and the tented field are places in which they excel. They are more Spartan than Athenian, men of action rather than men of ideas, personifying solidity, integrity, and simplicity. In such traits their code and their immortality are imbedded. Other Virginians were more brilliant and imaginative, but less revered. Intellectuals like Thomas Jefferson, John Taylor, John Marshall, and Woodrow Wilson belong more to the nation than to the Commonwealth. In their own state, they are admired more than they are loved.

Northern intellectuals have trouble understanding the Virginia preference. So it was when Henry Adams had as his Harvard College roommate Robert E. Lee's son Rooney. "The habit of command was not enough, and the Virginian had little else," wrote Adams. "He was simple beyond analysis; so simple that even the simple New England student could not realize him. No one knew enough to know how ignorant he was; how childlike; how helpless before the relative complexity of a school. He had no intellectual training; he could not analyze an idea; nor even conceive of one."

In this Adams was right: Virginians are not much given to analysis. The state, and indeed the whole South, has never produced an important school of thinkers, men of logic and metaphysics—perhaps because their deep-rooted tradition suggests that this is not how to arrive at the real truth.[1] Close, scientific analysis destroys but does not explain. The butterfly pinned to the wall does not explain the beautiful spectacle of the butterfly in flight. Don't think, believe.

In this Adams was wrong: Virginians are not helpless before complexities or weak in adversity. Their idol will not shine in a salon or soiree atmosphere; his writings will lack subtleties and nuances. Yet if asked to push on when others are exhausted, he will advance. If asked to risk his life by charging when others retreat, he will charge. If saddled with a job for which he is inadequate, he will somehow bear the load. With decency and determination he will toil without complaining and, in a supreme test, die without faltering.

To the outside observer, this determination smacks of stubbornness. Men did not enjoy running head on into a military opinion of Stonewall Jackson, or a political decision of Woodrow Wilson. Some have gone so far as to say Virginians are clan minded and snobbish. Mississippian William Faulkner made the allegation, but took the barb out, while at the University of Virginia in 1957 as writer-in-residence. "I came because I like your country, Virginia, and Virginians," the Nobel prize winner told reporters. "Virginians are all snobs. A snob spends so much time being a snob he has none left to bother other people."

Virginius Dabney, editor of the Richmond *Times-Dispatch*, knew no reason for Virginians to hide their light under a bushel basket. "We Virginians modestly admit our superiority to citizens of all other American states. We can handle a Northerner without half trying, whether it be inside the squared circle, at the brass rail, or with derringers at ten paces."[2] Such self-assurance allows Virginians to rationalize inconsistencies and perpetuate attitudes that otherwise might disappear. At times Virginians invoke the Deity as a witness that they are, and are meant to be, specially blessed. Speaking at the 1907 Jamestown Celebration, Thomas Nelson Page said: "It has been well said that God acts through His prepared agencies; that He prepared Virginia to place the seal of His favor on, and the Virginia colonists and their successors as His instruments to accomplish His mighty work."

Virginians may have set the national pattern in the seventeenth and eighteenth centuries; they certainly do not in the twentieth. Recent students of American character emphasize feverish pace, low political morals, two-party politics, and cult of the future. Reverse these and you have what Virginians stress: a leisurely pace, high political morals, one-party politics, and cult of the past. A. M. Schlesinger generalizes about our "mingled population"; but we cannot heed him in a state in which 98 per cent of the people are natives. Vertical mobility, mechanical inventiveness, wastefulness, and rebelliousness are not conspicuous in Virginia. Allan Nevins lists motor restlessness, passion for money, racial heterogeneity, and equalitarianism as American traits. Not so in Virginia. Henry Commager sees America as the land of experimentation, rudeness, and social equality. By reversing his list—lack of experimentation, studied politeness, and social inequality—we see Virginia. The standard accounts of America give little insight into the ways of the Old Dominion.

The reason for this cannot be put into a few, or many, words. It has to do not only with a people's economy and politics and history, but with their most precious possession, tradition. Tradition is the distilled essence of experience—what fathers tell sons and mothers whisper to daughters. Cherished memories are preserved not only by law or literature, but by beliefs and attitudes. Tradition is slow to form and slower to die. Men protect it like precious crown jewels.

Virginia's jewels are scattered far and wide. Each region has its own ecology, each town its local variations. Tidewater emphasizes colonialism, English ways, and Georgian building. Piedmont favors ante-bellum days, the Virginia Dynasty, and Greek Revival architecture. The Scotch-Irish and Germans in the Valley have their own historical patterns, family farms, and convictions. Southwestern Virginia stresses log cabin culture, mountain ballads, and new industries. Yet inhabitants of all these regions have something in common. They are *Virginians*.

The state is close-knit because the families are self-contained and clannish. These are parochial land-rooted people of a continuous social character composed of the same kind of families and attitudes. Virginia is a vast cousindom. Second and third cousins are known, visited, and accepted as a necessary part of life. Large families have always been the rule. A state-wide interlocking kinship does more to foster Virginia-centeredness than any other factor. Mass media notwithstanding, the favorite indoor sport in Virginia is still climbing about on the family tree.

Douglas Southall Freeman claimed, in a much-quoted passage, that Virginia practices "a mild form of Shintoism."[3] Not with the noun "Shintoism," but with the adjective "mild," would the student of Virginia quarrel. Dr. Freeman, who doffed his hat whenever he passed Lee's statue on Monument Avenue, hardly meant this as a criticism of his native state. Though Virginians admit dangers in ancestor worship, they are quick to point out satisfactions. It gives them a sense of belonging that the wealthiest newcomer can't buy. Never mind if grubbers in dusty archives "expose" family claims and "myths" about Cavalier ancestry. None of the documents can do away with the fact that Virginians have believed in their ancestors, and acted out their lives accordingly. Not Roland or Charlemagne or King Arthur himself behaved more like the medieval knight than did Lee, Jackson, and Stuart. Not all the ink in America can blot out their memory and achievement.

This is what Virginians believe, and what they tell their children. The vast majority of them have received their basic education without benefit of much formal schooling. Their English folk heritage—the language, King James Bible, home, agricultural and political folklore, sense of ritual and property—have sufficed. With these they have survived and increased despite all adversities; found prosperity and peace by grafting Indian shoots on the old English branches.

No story illustrates the prevailing attitude better than one about the education of Daniel Boone, hero of Virginia's frontier epoch. Uncle John Boone attempted to turn Daniel to bookish ways, but was forced to give up in despair. When he appealed to Daniel's father, Squire Boone took his son's side in the argument. "Let the girls do the spelling," said the father, "and Dan will do the shooting."[4]

Virginia's famous Revolutionary leaders, whose words and deeds lent glory to their times, are praised by many who do not realize that only two of these Founding Fathers (Jefferson and Madison) had much formal schooling.

The Virginia Dynasty wrought more change in their nation than in their state. In the 1830's almost a third of the adult white population of Virginia was illiterate. Teaching Negroes to read was prohibited by law. Not until 1870 was a state public school system adopted. The prevailing attitude toward it was summarized in the May, 1870, number of the *Virginia Educational Journal*: "The people of this state have consented under the persuasive influence of the bayonets of the U.S. government to make trial of a mode of education against which their judgment and observation have for years revolted. We must swallow the dose now."

Actually the dose was not swallowed in that year or generation. Only with the inclusion of a compulsory school provision in the 1902 state constitution was a true beginning made. The compulsory law applied to those "between the ages of eight and twelve years, except such as are weak in body or mind, or can read and write, or are attending private schools, or are excused for cause by the district trustees." Helping set out the tobacco plants or planting corn was often "cause" enough. In 1906 there were still only ten four-year high schools in the entire state.

Opposition to public instruction continued long after the law required it. The Reverend Robert Lewis Dabney, an intellectual leader of post-bellum Virginia, argued that free schools were unchristian and communistic. They would demoralize the Negroes, and make Virginians meaner than Mexicans and Yankees. Public instruction has always been an uphill battle in the state. As late as 1958, Dr. Ralph Cherry, dean of the graduate school of education at the University of Virginia, said in a public speech: "We're at the stage now in teacher education in Virginia where medical education was in 1910. They were in a mess."

Having surveyed the history of state education since Reconstruction, Francis B. Simkins concluded that the imported instructional devices and the imported dietary prescriptions have not altered the basis thought patterns or eating habits of Virginia's children. For example, Virginians' attitude toward the problem of race is basically the same in the day of Harry Bryd as it was in the day of Thomas Jefferson or Robert E. Lee. "The school has not lived up to the revolutionary intentions of Horace Mann and other reformers. It has not leveled off class distinctions. Fundamental changes of habits have not taken place among the millions of Virginians who go to public school."[5]

The reluctance to join the New Order may not be remedied by sending many teachers off to graduate school and changing textbooks. The people can be wiser than the educators. The instinctive drives to retain ancestral folkways may be Virginia's salvation. They are sound bases for happiness and creativity.

The pervasive tone of Virginia's thought for generations has been anti-intellectual. Poets, thinkers, logicians have never been admired like the soldier, politician, or preacher. "Why do you waste your time on a damned thing like poetry?" a neighbor demanded of Philip Pendleton Cooke. "A man of your position might be a useful man." In the spring of 1876, Ralph Waldo Emerson visited the University of Virginia to speak on "The Natural and Permanent Function of the Scholar." Soon the impatient students were squirming, sighing, and "making gestures indicative of pain." The pandemonium increased. Poor Mr. Emerson turned over six pages at a time. He found out, first hand, that young Cavaliers are not very scholarly fellows.

Public library statistics confirm this. When World War I ended, Virginia had no regional libraries, no county libraries, and only twenty-two town libraries. Five years later, the state public libraries contained an estimated 165,000 volumes, to which less than 2 per cent of the rural population had access. By World War II, that percentage had reached 30. Though this paid silent tribute to people who did fine work with meager resources, it also indicated that less than a third of the people in a rural state could draw readily upon any public library.

The history of the *Reviewer,* a literary journal published in Richmond during the 1920's, is a further illustration. The excellent review was acclaimed in New York, London, and Tokyo, but not in Richmond. One New York editor listed it among the dozen most important English or American reviews, and another saw in it "the beginning of a great Southern literary renaissance." Virginians were not impressed. The four editors, all members of upper-class Richmond society, let the magazine go by default to the richer literary soil of North Carolina. James Branch Cabell, a contributor, had the last word. "Our Virginia writers are not perfect, we may admit tentatively, inasmuch as we never went so far as to read their books; even so, these writers are ours, and we do not care to have them dispraised by outsiders."

His comment points up Virginia's pride which, in the final analysis, ranks as her cardinal sin. The state's history, politics, and landscape contain illustrations. Walk down that most Virginian of streets, Richmond's Monument Avenue, where the defeated Southern generals and their obstinate Confederate president sit majestically atop their marble pinnacles; it is as though they had learned nothing from the bloodletting. Pride shows through Virginia's interpretation of the war; for her citizens view operations in other theaters as a kind of side show. They fail to see that the hills around Chattanooga and Vicksburg were important, as were those around Richmond and Gettysburg. Pride enveloped the greatest Confederate soldier, Lee, who dressed impeccably with full trim and red sash when he went to surrender. Most incredible of all, one sees the pride of the men who fought under him, but would not come back to their native state when it needed them most. As a traveler in Texas pointed out in 1882, "It was not yet the fashion for young Virginians of good family to engage in hard, rough work near their homes."[6]

Here is a self-respect and honor complex that derives vicarious pleasure from tragedy and makes even the intelligentsia anti-intellectual. Here is the reason that so far as Virginians are concerned, their history is made not by men but gentlemen, and their Negroes (except for the "uppity" ones who had best go North) are quite happy under the old dispensation. Here is the closed communion, where new problems call forth rationalizations rather than solutions.

Such pride tends to destroy one's sense of humor and proportion. Any attempt to revise or reinterpret the Accepted Version is regarded not as good scholarship but as poor taste. An attempt at popular interest by the historian is often regarded as frivolous. What outsiders call folklore or legend has another name in Virginia—the truth.

Pride is not an unmixed evil, and may be a sinew of the soul. Without it, little is sustained in life or given a full measure of human meaning. Flourishing traditions rest on the land, the folk, and the relationship between the two. One strength is of the earth, one of the human spirit. Together they bring wholeness and meaning to life.

When the connection with the earth is lost, so is the power to feel deeply. Like trees that must be moved, men are uprooted. Virginians have held on to their land. They have not often intellectualized this love, but they have felt it. When necessary, they have defended the soil with their lives, making of pride the *amour propre*.

I hope this is not merely another rationalization. I would not deny that Virginians are as lonely and sinful as all men everywhere. Not only morally, but politically, are they tied inextricably to the world picture. What happens in Algiers and Tokyo affects Richmond and Big Stone Gap. Aspirins and anxieties heed no boundary lines.

Some Virginians have lined up for battle; many others line up in front of the A.B.C. (Alcoholic Beverage Control) stores to buy bottled solutions for their many problems. The historian of Virginia should point to the long A.B.C. lines, and the large percentage of Negroes in them. They have less to spend, but more to forget.

I have said too little of Virginians' shortcomings; too little of rusticity which becomes provincialism and tradition which becomes archaism. For all this, Virginia is a place of fascinating, struggling people, acting like one ingrown family, for better and (not infrequently) for worse.

They live in code country. Those who believe in it sometimes have a firm grip on their elusive mortality. They go about the business of living out their lives without whining or despairing. They die cherishing the one thing which cannot be taken away from them—an honorable ending.

Such a man was George Washington. In schoolbooks he became

a prudish paragon. In real life he was imperfect enough to swear like a trooper and fall in love with Sally Fairfax, wife of his good friend and neighbor. Whatever his faults, he proved that men can snatch victory from disaster, if only they will believe and persevere. Knowing this, Virginians have done what the father of their country did—built homes, tilled the fields, raised up succeeding generations, and ended their lives with hope of everlasting life.

They did this, and were content, because they believed not only in what had been, but what was and would be. A future worthy of them is to be gained not by doting on memories, but by doing those things which have been proven right and necessary.

Very few of us who purport to be historians know much about history; but everything we do know indicates that history is incapable of running backward. As we survey twentieth-century Virginia, we are not so concerned with the flaws as the inflexibility. How can leaders who know and intuit so much not realize that a constant posture of looking backward is a sign of stagnation? When the responsible default, the irresponsible take over. This will be the sad case if Virginia leaders continue to preach "massive resistance" and defiance of moderate alteration.

History and tradition should liberate, not enslave. This is the message, and the hope, of Virginia.

Appendix

CLIO IN BONDAGE: HISTORY WRITING IN VIRGINIA

Forging a tradition is a communal undertaking. Recording it is an act of faith. Virginia history has been written with the heart as well as the head, filled with "goodly trees and faire meadows." Since the audience of the state's early historians was partly an Old World audience, they wrote vividly, so they would be well received abroad. Colonial volumes were secular in tone, unmoved by questions which troubled New England divines.

Nor were their accounts ostentatious. As Louis B. Wright notes in *The First Gentlemen of Virginia,* it was no more proper for a gentleman to display his erudition (as did Cotton Mather, for example) than it was to appear at a dance stripped of his shirt. Their goal was broad and breathtaking history, which tended to read like fiction —and indeed sometimes was. Their books were bought, admired, and remembered. Not all the scientific historians of a later day can claim as much.

Virginia's historians up to the Civil War did not alter the basic premises which they inherited from their predecessors. In the late nineteenth century, however, ideas on history writing changed. The new program was imported from the seminars of Germany. History must be written, the scholarly and influential Leopold von Ranke

insisted, "as it actually happened." Facts must "speak for themselves." Although Ranke was never able to achieve such objectivity
himself, he sent his students away determined to find it. They would
dissect every scrap of information; produce somber, solid, and
definitive monographs. All available material must be exhausted.
As it turned out, the reader, not the material, was usually exhausted.

The Johns Hopkins University in Baltimore championed the new
methodology. Historian Herbert B. Adams trained many Virginians
in the graduate school there (sometimes called "Adams' Seminary"),
and wrote two Virginia monographs himself. By 1900, Hopkins-
trained historians had published over seven hundred books and
articles on the South. The *Virginia Magazine of History and Biography* was founded in 1892 partly at their instigation. A Johns Hopkins graduate, Henry McIlwaine, reorganized the Virginia State
Library in 1903. Objectivity became the new motto.

Alexander Brown and Philip A. Bruce were among the first successful practitioners of the new style. Brown, who lost his hearing
while serving with the Confederate army, spent much of his life
collecting historical documents. He specialized in the first decade
of the Jamestown settlement. In order to do so, he practiced a rigid
economy and exemplified unselfish devotion to his self-appointed
task. His mountain of information did not make him objective, however.[1] He came to feel that the liberals in the London Company had
been badly treated by members of the King and Court party, who
falsified records, discredited well-meaning colleagues, and suppressed
the truth. Sir Edwin Sandys was Brown's special hero; he came to
write of Sandys' enemies as though they were his personal opponents.
Brown could be as caustic as Captain John Smith, whom he disliked
intensely. *New Views of Early Virginia History* and *English Politics
in Early Virginia History* summarize Brown's opinions. Not only
was he a collector, but an interpreter, of the beginnings of the Old
Dominion.

More influential was Philip A. Bruce, the father of scientific history in Virginia. Bruce, a man of independent means, wanted to describe "the purely economic condition of Virginia in detail." His
ponderous *Economic History of Virginia in the Seventeenth Century*
and *Institutional History of Virginia in the Seventeenth Century*
typify Germanic scholarship at its best. Although he did not accept
the Cavalier myth, Bruce pointed to "many evidences that a large
number of the immigrants sprang from English families of substance." Behind his well-mustered facts dwells the nostalgia for

"spacious days of the old landed aristocracy."

Like many Virginians, Bruce had a habit of moving off into "if only" land. If only Charles I had come to Virginia . . . if only Virginia had freed her slaves . . . if only Longstreet had moved quickly at Gettysburg. If only the Indians had not perpetrated the Great Massacre of 1622, Bruce stated, Virginia would have had a college much older than Harvard. Then, as he speculated in his *Institutional History,* "Virginia would have possessed a foundation that would have been clothed with the deeply romantic interest thrown around the college of the Old World by the beautifying touch of time and by the glorious achievements of their sons on every stage of action." If only—

The Virginia Plutarch, considered Bruce's masterpiece, proves that he was a hero-worshiper, and that Virginia was his Olympus. He claims for his paragons the homage he felt was rightfully theirs, giving classic dignity to lives he thought "Plutarchian in proportion." Neither in conception nor execution is this volume "scientific."

A number of younger "objective" historians were dubious about Bruce's stress on heroes and his pious conclusions. Among these was Thomas Jefferson Wertenbaker, who after World War I specialized in the history of colonial Virginia. A native of Charlottesville, he attended Mr. Jefferson's University and received one of its first doctorates in history. A chief target in his early books was the Cavalier myth. He maintained the early Virginians were not aristocrats by birth; the aristocracy which rose up was grown from New World soil: "On its economic side it was built up by the system of large plantations; politically it was engendered by the lack of a vigorous middle class and sustained by the method of appointment to office; socially it was fostered by the increasing wealth of the planters and by the ideal of the English gentleman."[2]

Patrician and Plebeian in Virginia, Planters of Colonial Virginia, and *Virginia Under the Stuarts* dispelled the romantic haze in which earlier writers had encompassed Virginia's beginning. Because his style was better than that of most of his contemporaries, and because his material was jarring, Wertenbaker was much read and quoted.

Virginians were less vocal now about their blue-blooded past. What a shame that the early writers had to be refuted by document-diggers. William Byrd had said the inhabitants of Virginia "consist mostly of English gentlemen, who keep many farm laborers and slaves." John Fiske called them "picked men and women of excellent sort," who had Drake's daring, Elizabeth's shrewdness, and Shakespeare's wit. Ships bound for Virginia, romantic historians had implied, were packed to the bowsprits with Prince Rupert's men, lads who would sheath their swords only for lack of argument. Now these romantic illusions were being shattered by irreverent scholars who were searching out distasteful facts.

Having swung too far to the right, the pendulum now veered to the left. Writers trained to see trees, but not forests, drew wrong conclusions from right evidence. "If we work with particular attention to things as they were," wrote researcher George Willison, "we will find they were seldom what they seemed, and almost never as first reported." Facts would be forced to do what facts never have done and never can do—speak for themselves.

Willison marshaled his researches. The first Virginians were dissipated sots, still smelling of the stews and grogshops of London; or they were "homeless children picked up on London streets, lewd women from the Bridewell and other houses of correction, 'mayds' gathered for sale as wives, vagrants and unemployed."[3] Proud of his discovery of specific and little-known materials about their past, Willison missed the drama and gamble of their voyage. He called their safe arrival "an incredible stroke of luck," failing to note Admiral Newport's demonstrable achievement. Under Captain John Smith, Willison says, the story passes beyond belief to the point of madness. Smith is too complex, and too inconsistent, for him to handle. So, indeed, is the whole spirit of the Elizabethan age.

The next step was to revise the revisionists. Working at Wertenbaker's Charlottesville alma mater, John Manahan produced a doctoral thesis which challenges the claims of *Patrician and Plebeian in Virginia*.[4] Studies by Wilcomb Washburn, Edna Jensen, and others point to serious errors in the "objective" summary of recent years.[5] Perhaps, as Manahan suggests, the Cavalier will be remounted. The day may come when the dusty volumes by the romantics will be brought down from the attic and placed in the parlor.

If that happens, they must find a place beside sets by Douglas Southall Freeman, a man of huge reputation. Freeman was the authority on *the* war, and on *the* general who led the "Lost Cause." No scientific historian has been so carefully read and readily believed. He dwelt in Richmond, Plutarch on the James, surrounded by a vast and uncritical admiration unparalleled in modern historiography.

Freeman, too, was trained at the Johns Hopkins seminars. Journalism was his vocation, and he edited the Richmond *News-Leader*.

Real fame came from his avocation, history. His first books were those of the apprentice learning his trade: *Calendar of Confederate Papers* and *Lee's Dispatches.* After years of collecting and studying, he was ready to write his life of Lee.

The resulting four-volume *R. E. Lee,* supplemented by his three-volume *Lee's Lieutenants,* made Freeman an undisputed authority. The detailed volumes revivified, lastingly and lovingly, a major figure in America's past. Unlike his less gifted colleagues, Freeman had a theory and a model for his work: "My own theory of historical presentation is the result of many reflections and the study of many models. I owe most to Boswell's life of Johnson."[6]

He also had a decided opinion about biographers who let their opinions color the story: "The biographer, like the dramatist, has no place on the stage. When he has made his bow to his audience and has spoken his prelude, telling what he will try to exhibit, he must retire to the wings, to raise the curtain and to leave the play to the actors."[7]

Yet Dr. Freeman did not leave the stage, and he did not write objectively. Gracefully, eloquently, powerfully—but not objectively. Indeed, he was the most Virginian of them all.

His many admirers would disagree with this, and point to his detached "fog of war" technique. This device required the writer to relate only what his subject knew at that time. Since the general couldn't see over the hill or into the future, neither should the reader. Historical figures cannot jump back and fourth from one city or one battle to another; neither should historians. The fog of the unknown must not be lifted. The reader should see just what Lee saw, and no more. This, his supporters argue, is Freeman's great contribution to military history.

But this technique may confuse and mislead. "By insisting on remaining at headquarters with Lee," T. Harry Williams notes, "Freeman fails to give a clear and complete picture of Lee's campaign, and hence of Lee himself."[8] Even well-informed readers can get lost in the fog of Freeman's presentation.

Freeman defenders insist that he is writing biography, not history; that he wants to show Lee in action, rather than the battle of Gettysburg. The "fog of war" should be evaluated, therefore, on how well it shows Lee in action. So insists historian Joseph Harrison, Jr., who rose in shocked wrath when Professor Williams' criticism was published.[9]

Like Lee, Freeman held to the tournament notion of war; but

the Civil War was actually a modern conflict involving total production and whole populations. He was a Virginia gentleman writing movingly about a Virginia gentleman. The result was vivid and perceptive, but hardly objective. There are times when Freeman comes close to saying that what Lee did was right because he was Lee. At critical points in the story, the biographer was not content to stay on the wings of the stage. He violated his own canons.

To point to Freeman's flaws does not diminish his stature or achievement. Everybody has a side in war. Freeman sincerely believed in the greatness of Lee and the valor of Confederates. Virginia may not see his equal in history writing for many a day.

Some of Freeman's conviction was shared by a younger Richmonder, Clifford Dowdey. After graduation from the John Marshall High School after World War I, he spent most of the time between the ages of seventeen and forty in New York City. "Yet, I never wrote about anything except Virginia's past," he has said.[10] "Living in the North so long stimulated the urge to articulate, to define, to preserve the essence of my own people's past. The past of dead people was more compelling to me than the blandness of Hollywood or intellectualism of New York. Such a compulsion would scarcely make for objectivity."

Eventually this self-styled "reformed fiction-writer and fugitive from the money salt-mines" came home, where he now edits *Virginia Record* and acts as semiofficial spokesman for his state in magazines and anthologies. His research, by his own say, is in breadth rather than depth. "I have a passionate feeling about my own people; I've tried in novels, stories, articles, and history to present their story as truly as God gave me the vision to see truth. I don't write to impress historians; I write to be read." A diligent worker, currently Clifford Dowdey is at work on a trilogy on the personalities of Lee's armies. The first volume, *Death of a Nation,* appeared in 1958.[11]

History, being a communal concern, must be written and read by many people less articulate than Bruce, Wertenbaker, Freeman, or Dowdey. These are soldiers who carry out the plans of the general staff. They write state, county, local, or family histories, or merely attend meetings in which these matters are discussed. Week after week, in their unspectacular way, they wage war against oblivion and forgetfulness.

Two striking facts about historical and patriotic organizations in Virginia are that they have grown rapidly in the twentieth century and that the control of them to a large extent is wielded by their female members.

The most venerated organization is the Association for the Preservation of Virginia Antiquities, founded in 1889 "to acquire, restore, and preserve the ancient historic grounds, monuments, and tombs in the Commonwealth of Virginia." Mrs. Fitzhugh Lee was the first of a line of ladies who have served as president. The A.P.V.A. owns the historical tip of Jamestown Island, the Mary Washington house, the John Rolfe property, the Williamsburg Powder Horn, the Cape Henry lighthouse, and other shrines. A sister organization, the Society of Colonial Dames in Virginia, has somewhat similar objectives: "to preserve manuscripts, traditions, relics, and mementos of bygone days, to restore buildings connected with our early history, and to teach the sacred obligation of honoring the memory of historic ancestors." Only those who are descended from "ancestry of worthy life who resided in an American colony prior to 1750" are eligible for membership.

The founding of the Daughters of the American Revolution in 1890 was a milestone both in the growth of interest in history and in the battle of the sexes. The Sons of the American Revolution precipitated a crisis by voting to exclude women. "Were there no mothers in the Revolution?" became the rhetorical battle cry of the excluded feminine patriots. Their answer was the D.A.R., which soon overshadowed the parent organization in self-assertion and power.

Nor could the United Confederate Veterans maintain their position once the ladies took the offensive. At the 1906 U.C.V. annual convention, General Stephen Lee reported that 412 of the 569 local clubs were in arrears, lost beyond recovery.

But the Lost Cause had been found by other champions. The newly formed United Daughters of the Confederacy moved their batteries of speakers, fund raisers, and apologists into position. Towns which were only railroad whistle stops supported two U.D.C. chapters, carrying on a friendly but brisk rivalry. Only the bravest of men dare cross the path of the U.D.C., which in 1958 could boast of over a hundred Virginia chapters and 5,000 dues-paying, Confederacy-proud members.

These ladies, like the Vestal Virgins of ancient times, have been the keepers of the sacred flame. Women's clubs have fought the local skirmishes while larger state organizations have fought the major battles. Grass-roots meetings are critical; tradition is no stronger than the local groups which study and record it. Madam Chairman is an important personage in Virginia society.

Women have been especially effective when a shrine has been in danger. They "rescued" Monticello, Stratford, and many lesser places from remodeling or destruction, just as they saved Mount Vernon in the generation before the Civil War. Pamela Cunningham, founder of the Mount Vernon Ladies Association, spoke proudly and definitely about what the gentle sex could do to preserve Virginia's shrines when she retired in 1874: "Let visitors see that though we slay our forests, remove our dead, pull down our churches, move from home to home, let them see that we know how to care for the homes of our heroes."

If Clio has been in bondage, she has had lady jailers. Still, her most widely read captor is Hamilton J. Eckenrode, who wrote many of the state highway-marker texts. Eckenrode was trained at Johns Hopkins University, but the idea for the markers originated in politics rather than in the seminar. Harry F. Byrd's campaign manager during his 1925 gubernatorial campaign was William E. Carson. The two men, lunching at Cuckoo Tavern in Louisa County, noticed a tablet honoring Jack Jouett, whose daring ride saved Jefferson from capture by approaching British cavalrymen. Carson suggested that such markers be erected throughout the state, not only for the benefit of natives but also to accommodate the many tourists. Good markers would be good business.[12]

The future Governor agreed. After his election, he appointed William Carson chairman of the newly created state Commission on Conservation and Development. Subsequently Carson chose Dr. Eckenrode to prepare the marker inscriptions.[13] Merchants, real estate agents, and local historians were enthusiastic. The program expanded during the Depression. That a state which lagged so far behind in social and governmental services would lead in erecting iron markers is a telling comment. There are a lot of projects her politicians will scrimp on—but not on commemorating and extolling the past. On this all parties and cliques agree. Tradition is the Old Dominion's most valuable natural resource.

Thus the state highways have become open-air classrooms; all those who use automobiles must attend. Even the conservatives who have no admiration for the Age of Asphalt insist that the hard-surfaced roads be flanked with historic inscriptions.

It would be interesting to know how many of them are literally true. The past hides its tracks well in the labyrinth of time. While historians side with Pontius Pilate to ask yet again what is truth, most Virginians believe what they want to believe. New techniques and theories arise; they remember the old and venerable legends.

At least two hundred state histories, excluding memoirs, biographies, and genealogies, have been published since 1900. None seemed adequate for public schools to the Virginia History and Government Textbook Commission, established by the General Assembly in 1950. After years of labor by many people, "suitable" texts for the fourth, seventh, and eleventh grades were completed in 1956.

Just what they were suitable for was debatable. Dr. Lawrence Burnette, Jr., a Ph.D. in history from the University of Virginia who served as field editor for the publishing firm which produced two of these textbooks, raised the question in 1957, after his job was completed. Speaking at the Institute of Southern Culture in Farmville, he suggested that the Old Dominion viewed history "as its personal story rather than an impersonal chronicle, equating its own understanding of history with truth. If Virginia is to read a history of itself, this understanding must not be contradicted. Virginia will not listen to self-criticism; it is regarded as a form of mental disorder."[14]

Dr. Burnette went on to point out what careful readers of Virginia history books had already suspected. "The Virginia historical tradition has its own rites and taboos that suggest a religion of narcissism. The goal of the historian has often been to perpetuate past glories and suppress all forms of heresy and schism. Writers and editors of Virginia's missals, apologias, and chronicles would do well to remember that sycophancy is a sin, but apostasy is a mortal sin."

Most of Clio's captors have sinned unintentionally. They have done what they thought right, and have approved of steeping history in romance. Though many ideas and reforms have been trampled upon, their state, captured for the world by swashbuckling Elizabethans, remains the symbol for romance throughout the English-speaking world. The silver thread which unites earth to heaven is still unbroken.

Bibliographical Note

Whole volumes, and very substantial ones, have been prepared about the library of Virginiana which has grown up over the centuries. E. G. Swem's *A Bibliography of Virginia* (Richmond, 1916-17) and *Virginia Historical Index* (Roanoke, 1934-36), and Lester Cappon's *Bibliography of Virginia History Since 1865* (Charlottesville, 1930) are the best of these.

The general reader might find "A Reading List of Selected Books about Virginia," an eleven-page mimeographed list put together by William Rachal, Elizabeth Coleman, and Edwin Hemphill in 1948 for the Virginia Department of Conservation and Development, a better place to begin. This reading list attempts a comprehensive selection of books covering the development of virginia, its people, and its civilization. All periods of time, all sections of the state, and broad aspects of the state's life are included.

As for one-volume histories of the Old Dominion, there has been none in the last half-century to match in literary flavor and charm John Esten Cooke's *Virginia, A History of the People* (Boston, 1884) and Thomas Nelson Page's *The Old Dominion, Her Making and Her Manners* (New York, 1908). The best general summary was made by the Virginia Writers' Project and published in the American Guide Series as *Virginia: A Guide to the Old Dominion* (New York, 1940). Matthew Page Andrews' *Virginia, the Old Dominion,* which appeared three years earlier, is good for the colonial period. In a more popular vein are Agnes Rothery's *Virginia: the New Dominion* (New York, 1940) and Virginia Moore's *Virginia Is a State of Mind* (New York, 1942).

The Old Dominion Foundation sponsored Jean Gottman's *Virginia at Mid-Century* (New York, 1955). The French geographer, who had done studies of various European countries, was asked to "take stock" of Virginia, and has done so in a thoroughly documented study. Meanwhile, Francis B. Simkins, Spotswood Hunnicutt, and Sidman Poole were at work on a state history book for the public schools, which appeared as *Virginia: History, Government, Geography* (New York, 1957). It is an accurate and comprehensive textbook.

Of the various state magazines, the historian will find three that deserve special attention: the *Virginia Quarterly Review*, the *William and Mary Quarterly*, and the *Virginia Magazine of History and Biography*. They are published in Charlottesville, Williamsburg, and Richmond, respectively. In these three cities one finds the only significant libraries and research facilities in the Old Dominion. To them anyone interested in studying the not always predictable actions and attitudes of the *Homo Virginianus* must eventually go.

Among the more specialized publications *Commonwealth* (the monthly journal of the state Chamber of Commerce), *The Virginia Economic Review*, and the *University of Virginia Newsletter* are outstanding. The Richmond *News-Leader* (a 1903 consolidation of the *Evening News* and the *Evening Leader*) and the Richmond *Times-Dispatch* (a 1903 consolidation of the *Times* and the *Dispatch*) give comprehensive news coverage, though the Roanoke *Times* does better by the western counties. See Lester Cappon's *Virginia Newspapers, 1821-1935* (New York, 1936) for earlier newspapers.

Once one starts to choose titles of special studies of periods and figures of Virginia history, the titles quickly mount; since such a list has been prepared, as we pointed out in the second paragraph of this note, there is no point in duplicating it here.

It is hoped that the books mentioned in the notes of this volume will prove valuable to the reader who wants to know more of Virginia. They have been chosen with care, and seem to me the best on the subject under discussion.

Notes

Chapter 1 Into Denser Green

1. See Jarvis M. Morse, "John Smith and his Critics: A Chapter in Colonial Historiography," *Journal of Southern History*, vol. L, 1935. Smith's own writings were edited by Edward Arber and published in 1884. The early years are analyzed in great detail in Alexander Brown's *The First Republic in America* (Boston, 1898) and *The Genesis of the United States* (Boston, 1890), and in Philip A. Bruce's *Institutional History of Virginia in the Seventeenth Century* (New York, 1910). Another excellent study is Herbert L. Osgood's *The American Colonies in the Seventeenth Century* (New York, 1904–7).

2. See especially Dr. Laura Polanyi Striker's study of the Hungarian years, which is printed as Appendix I of Bradford Smith's *Captain John Smith: His Life and Legend* (New York, 1953); and Philip L. Barbour's "Captain John Smith's Route through Turkey and Russia," *William and Mary Quarterly*, vol. XIV, no. 3, July, 1957, pp. 358 f.

3. Carl Carmer, *The Susquehanna* (New York, 1955), Chapter I.

4. George Percy insisted that the man killed her for adultery and ate her to conceal the crime, foreshadowing Lord Dunsany's "Two Bottles of Relish." He had an adequate supply of grain in the house, although he was out of meat.

5. William Strachey, *The Historie of Travaile into Virginia Britannia*, edited by R. H. Major for the Hakluyt Society Publications, no. 6 (London, 1849), p. 53.

6. See Lyman Carrier, *Agriculture in Virginia, 1607–1699* (Richmond, 1957).

7. So concludes George F. Willison in *Behold Virginia: the Fifth Crown* (New York, 1951).

Chapter 2   A Second Start

1. "Good Newes from Virginia, 1623," in *William and Mary Quarterly,* vol. V, April, 1948, pp. 351 f.

2. See Thomas Jefferson Wertenbaker, *The First Americans, 1607–1690* (New York, 1929), and Wesley Frank Craven, *The Southern Colonies in the Seventeenth Century, 1607–1689* (Baton Rouge, 1949).

3. Wilcomb E. Washburn, *Virginia Under Charles I and Cromwell, 1625–1660* (Richmond, 1957), pp. 20 f. See also Edna Jensen, "Sir John Harvey: Governor of Virginia," M.A. thesis, University of Virginia, 1950. Dr. Marvin Schlegel argues that it was the governors, not the councils, that were hamstrung in colonial days; and that Harvey was a bad Governor in the Virginia mythology because he tried to enforce the authority he was supposed to have.

4. These papers were uncovered and used by Wilcomb E. Washburn, who also utilized material in the Pepysian Library, Magdalene College, Cambridge, and the little-known account in the February 23, 1769, *Virginia Gazette.* The above summary of his findings is used with Dr. Washburn's permission.

5. See Abernethy's introduction to the facsimile edition of William Harris' *More News from Virginia* (Charlottesville, 1943).

6. Quoted by Richard B. Davis, "The Devil in Virginia in the Seventeenth Century," *Virginia Magazine of History and Biography,* vol. 65, April 1957, pp. 131 f.

7. See the anonymous pamphlet entitled *Trial of Grace Sherwood for Witchcraft, in Princess Anne Co., Va., 1705-06* (Norfolk, 1854) and "The Witchcraft Delusion Refected" in *Virginia Cavalcade,* summer, 1956, pp. 28 f.

8. So reports Matthew Page Andrews in *Virginia, the Old Dominion* (New York, 1937), Chapter X. The story may well be apocryphal.

9. Quoted by Louis B. Wright in *The First Gentlemen of Virginia* (San Marino, Calif., 1940), p. 109.

Chapter 3   Eden, in Fact

1. Richmond Croom Beatty, *William Byrd of Westover* (Boston, 1932), p. 35. Byrd himself published only a few scattered pieces during his lifetime. He had been dead almost a century when Edmund Ruffin brought out some Byrd pieces in the 1841 *Virginia Farmers' Register.* His secret diaries had to wait even longer for publication.

2. See *The London Diary (1717–1721) and Other Writings,* edited by Louis B. Wright and Marion Tinling (New York, 1958), especially Dr. Wright's introductory essay.

3. Hugh Morrison, *Early American Architecture* (New York, 1952), p. 283.

4. Quoted by Edmund S. Morgan, *Virginians at Home* (Williamsburg, 1952), p. 77.

5. For a catalogue of this remarkable library, the largest in the colonies, see J. S. Bassett's *Writings of Colonial William Byrd,* Appendix A.

6. Louis B. Wright, *The Cultural Life of the American Colonies, 1607–1763* (New York, 1957).

7. Such is the conclusion of Charles S. Sydnor in *Gentlemen Freeholders: Political Practices in Washington's Virginia* (Chapel Hill, 1952).

8. For a detailed account, see T. T. Waterman's *The Mansions of Virginia* (Chapel Hill, 1946).

9. Carl Bridenbaugh, *Myths and Realities* (Baton Rouge, 1952), pp. 17 f.

10. "Quincy Journal," pp. 466–67, quoted *ibid.,* p. 52.

11. See Thomas Jefferson Wertenbaker, *Planters of Colonial Virginia* (Princeton, 1922), p. 160.

12. For an analysis of this apprenticeship, and Byrd's literary views, see Willie T. Weathers, "William Byrd: Satirist," *William and Mary Quarterly,* vol. IV, January, 1947, pp. 27 f.

13. Richmond Beatty, *William Byrd's Natural History of Virginia* (Richmond, 1940), p. xxiv.

14. Douglas Southall Freeman, *George Washington, A Biography* (New York, 1948), vol. I, p. 73.

Chapter 4   The Lonesome Valley

1. Lederer's story is told in John Wayland's *The German Element of Shenandoah Valley of Virginia* (Charlottesville, 1907).

2. D. H. Zigler, *A History of the Brethren in Virginia* (Elgin, Ill., 1908), p. 31.

3. See Willit H. Foote's *Sketches of Virginia, Historical and Biographical* (Philadelphia, 1850), Chapter V.

4. Robert Bailey, *The Life and Adventures of Robert Bailey . . . Interspersed with Anecdotes, and Religious and Moral Admonitions* (Richmond, 1822).

5. R. W. Pettengill, *Letters from America*, quoted in Freeman H. Hart, *The Valley of Virginia in the American Revolution, 1763–1789* (Chapel Hill, 1942), p. 29.

Chapter 5   Liberty or Death

1. Fauquier to Board of Trade, July 8, 1764. A detailed history of this period and its documents may be found in George Bancroft's *A History of the United States, from the discovery of the American Continent* (Boston, 1834–75), vol. II.

2. For a detailed account of the last days of English rule, see W. Hugh Moomaw, "The British Leave Colonial Virginia," *Virginia Magazine of History and Biography*, vol. 66, April, 1958, pp. 147 f.

3. Charles S. Sydnor, *Gentlemen Freeholders* (Chapel Hill, 1952), p. 8. Three other provocative studies are John F. Jameson, *The American Revolution Considered as a Social Movement* (Princeton, 1926); John R. Alden, *The American Revolution, 1775–1783* (New York, 1954); and Edmund S. Morgan, *The Birth of the Republic* (Chicago, 1956).

4. This idea is fully developed by Curtis P. Nettels, *George Washington and American Independence* (Boston, 1951).

5. A comprehensive biography of Mason is badly needed. Until it appears, we must depend on Kate Rowland, *The Life of George Mason, 1725–1792* (New York, 1892), and Helen Miller, *George Mason, Constitutionalist* (Cambridge, 1938).

6. No one has dealt with Madison more astutely than Henry Adams in his *History of the United States of America* (New York, 1909–11), vols. V–IX. Irving Brant's four-volume *James Madison* (New York, 1941–53) is outstanding.

7. See Irving Brant's summary in "Madison: On the Separation of Church and State," *William and Mary Quarterly*, vol. VIII, no. 1, January, 1951.

Chapter 6   The Squire of Mount Vernon

1. *Washington's Journal, 1747–48*, edited by J. M. Toner (Albany, 1892), p. 45.

2. Douglas Southhall Freeman, *George Washington, A Biography* (New York, 1948), vol. 1, p. 203.

3. This computation was made by Freeman, *ibid.*, vol. II, pp. 320–21.

4. Quoted by John Tebbel in *George Washington's America* (New York, 1954), p. 178.

5. *Ibid.*, p. 192.

6. Quoted by Francis R. Bellamy, *The Private Life of George Washington* (New York, 1951), p. 353.

7. W. E. Woodward, *George Washington, The Image and the Man* (New York, 1926), p. 401.

8. Marcus Cunliffe, *George Washington: Man and Monument* (Boston, 1958).

9. According to visitor James Kemper, Weems' son Jesse was "exceeding forward." When Mrs. Weems cautioned him, "he replied with airs of levity and rashness that he was determined to go on, and that the Scripture required us to 'leave Father and Mother to follow Christ.'" Kemper's other observations are mentioned in my article "Journey Through the Wilderness," *Virginia Magazine of History and Biography*, vol. 57, no. 2, April, 1949, pp. 133 f. A fuller analysis of Washington's hero-makers appears in my *American Heroes: Myth and Reality* (Washington, 1954).

10. See *Report of the United States George Washington Bicentennial Commission* (Washington, 1932), vol. V, p. xii.

Chapter 7   The Sage of Monticello

1. John Summerson, *Architecture in Britain, 1530-1830* (Baltimore, 1954), p. 343.

2. See Grant McConnell, *The Decline of Agrarian Democracy* (Los Angeles, 1953), Chapter 1.

3. See Jean Gottman, *Virginia at Mid-Century* (New York, 1955), Chapter 2.

4. See the chapter on "Jefferson and the Democratic Aristoi" in Edwin H. Cady's *The Gentleman in America* (Syracuse, 1949).

5. Henry Nash Smith, *The Virgin Land* (Cambridge, 1950), p. 18.

6. Reawakened interest in Jefferson's life and principles is everywhere evident. Not until our day were his voluminous papers and letters collected; that job is now being done under the direction of Julian P. Boyd; the publication by the Princeton University Press began with Volume I in 1950. Perhaps the most satisfactory biographical study in recent years is Dumas Malone's *Jefferson and His Time* (Boston, 1948–51).

Chapter 8   Bountiful Harvests and Bad Seeds

1. Henry Adams, *History of the United States* (New York, 1909–11), vol. IX, p. 220. Two other comprehensive summaries of this period are John B. McMaster's eight-volume *History of the People of the United States from the Revolution*

to the *Civil War* (New York, 1914), and John A. Krout, *The Completion of Independence, 1790–1830* (New York, 1944).

2. See Perceval Reniers, *The Springs of Virginia* (Chapel Hill, 1941).

3. Thomas J. Wertenbaker, *Norfolk, Historic Southern Port* (Durham, N. C., 1931), p. 181.

4. Jesse Burton Harrison, *Ars Sonis Focisque,* edited by Fairfax Harrison (Richmond, 1910), pp. 126-27.

5. So argues Jean Gottman in *Virginia at Mid-Century* (New York, 1955), pp. 113 f.

6. See W. S. Drewry, *Slave Insurrections in Virginia, 1830–1865* (Washington, 1900), and Benjamin Brawley, *Negro Builders and Heroes* (Chapel Hill, 1937).

Chapter 9   Lean Men and Long Rifles

1. Quoted by William C. Pendleton in *Political History of Appalachian Virginia* (Dayton, Va., 1927), p. 8.

2. See William Taylor Thom, *The Struggle for Religous Freedom in Virginia: the Baptists* (Baltimore, 1900). Surviving mountain superstitions are described in Alfreda Peel's *Witch in the Mill* (Richmond, 1947).

3. A vivid description of the life that confronted "a stout young Irishman and his bride who moved upcountry about 1800" may be found in Wilbur J. Cash's *The Mind of the South* (New York, 1941), pp. 27 f.

4. J. T. Dorris, "Transylvania Colony," *Kentucky School Journal,* vol. XIII, no. 1, September, 1934, p. 29.

5. Daniel Bryan, *The Mountain Muse* (Harrisonburg, Va., Davidson and Bourne, 1813), p. 136.

6. *Ibid.,* p. 180.

7. See Edmund P. Tompkins, *Rockbridge County, Virginia, An Informal History* (Richmond, 1952) Chapter 13; and my article on John Jordan in *The Iron Worker* for October, 1957.

8. Talbot Hamlin, *Greek Revival Architecture* (New York, 1935), pp. 210–11.

Chapter 10   Eden, in Fiction

1. Four monographs on this subject are H. J. Eckenrode, "Sir Walter Scott and the South," *North American Review,* October, 1917, pp. 559 f.; Grace W.

Landrum, "Sir Walter Scott and his Literary Rivals in the U. S.," *American Literature,* November, 1930, pp. 256 f.; David A. Randall, "Waverly in America," *The Colophon,* vol. I, summer, 1935, pp. 27 f.; and G. Harrison Orians, "Walter Scott, Mark Twain, and the Civil War," *South Atlantic Quarterly,* October, 1941, pp. 342 f. Good summaries of the subject may be found in Jay B. Hubbell, *The South in American Literature, 1607–1900* (Durham, 1954), and Robert A. Lively, *Fiction Fights the Civil War* (Chapel Hill, 1957).

2. George Trevelyan, "History and Fiction," *Living Age,* vol. CCCXIII, June, 1922, p. 565.

3. Captain Robert E. Lee, *Recollections and Letters of General Robert E. Lee* (New York, 1924), p. 10.

4. James Hogg, *The Domestic Manners and Private Life of Sir Walter Scott* (Glasgow, 1834), p. 67.

5. See Willard Thorp, *A Southern Reader* (New York, 1955), pp. 260 f.

6. John M. Turner, "Tournament Riding in the South," *South Atlantic Quarterly,* vol. XXXV, 1936, pp. 400 f.

7. This is not to imply that the ensuing fiction has no basis in fact. John E. Manahan's "The Cavalier Remounted: A Study of the Origins of Virginia's Population, 1607–1700," unpublished 1946 doctoral dissertation at the University of Virginia, demonstrates that some of the early Virginia blood was bluer than recent historians have implied. See also William R. Taylor's study of "Cavalier and Yankee. The Origins of the Old South as a Cultural Ideal," unpublished 1956 Harvard dissertation.

8. The question of Cooper's use of Boone material is discussed in Henry Nash Smith, *Virgin Land* (Cambridge, 1950), Chapter VI.

9. Wesley F. Craven, *The Legend of the Founding Fathers* (New York, 1956).

10. Arthur A. Link, *Pioneers of Southern Literature* (Nashville, 1913), p. 240.

11. Richmond Croom Beatty, *William Byrd of Westover* (Boston, 1932), p. xii.

12. Francis P. Gaines, *The Southern Plantation: A Study in the Development and the Accuracy of a Tradition* (New York, 1925), p. 4.

13. A detailed account of Caruthers may be found in Curtis Carroll Davis, *Chronicler of the Cavaliers* (Richmond, 1953).

14. Katherine M. Jones, *The Plantation South* (New York, 1957), p. 12.

15. *Ibid.,* pp. 24 f.

16. Jay Hubbell, *Virginia Life in Fiction* (Dallas, 1922), p. 10.

17. Quoted by Frederick Olmstead, *Seaboard Slave States* (New York, 1859) vol. II, p. 186.

18. Stark Young, "Not in Memoriam, But in Defense," in *I'll Take My Stand* (New York, 1930), p. 350.

Chapter 11   Washington to Richmond, Via Air

1. Of the making of Civil War books, there is no end. As early as 1866, John R. Bartlett published a 477-page book on the *Literature of the Rebellion*. Listing bibliographies about the War—or the President who reunited the divided nation—is a sizable task. Choosing a few titles is difficult because many accounts are violently partisan. Southerners joke about the local lady who has devoted herself to writing *A True and Impartial Account of the War Between the States —from a Southern Viewpoint*. On the other hand, one suspects that a book with a title like *The Adder's Den; or, Secrets of the Great Conspiracy to Overthrow Liberty in America* (New York, 1866) may not be a model of objectivity, either.

Professional historians square off and do battle. One can either begin with Arthur Cole's *The Irrepressible Conflict* (New York, 1934) and move on to Avery Craven's *The Repressible Conflict* (Baton Rouge, 1939), or vice versa. Or he can take off a month and try to decide what happened to Longstreet on July 3, 1863.

Since this is presumably a footnote, not an essay, I shall suggest six Civil War titles and be done. The first, Stephen Crane's *Red Badge of Courage*, is fiction; but it is real in the sense that few histories are real. My other five titles represent different points of view and interests; but each is well-conceived and well written: William E. Dodd, *Lincoln or Lee* (New York, 1928); Allan Nevins, *Ordeal of the Union* (New York, 1947–); James G. Randall, *The Civil War and Reconstruction* (Boston, 1953); Clement Eaton, *A History of the Southern Confederacy* (New York, 1954); and Bruce Catton, *A Stillness at Appomattox* (New York, 1954).

Chapter 12   The Man in the Crimson Field

1. Honorable Henry T. Wickham, *Address*, Senate Document No. 10, 1940 (Richmond, State Printing Office, 1940), p. 14.

2. James Branch Cabell, *Let Me Lie* (New York, 1947), p. 178.

3. John S. Wise, *The End of an Era* (Boston, 1900), p. 434.

4. Douglas Southall Freeman, no debunker of Lee, admits this. See his account in the *Dictionary of American Biography* (New York, 1933), XI, pp. 120–29.

5. The question of Lee's postwar reputation is discussed in my *Virginians on Olympus* (Richmond, 1951).

6. Edwin A. Alderman, *Virginia, An Address Delivered in Petersburg, Virginia* (Charlottesville, 1909), p. 10.

Chapter 13 Reconstruction

1. Whitelaw Reid, *After the War: A Southern Tour* (Cincinnati, 1866), p. 128.

2. A. G. Bradley, "An Old American Turnpike," *Fortnightly Review,* 1 August, 1896, pp. 103–4.

3. Lewis Mumford, *The Brown Decades: A Study of the Arts in America, 1865–95* (New York, 1931).

4. *American Annual Cyclopedia and Important Events of the Year, 1867* (New York, 1868) p. 763. Quoted by Matthew Page Andrews, *Virginia, the Old Dominion* (New York, 1937) p. 541.

5. John M. Schofield, *Forty-Six Years in the Army* (New York, 1897), pp. 400–401.

6. Such practices are discussed in James A. Bear Jr.'s unpublished M.A. thesis, "Thomas Staples Martin: A Study in Virginia Politics, 1883–1896," University of Virginia, 1952.

7. See Nelson M. Blake, *William Mahone of Virginia: Soldier and Political Insurgent* (Richmond, 1935), and Allen W. Moger, *Rebuilding of the Old Dominion: A Study in Economic, Social, and Political Transition from 1880–1902* (Ann Arbor, 1940).

8. Richmond *Weekly-Whig,* July 25, 1883.

9. Allen W. Moger, "The Origin of the Democratic Machine in Virginia," *Journal of Southern History,* vol. VIII, May, 1942, p. 202.

10. Walter Watson to Francis Lassiter, June 9, 1892, Francis Rives Lassiter Papers, Duke University Library.

11. See Moger, *op. cit.,* pp. 208–9.

12. F. A. Magruder, *Recent Administration in Virginia,* Johns Hopkins Studies, series XXX, no. 1, p. 102.

Chapter 14 Civil War II

1. For a summary of this conflict, see Robert A. Lively, *Fiction Fights the Civil War* (Chapel Hill, 1957); Louis D. Rubin's "Lee's Surgeon's Horse: A Plea for Historiography," *Civil War History,* vol. III, December, 1957; and Sheldon Van Auken's "The Southern Historical Novel in the Early Twentieth Century," *Journal of Southern History,* vol. XIV, no. 2, May, 1948.

2. Paul H. Buck, *The Road to Reunion, 1865–1900* (Boston, 1938), p. 235.

3. Quoted by John O. Beaty, *John Esten Cooke, Virginian* (New York, 1922), p. 89.

4. See Jay B. Hubbell, *Virginia Life in Fiction* (Dallas, 1922), pp. 27 f.

5. Robert L. Scribner, "Father John B. Tabb," *Virginia Cavalcade*, vol. VI, no. 1, 1956, p. 5.

6. William McDevitt, *My Father, Father Tabb* (New York, 1945), p. 25.

7. See my study of *General Lee's Photographer: The Life and Work of Michael Miley* (Chapel Hill, 1954).

8. An abstract of Miley's process is published in the *Journal of the Franklin Institute*, vol. CLIX, June, 1905, pp. 470–72.

9. Arnold J. Toynbee, *A Study of History*, Somervell abridgment (New York, 1947), p. 315.

Chapter 15   John Bull vs. Uncle Sam

1. Winston Churchill, *The World Crisis, 1911–1914* (London, 1923), p. 272.

2. See Louis B. Wright's chapter on "English Patterns for Virginia Planters" in *The First Gentlemen of Virginia* (San Marino, 1940).

3. See William E. Garnett, "The Virginia Rural Church and Related Influences," *Virginia Agricultural Experiment Station Bulletin No. 478* (Blacksburg, 1954).

4. See Francis Simkins, "The Rising Tide of Faith," in *The Lasting South*, edited by Louis D. Rubin, Jr., and James J. Kilpatrick (Chicago, 1957).

5. Edwin M. Poteat, Jr., "Religion in the South," in William T. Couch's *Culture in the South* (Chapel Hill, 1935). See also Wesley Gewehr, *The Great Awakening in Virginia, 1740–1790* (Durham, 1930); Twelve Southerners, *I'll Take My Stand* (New York, 1930); and Virginius Dabney, *Dry Messiah, The Life of Bishop Cannon* (New York, 1945).

6. "Letters to the Editor," *Rockbridge County News*, June 11, 1953.

Chapter 16   You-All Hurry Back

1. See Kathleen Bruce, *Virginia Iron Manufacturing in the Slave Era* (New York, 1931), Chapter VIII.

2. For details see Allen W. Moger's *Rebuilding of the Old Dominion* (Ann Arbor, 1940).

3. See *Roanoke, Story of County and City* (Roanoke, 1942), compiled by the Writers' Program of the Work Projects Administration, especially Part II, "Panorama of Progress."

4. See *ibid.*, Chapter III; E. P. Tompkins, *Rockbridge County, Virginia, An Informal History* (Richmond, 1952), Chapter XI; and Hugh White's account in the *Rockbridge County News*, April 21 and 28, 1938.

5. C. N. Berkeley, *Why is Virginia Poor?* (Richmond, 1884). Quoted by Moger, *op. cit.*, p. 54.

6. See *A Report on Virginia's Economy*, prepared by the Fiscal Study Committee of the Advisory Council on the Virginia Economy (Richmond, 1957).

7. Julian Meade, *I Live in Virginia* (New York, 1935), p. 46.

8. Lyon G. Tyler, *Virginia Principles* (Richmond, 1927), p. 23.

Chapter 17 Tradition in Search of Meaning

1. Dorothy B. Schlegel, "James Branch Cabell and Southern Romanticism," typescript of a paper read at the Institute of Southern Culture, Farmville, Virginia, April 18, 1958.

2. Ellen Glasgow, *The Woman Within* (New York, 1954), p. 133.

3. Edmund Wilson, "The James Branch Cabell Case Reopened," *The New Yorker*, April 21, 1956, pp. 129 f.

4. This analogy is fully developed by Desmond Tarrant in an unpublished manuscript entitled "Towards Jerusalem: A Study of the American Romanticist, James Branch Cabell." An earlier version was submitted as a master's thesis at the University of London in 1956.

5. James Branch Cabell, *Beyond Life* (London, n. d.), p. 139.

6. James Branch Cabell, *Preface to the Past* (New York, 1936), p. 158.

7. James Branch Cabell, *Let Me Lie* (New York, 1947), p. 74.

8. Edmund Wilson, "James Branch Cabell:1879–1958," *Nation*, June 7, 1958, p. 520.

9. Ellen Glasgow, *A Certain Measure* (New York, 1938), p. 11.

10. Elizabeth Monroe, *The Novel and Society* (Chapel Hill, 1941), p. 140.

11. Ellen Glasgow, "Personal Philosophy," in *I Believe*, edited by Clifton Fadiman (New York, 1939), p. 109.

12. For this division I am indebted to William W. Kelly, whose unpublished doctoral dissertation, "Struggle for Recognition: A Study of the Literary Reputation of Ellen Glasgow," Duke University, 1957, is used with his permission.

13. Ellen Glasgow, *Virginia* (New York, 1913), Preface, p. ix.

14. This review of *Letters of Ellen Glasgow* (New York, 1957) appeared in *The New York Times* for January 19, 1958.

15. Letter to the author, dated April 17, 1958.

16. John W. Aldridge, *In Search of Heresy* (New York, 1956), pp. 59 f. For the interview mentioned, see *Writers at Work: The Paris Review Interviews* (New York, 1958).

Chapter 18   F.F.V.'s

1. *Letters of John Randolph to a Young Relative; Embracing a Series of Years, from Early Youth to Mature Manhood* (Philadelphia, 1834).

2. Walter B. Hill, "Address," in *The University of Virginia in the Life of the Nation* (New York, 1905), p. 45.

3. Thomas Sugrue, *Stranger in the Earth* (New York, 1948), p. 164.

4. This gay little poem, by James McClurg and St. George Tucker, is reprinted in A. C. Gordon's *Lyric Virginia Today* (New York, 1932).

5. Quoted by Edmund S. Morgan, *Virginians at Home, Family Life in the Eighteenth Century* (Williamsburg, 1952), p. 45.

6. See Constance C. Harrion, "Colonel William Byrd of Westover," *Century*, vol. XLII, 1891, p. 171.

7. Allen Tate, *The Fathers* (New York, 1938), p. 210.

8. See William H. Gaines, Jr., "John Peel in Virginia," *Cavalcade*, autumn, 1953.

9. See Jean and Tony Walker's article on "Virginia's Big Stake in Horse Racing," *Commonwealth*, August, 1954.

10. Quoted by Robert M. Denhardt, *The Horse of the Americas* (Norman, Okla., 1948), p. 179.

11. The army of Napoleon used a similar roll call. See William Couper, *The V.M.I. New Market Cadets* (Charlottesville, 1933).

12. Dixon Wecter, *The Saga of American Society* (New York, 1937), p. 23.

13. Jean Gottman, *Virginia at Mid-Century* (New York, 1955), p. 561.

Chapter 19   Poor White

1. The best summary of this literature is found in Shields McIlwaine, *The Southern Poor-White from Lubberland to Tobacco Road* (Norman, Okla., 1939).

2. William A. Caruthers, *The Kentuckian in New York* (New York, 1834), vol. I, pp. 78–79.

3. These figures were supplied by J. A. Simpson, chief of the Bureau of Research and Statistics of Virginia's Department of Welfare and Institutions.

4. Arnold J. Toynbee, *A Study of History,* Somervell abridgment (New York, 1947), p. 149.

5. William E. Garnett and Allen D. Edwards, *Virginia's Marginal Population— A Study in Rural Poverty* (P.P.I. Bulletin No. 335, 1941), pp. 5 f. See also Dorothy Scarborough, *A Song Catcher in Southern Mountains* (New York, 1937), and Charles M. Wilson, *Corn Bread and Creek Water* (New York, 1940).

Chapter 20   Marse Chan vs. the N.A.A.C.P.

1. Ulrich B. Philips, "Slave Crime in Virginia," *The American Historical Review,* vol. XX, 1914, pp. 336–40.

2. James S. Buchingham in Ulrich B. Phillips, *American Negro Slavery* (New York, 1918), p. 416.

3. B. A. Botkin, *Lay My Burden Down* (Chicago, 1945), p. 134. This book is a group of excerpts from the seventeen-volume collection.

4. Paul Lawrence Dunbar, *Complete Poems* (New York, 1913), p. 45.

5. This capitulation is fully discussed by C. Vann Woodward in *The Strange Case of Jim Crow* (New York, 1957).

6. Richmond *Times-Dispatch,* June 1, 1955, p. 14.

7. Francis B. Simkins, *A History of the South* (New York, 1953), p. 536.

8. See Woodward, *op. cit.,* p. 161.

Chapter 21   Mountain Music

1. H. Fox Strangways, *Cecil Sharp* (London, 1933), p. 148.

2. Evelyn K. Wells, *The Ballad Tree* (New York, 1950). Chapter 14, on "Some Characteristics of Folk Tunes," is recommended for the person interested in knowing more about this subject.

3. Both the version and the parody are given in A. K. Davis' *Traditional Ballads of Virginia* (Cambridge, Mass., 1929), pp. 141 and 145.

4. See the introduction to Jackson's *Spiritual Folk-Songs of Early America* (New York, 1937).

5. Despite the influence of juke boxes and radio, hymns like this may still be heard in many rural churches.

6. Edmund P. Tompkins, *Rockbridge County, Virginia, An Informal History* (Richmond, 1952), p. 92.

7. F. O. Mattheissen, *American Renaissance* (New York, 1941), p. 641.

8. Louis W. Chappell, *John Henry, A Folklore Study* (Jena, Germany, 1933).

Chapter 22   Restoration Blues

1. Quoted by Alfred Bagby, *King and Queen County, Virginia* (New York, 1908), p. 247.

2. Warren Hall, *Tangier Island* (Philadelphia, 1932), p. 77.

3. Elizabeth V. Huntley, *Peninsula Pilgrimage* (Richmond, 1941), p. 5.

4. Helen Campbell, *Diary of a Williamsburg Hostess* (New York, 1946).

5. Wallace Nutting, *Virginia Beautiful* (Norwood, Mass., 1930), p. 50.

6. James Branch Cabell, *Let Me Lie* (New York, 1947), p. 92.

7. The state's voting record is analyzed by V. O. Key, Jr., in *Southern Politics* (New York, 1949), Chapter 2.

8. See Edward T. Folliard's perceptive summary in eleven consecutive articles in the Washington *Post*, beginning June 9, 1957.

9. See *Public Welfare Statistics, vol. XVII, no. 2* (Richmond, 1957).

10. Albert O. Porter, *County Government in Virginia* (New York, 1947).

Chapter 23 The Virginia Lady

1. I am indebted to Dr. Marvin Schlegel's paper on Virginia history, read before the 1956 annual meeting of the Virginia Social Science Association, for the notion of the "three Johns" used in this chapter. Two recent books that express the outlook of upper-class Virginia ladies are Virginia Moore's *Virginia Is a State of Mind* (New York, 1942) and Rebecca Y. Williams' *The Vanishing Virginian* (New York, 1940).

Chapter 24 Jamestown Revisited

1. Richard Weaver, "Aspects of the Southern Philosophy," *Southern Renascence* (Baltimore, 1953), p. 15.

2. Virginius Dabney, "An Approach to Virginia," *Saturday Review of Literature,* Jan. 23, 1943, p. 18.

3. Douglas Southall Freeman, "The Spirit of Virginia," in *Virginia, A Guide to the Old Dominion* (New York, 1940), compiled by workers of the Writers' Program of the Works Projects Administration in the State of Virginia. For a more recent comment on the same subject, see Cabell Phillips' "Virginia—The State and the State of Mind," *The New York Times Magazine,* July 28, 1957, pp. 18 f.

4. There was an interesting paradox in the attitudes and career of Boone and the other frontier scouts. To find the true values of nature, they left civilization behind; yet they broke trails for others to follow, thus reducing the savage wilderness for civilization. This paradox, and the frontier folk mind, is analyzed by Henry Nash Smith in *Virgin Land; the American West as Symbol and Myth* (Cambridge, 1950).

5. Francis B. Simkins, "The Education That Doesn't Educate; the Persistence of Virginia Folkways," in *Virginia in History and Tradition* (Farmville, 1958), p. 9.

6. Anonymous, "Studies in the South, III," *Atlantic Monthly,* vol. XLIX, May, 1882, p. 683.

Appendix Clio in Bondage: History Writing in Virginia

1. Wesley F. Craven analyzes Brown's work in *Dissolution of the Virginia Company: the Failure of a Colonial Experiment* (New York, 1932).

2. T. J. Wertenbaker, *Patrician and Plebeian in Virginia* (New York, 1916), p. 54.

3. George F. Willison, *Behold Virginia: the Fifth Crown* (New York, 1951), p. 6.

4. John E. Manahan, "The Cavalier Remounted: A Study of the Origins of Virginia's Population, 1607–1700," unpublished doctoral dissertation, University of Virginia, 1946.

5. Wilcomb E. Washburn, "Bacon's Rebellion, 1676–1677," unpublished doctoral dissertation, Harvard University, 1955; and Edna Jensen, "Sir John Harvey, Governor of Virginia," unpublished master's thesis, University of Virginia, 1950.

6. Douglas S. Freeman, letter to the author, dated November 2, 1947.

7. *Ibid.*

8. T. Harry Williams, "Freeman, Historian of the Civil War: An Appraisal," *Journal of Southern History,* vol. XXI, 1955, p. 96.

9. Joseph H. Harrison, Jr. "Harry Williams, Critic of Freeman: A Demurrer," *Virginia Magazine of History and Biography,* LXIV, 1956, pp. 70–77.

10. Letter to the author, dated May 28, 1958.

11. Clifford Dowdey, *Death of a Nation, The Story of Lee and His Men at Gettysburg* (New York, 1958). The publisher's announcement pointed out the book was written "from the Southern viewpoint."

12. This story was confirmed in a letter from Mr. Byrd to the author, dated November 4, 1948.

13. Eckenrode, holder of strong racial views, maintained in his biography of *Jefferson Davis* (New York, 1923) that "the victory of the North meant the predominance of the non-Nordic elements in American life" (p. 361).

14. "Editorial Problems in Virginia History," in *Virginia in History and Tradition,* edited by R. C. Simonini (Farmville, 1958), p. 116.

Index

Fishwick, Marshall William.
 Virginia: a new look at the Old Dominion. ₁1st ed.₎
New York, Harper ₁1959₎
   305 p. illus. 22 cm. (A Regions of America book)
   Includes bibliography.

   1. Virginia—Hist.   I. Title: A new look at the Old Dominion.

F226.F49   975.5   58–6148

Library of Congress

VIRGINIA
THE OLD DOMINION STATE

J.O'N.COSGRAVE II

White Sulphur Springs •   • Clifton
•Covington

ALLEGHENY M

Bluefield •   • Pearisburg

• R

•Radford
•Pulaski

Appalachia •Norton   Wytheville •

Harlan •   •Big Stone Gap

MOUNTAIN EMPIRE

Martinsville •

• Bristol

Clinch River   • Kingsport   Mt. Airy •

SCALE OF MILES

0   10   20   30   40   50 MILES